OKLAHOMA POLITICS AND POLICIES

D0864679

*Politics and Governments
of the American States*

General Editor

John Kincaid
U.S. Advisory Commission on
Intergovernmental Relations
and the University of North Texas

Founding Editor

Daniel J. Elazar
Temple University

Editorial Advisory Board

Thad L. Beyle
University of North Carolina at
Chapel Hill

Diane D. Blair
University of Arkansas

Ellis Katz
Temple University

Charles Press
Michigan State University

Stephen L. Schechter
Russell Sage College

Published by the University of
Nebraska Press in association
with the Center for the Study
of Federalism

DAVID R. MORGAN, ROBERT E. ENGLAND,
AND GEORGE G. HUMPHREYS

Oklahoma Politics & Policies: Governing the Sooner State

Foreword by

ROBERT H. HENRY,

ATTORNEY GENERAL OF OKLAHOMA

UNIVERSITY OF NEBRASKA PRESS

LINCOLN AND LONDON

Copyright © 1991 by the
University of Nebraska Press
All rights reserved
Manufactured in the
United States of America

The paper in this book
meets the minimum requirements of
American National Standard
for Information Sciences – Permanence of
Paper for Printed Library Materials,
ANSI Z39.48-1984.

Library of Congress
Cataloging in Publication Data
Morgan, David R.
Oklahoma politics and policies:
governing the Sooner State /
by David R. Morgan,
Robert E. England, and George G. Humphreys;
foreword by Robert H. Henry.
p.   cm. – (Politics and governments
of the American states)
Includes bibliographical references
(p.) and index.
ISBN (invalid) 0-8032-3106-7 (cl) (alk). –
ISBN 0-8032-8136-6 (pa) (alk)
1. Oklahoma – Politics and government.
1. England, Robert E.
II. Humphreys, George G., 1949-
III. Title. IV. Series.
JK7116.M67   1991   320.9766—dc20   90-13044   CIP

To
My wife, Carolyn, and my four children,
Marilyn, Steve, Lisa, and Greg
D.R.M.

Two of my best friends, Bill and Loyce England,
my loving father and mother
R.E.E.

Oklahoma Secretary of State Hannah D. Atkins,
in appreciation of our friendship
G.G.H.

CONTENTS

TABLES, MAPS, AND FIGURES

ROBERT H. HENRY

Foreword

A young man returned to rural Oklahoma after completing college and law school. Armed with his law degree, he set about to open an office. Realizing that he was largely unknown after his scholastic absence, he decided, as any knowledgeable rural Oklahoman would, that the best way to get his name known was to run for political office.

He knew he wouldn't win; it was the publicity that was important. So, to the amazement of all, he filed against the long-time, incumbent county commissioner, the most powerful politician in the area.

At the first "speakin'," virtually the entire county gathered to see what the young upstart with no experience or organization could possibly have to say. The lad knew it would be an uphill battle, so he closed his speech with a powerful peroration appealing to the presumed universal disdain for corruption: "Ladies and gentlemen, good voters of this county, I remind you that there is only *one,* only one hard-paved road in the entire county, and that runs straight from the incumbent's farm right to the county seat. Now is that the kind of county commissioner you want?" "It damn sure is!" a voice cried from the back. "Why, he's already got his road."

As shown by this story, Oklahomans are afflicted with what historian Danney Goble might call a "bucolic tradition of negativism";[1] they frequently display a defensive cynicism produced by their often painful history of strife, overburdened land, and poverty. These hardships, perhaps allied with a failure of vision by early leaders, conspired to create political and economic systems that frequently broke down. The Sooner story is unquestionably one of conflict— conflict between people, between Sooners and their environment, and now, as this book clearly explains, between Oklahoma's past and its present.

The conflict that began with the forced relocation of the Five Tribes, and the resultant fratricide, continued as the Civil War further divided the tribes. Later, as thousands of poor settlers moved in, lured by "free land" and not understanding the massive overpopulation such settlement without economic markets would create, the conflict continued. Cultures collided as the Republican, Methodist wheat farmers from Kansas moved in from the Northwest, meeting the Democratic, Baptist cotton farmers from Texas and Arkansas. The poverty that resulted from overpopulation (too many people for undeveloped lands and markets to support) was lyrically described by Socialist newspaperman Oscar Ameringer when he recounted what he saw on his first trip to Oklahoma in 1907:

> I found toothless old women with sucking infants on their withered breasts. I found a hospitable old hostess, around thirty or less, her hands covered with rags and eczema, offering me a biscuit with those hands, apologizing that her biscuits were not as good as she used to make because with her sore hand she no longer could knead the dough as it ought to be. I saw youngsters emaciated by hookworms, malnutrition, and pellagra, who had lost their second teeth before they were twenty years old. I saw tottering old male wrecks with the infants of their fourteen-year-old wives on their laps. I saw a white man begging a Choctaw squaw man who owned the only remaining spring in that neighborhood to let him have credit for a few buckets of water for his thirsty family. I saw humanity at its lowest possible level of degradation and decay. I saw smug, well dressed, overly well fed hypocrites march to church on Sabbath day, Bibles under their arms, praying for God's kingdom on earth while fattening like latter-day cannibals on the share croppers. I saw wind-jamming, hot-air-spouting politicians geysering Jeffersonian platitudes about equal rights to all and special privileges to none; about all men born equal with the rights to life, liberty and the pursuit of happiness without even knowing, much less caring, that they were addressing as wretched a set of abject slaves as ever walked the face of the earth, anywhere or at any time. The things I saw on that trip are the things you never forget.[2]

After the ecological disaster of the Dust Bowl era of the 1930s and World War II, Oklahoma continued its struggle, making uneven but uphill progress, primarily fueled by the petroleum under its soil. In 1982, after finally reaching the national average on per capita income, Oklahoma saw that prosperity wither with a crash in oil prices, followed by declining agriculture prices, which together caused the collapse of more than one hundred banks in seven years.

But despite this remarkable history of conflict and adversity, Oklahomans have accomplished much in very little time. Tempered by hardship and accustomed to hard work, we Oklahomans have gone about as far as hard work alone can take us. It is time to transcend the politics of negativism, of preservation of a dismal status quo, of a populism that preaches, "If I can't have it, I don't want anybody else to," of a conservatism that decries the spending of tax money for any reason. As our authors state, "Perhaps more than most states, Oklahoma struggles to reconcile its traditional rural past with the demands of a postindustrial service economy."

Oklahoma, as these authors suggest, is clearly in a transitional phase. It is too early to tell in which direction and how far the state will evolve. Will we blend the virtues of our rural past (such as the ability and drive to work hard, the understanding of the necessity of sacrifice) with thoughtful and realistic consideration of the modern world and our global competitors? Or will we, fettered by inaction and negativism, retain a status quo that allows only a few big fish in a few small ponds? It is my hope that our decision will be one of investment in the education of our talented people, of stewardship of our beautiful lands and waters, of commitment to tolerance and the rule of law.

This important book, unquestionably reformist in outlook yet appreciative of the many unique features about Oklahoma, gives a clear picture of the past and describes the outlines of various transitional futures. Addressing a question basically undiscussed since Angie Debo's 1949 *Oklahoma: Footloose and Fancy-Free*, it will be controversial to some; it will make the gods angry.

For you who want to understand Oklahoma, whether as students of American state governments, historians of Oklahoma, or policy makers public or private, this book is vital. And if we Oklahomans want to build *our* road—linking town and country, past and future—it is for us, too.

JOHN KINCAID

Series Preface

The purpose of this series is to provide intelligent and interesting books on the politics and governments of the fifty American states, books that are of value not only to the student of government but also to the general citizen who wants greater insight into the past and present civic life of his or her state and of other states in the federal union. The role of the states in governing America is among the least well known of all the 83,217 governments in the United States. The national media focus attention on the federal government in Washington, D.C., and local media focus attention on local government. Meanwhile, except when there is a scandal or a proposed tax increase, the workings of state government remain something of a mystery to many citizens—out of sight, out of mind.

In many respects, however, the states have been, and continue to be, the most important governments in the American political system. They are the main building blocks and chief organizing governments of the whole system. The states are the constituent governments of the federal union, and it is through the states that citizens gain representation in the national government. The national government is one of limited, delegated powers; all other powers are possessed by the states and their citizens. At the same time, the states are the empowering governments for the nation's 83,166 local governments—counties, municipalities, townships, school districts, and special districts. As such, states provide for one of the most essential and ancient elements of freedom and democracy, the right of local self-government.

Although, for many citizens, the most visible aspects of state government are state universities, some of which are the most prestigious in the world, and state highway patrol officers, with their radar guns and handy ticket books, state governments provide for nearly all domestic public services. Whether elements of those services are enacted or partly funded by the federal government and actually carried out by local governments, it is state government that has the ultimate responsibility for ensuring that Americans are well served by all of their governments. In so doing, all of the American states are more democratic, more prosperous, and better governed than most of the world's nation-states.

This is a particularly timely period in which to publish a series of books on the governments and politics of each of the fifty states. Once viewed as the "fallen arches" of the federal system, states today are increasingly seen as energetic, innovative, and fiscally responsible. Some states, of course, perform better than others, but that is to be expected in a federal system. Each state is unique in its own right. It is our hope that this series will shed light on the public life of each state and that, taken together, the books will contribute to a better, more informed understanding of the states themselves and of their often pivotal roles in the world's first and oldest continental-size federal democracy.

DANIEL J. ELAZAR

Series Introduction

The more than continental stretch of the American domain is given form and character as a federal union of fifty states whose institutions order the American landscape. Most of the American states are larger and better developed than most of the world's nations. Each has its own story; each is a polity with its own uniqueness. The American states exist because they are civil societies. They were first given political form and then acquired their own characteristics. Each has its own constitution, its own political culture, its own relationship to the federal union and to its section. These elements in turn have given each its own law and history; the longer that history, the more distinctive the state.

It is in and through the states, no less than the nation, that the great themes of American life play themselves out. The advancing frontier and the continuing experience of Americans as a frontier people, the drama of American ethnic blending, the tragedy of slavery and racial discrimination, the political struggle for expanding the right to vote—all found, and find, their expression in the states.

Oklahoma Politics and Policies is the fourth book in The University of Nebraska Press and the Center for the Study of Federalism series: Politics and Governments of the American States. Each book in the series reviews the political development of the state to demonstrate how its political institutions and characteristics have evolved from the first settlement to the present. Each presents the state in the context of the nation and section of which it is part and reviews the roles and relations of the state vis-à-vis its sister states and the federal government. Although the books in the series are not expected to be uniform, they do focus on the common themes of federalism, constitutionalism, political culture, and the continuing American frontier, to provide a framework within which to consider the institutions, routines, and processes of state government and politics.

FEDERALISM

American federalism has been characterized by several basic tensions. One is between state sovereignty—the view that in a proper federal system, authority and power over most domestic affairs should be in the hands of the states—and national supremacy—the view that the federal government has a significant role to play in domestic matters affecting the national interest. The other tension is between dual federalism—the idea that a federal system functions best when the federal government and the states function as separately as possible, each in its own sphere—and cooperative federalism— the view that federalism works best when the federal government and the states, while preserving their own institutions, cooperate closely on the implementation of joint or shared programs.

Oklahoma, although a relatively young state, formed entirely out of the federal domain, has traditionally held to ideas of state sovereignty and dual federalism as part of its identification with the South. In practice, however, it has consistently cooperated with the federal government and sought federal aid when such a partnership has suited its purposes. From the days when Oklahoma was Indian Territory through the great post–World War II Corps of Engineers projects to create an Arkansas River channel navigable to the sea and thereby open Oklahoma to industrial development, the state has not only benefited from, but even has been dependent on, direct federal activities mobilized by the state's congressional delegation.

At the same time, on racial issues Oklahoma took a traditional "states' rights" position vis-à-vis the federal government until that issue was swept aside by the U.S. Supreme Court and the civil rights revolution. Unlike the case in other segregationist states, the civil rights revolution was fought in Oklahoma with only minor skirmishes, not with massive resistance, so that it was relatively easy for the state to put that particular problem with the federal government behind it.

Nor are direct federal benefits as important to the state today as they were in the days of the powerful Senator Robert Kerr, the father of the nine-foot channel, who was able to secure many other benefits for his state as well. Still, Oklahoma is institutionally very alert to the realities of American federalism and has done well to mobilize its governmental institutions to secure the maximum amount of assistance from federal sources, even as it has preserved its sense of distinctiveness as a state.

CONSTITUTIONALISM

State constitutions are potentially far more comprehensive than the federal constitution, which is one of limited, delegated powers. Because states are plenary governments, they automatically possess all powers not specifically denied them by the U.S. Constitution or their citizens. Consequently, a state constitution must be explicit about limiting and defining the scope of governmental powers, especially on behalf of individual liberty. So state constitutions normally include an explicit declaration of rights, almost invariably broader than the first ten amendments to the U.S. Constitution.

Overall, six different state constitutional patterns have developed. One is the commonwealth pattern, found in New England, which emphasizes Whig ideas of the constitution as a philosophic document designed first and foremost to set a direction for civil society and to express and institutionalize a theory of republican government. A second is the constitutional pattern of the commercial republic. The constitutions fitting this pattern reflect a series of compromises required by the conflict of many strong ethnic groups and commercial interests generated by the flow of heterogeneous streams of migrants into particular states and the early development of large commercial and industrial cities in those states.

The third, found in the South, can be described as the southern contractual pattern. Southern state constitutions are used as instruments to set explicit terms governing the relationship between polity and society, such as those that protected slavery or racial segregation or sought to diffuse the formal allocation of authority in order to accommodate the swings between oligarchy and factionalism characteristic of southern state politics. Of all the southern states, only Louisiana stands somewhat outside this pattern, since its legal system was based on the French civil code. Its constitutions have been codes—long, highly explicit documents that form a fourth pattern in and of themselves.

A fifth pattern is that found frequently in the less populated states of the Far West, where the state constitution is primarily a frame of government explicitly reflecting the republican and democratic principles dominant in the nation in the late nineteenth century, but emphasizing the structure of state government and the distribution of powers within that structure in a direct, businesslike manner. Finally, the two newest states, Alaska and Hawaii, have adopted constitutions following the managerial pattern developed and promoted by twentieth-century constitutional reform movements in the United States. Those constitutions are characterized by conciseness, broad grants of power to the executive branch, and relatively few structural restrictions on the legislature. They emphasize natural resource conservation and social legislation.

Oklahoma, straddling as it does the South and the West, shares the Far Western constitutional tradition. Its constitution is a frame of government first and foremost. Perhaps the most distinctive aspect of Oklahoma's constitutional tradition is the semiplace that it assigns to the Indians. Eastern Oklahoma was originally divided among the Five Civilized Tribes, each of which adopted a tribal constitution of its own. Together they developed what would have become a seventh constitutional tradition had it not been destroyed in the very founding of Oklahoma when the tribes were deprived of their autonomy in what was probably the ultimate white assault on Native Americans. (Here were five Indian tribes that had adopted American ways to the point of functioning like states within the Union, albeit without representation in federal institutions, but that were even denied the right to adapt by greedy and ethnocentric Americans.) Because of the extensive Native American population in Oklahoma and the prior existence of the Five Civilized Nations, the Oklahoma Constitution makes some provision for group rights for the Native Americans, rare in American constitutionalism.

THE CONTINUING AMERICAN FRONTIER

The United States was founded with a rural-land frontier that persisted until World War I, more or less, spreading farms, ranches, mines, and towns across the land. Early in the nineteenth century the rural-land frontier generated the urban frontier based on industrial development. The creation of new wealth through industrialization transformed cities from mere regional service centers into generators of wealth in their own right. The frontier persisted for more than one hundred years as a major force in American society as a whole and perhaps another sixty years as a major force in various parts of the country. The population movements and attendant growth of the urban-industrial frontier brought about the effective settlement of the United States in freestanding cities from coast to coast.

Between the world wars the urban-industrial frontier gave birth in turn to a third frontier stage, one based on the new technologies of electronic communication, the internal combustion engine, the airplane, synthetics, and petrochemicals. These new technologies transformed every aspect of life and turned urbanization into metropolitanization. This third frontier stage generated a third settlement of the United States, this time in metropolitan regions from coast to coast, involving a mass migration of tens of millions of Americans in search of opportunity on the rurban frontier.

In the 1970s the first post–World War II generation came to a close. Many Americans began speaking of the "limits of growth." Yet despite that anti-frontier rhetoric, there was every sign that a fourth frontier stage was begin-ning in the form of the rurban, or citybelt-cybernetic, frontier generated by the metropolitan-technological frontier just as the latter had been generated by its predecessor.

The rurban-cybernetic frontier first emerged in the Northeast, as did its predecessors, as the Atlantic Coast metropolitan regions merged into one an-other to form a six-hundred-mile-long megalopolis (the usage is Jean Gott-man's)—a matrix of urban and suburban settlements in which the older cen-tral cities came to yield importance if not prominence to smaller ones. Although the Northeast was first, the new rurban-cybernetic frontier, like its predecessors, is finding its true form in the South and West, where these city-belt matrices are not being built on the collapse of earlier forms, but are de-veloping as an original form. The present sunbelt frontier—strung out along the Gulf Coast, the southwestern desert, and the fringes of the California mountains—is classically megalopolitan in citybelt form and cybernetic with its aerospace-related industries and sunbelt living made possible by air conditioning and the new telecommunications.

Before the land rushes of 1889 and the 1890s, Oklahoma was the ultimate backwater of the rural-land frontier, set aside for American Indians who had been driven out of the rest of the country as part of the white advance yet still were subject to the white man's whims, even where the Indians did their best to adapt to the white man's ways. Just about the last territory opened for white settlement in the continental United States, for approximately two de-cades beginning in 1889, Oklahoma contributed something special to the legend of the land frontier—the land rush.

Integral to the land frontier in Oklahoma was the discovery of oil. The booms that resulted tied in well with the next two frontier stages, particularly the metropolitan-technological frontier, which rested heavily on the auto-mobile and the use of petroleum and its by-products. Thus in one giant step Oklahoma went from Indian Territory to a major factor in the great techno-logical revolution that accompanied the metropolitan frontier, creating a new set of legends that have become part of American lore, captured at the time by Hollywood in a series of early twentieth-century neo-Westerns.

The last stage of this effort was manifested in the great river development projects that made Tulsa a seaport one thousand miles inland. Oil transformed the central third of the state. This two-generation-long boom came to an end in the petroleum industry's upheavals of the 1970s.

As of 1990, Oklahoma has not really moved on into the rurban-cybernetic frontier. Indeed, even during the metropolitan-technological frontier its cities behaved more like those of the previous frontier stage, expanding their city limits to embrace population growth as had the cities of the Northeast two generations earlier, rather than falling into the conventional patterns of metropolitanization. Still, an Oklahoma citybelt is emerging, cutting diagonally across the state from the northeast to the southwest along Interstate 44.

THE PERSISTENCE OF SECTIONALISM

The nation's sectional alignments are rooted in the three great historical, cultural, and economic spheres into which the country is divided: the greater Northeast, the greater South, and the greater West. Following state lines, the greater Northeast includes all those states north of the Ohio and Potomac rivers and east of Lake Michigan. The greater South includes the states below that line but east of the Mississippi plus Missouri, Arkansas, Louisiana, Oklahoma, and Texas. All the rest of the states compose the greater West. Within that framework there are eight sections: New England, Middle Atlantic, Near West, Upper South, Lower South, Western South, Northwest, and Far West.

From the New Deal years through the 1960s, Americans' understanding of sectionalism was submerged by their concern with urban-oriented socioeconomic categories, such as the struggle between labor and management or between the haves and have-nots in the big cities. Even the racial issue, once the hallmark of the greater South, began to be perceived in nonsectional terms as a result of black immigration northward. This is not to say that sectionalism ceased to exist as a vital force, only that it was little noted in those years.

Beginning in the 1970s, however, there was a resurgence of sectional feeling as economic cleavages increasingly came to follow sectional lines. The sunbelt-frostbelt contribution is the prime example of this new sectionalism. "Sunbelt" is the new code word for the Lower South, Western South, and Far West; "frostbelt" is the code word for the New England, Middle Atlantic, and Great Lakes (Near Western) states. Sectionalism promises to be a major force in national politics, closely linked to the rurban-cybernetic frontier.

From a sectional perspective, Oklahoma is one of the most marginal of states. Not only does it lie at the intersection between the South and the West, the fault line between those two spheres runs right through the heart of the state. Oklahoma is sufficiently southern so that during the Civil War, before there actually was an Oklahoma, the more powerful of the Five Civilized Tribes effectively joined the South as slaveholding states. At the same time, western Oklahoma is classic cowboy country, and its Indian culture is part of that of the Great Plains.

THE VITAL ROLE OF POLITICAL CULTURE

The same locational factors place Oklahoma on the border between the traditionalistic and individualistic political culture areas. The United States as a whole shares a general political culture that is rooted in two contrasting conceptions of the American political order which can be traced to the earliest settlement of the country. In the first the polity is conceived as a marketplace in which the primary public relationships are products of bargaining among individuals and groups acting out of self-interest. In the second the political order is conceived to be a commonwealth—a polity in which the whole people have an undivided interest—in which the citizens cooperate in an effort to create and maintain the best government in order to implement certain shared moral principles. These two conceptions have exercised an influence on government and politics throughout American history, sometimes in conflict and sometimes complementing each other.

The national political culture is a synthesis of three major political subcultures. All three are of nationwide proportions, having spread, in the course of time, from coast to coast. At the same time, each subculture is strongly tied to specific sections of the country, reflecting the streams and currents of migration that have carried people of different origins and backgrounds across the continent in more or less orderly patterns. Based on their central characteristics, the three may be called individualistic, moralistic, and traditionalistic. Each reflects its own particular synthesis of the marketplace and the commonwealth.

The *individualistic political culture* emphasizes the democratic order as a marketplace in which government is instituted for strictly utilitarian reasons, to handle those functions demanded by the people it is created to serve. Beyond the commitment to an open market, a government need not have any direct concern with questions of the good society, except insofar as it may be used to advance some common view formulated outside the political arena just as it serves other functions. Since the individualistic political culture emphasizes the centrality of private concerns, it places a premium on limiting community intervention—whether governmental or nongovernmental—into private activities to the minimum necessary to keep the marketplace in proper working order.

The *moralistic political culture* emphasizes the commonwealth conception as the basis for democratic government. Politics is considered one of the great activities of humanity in its search for the good society—a struggle for power, it is true, but also an effort to exercise power for the betterment of the commonwealth. Consequently, both the general public and the politicians conceive of politics as a public activity centered on some notion of the public good and properly devoted to the advancement of the public interest.

The *traditionalistic political culture* is rooted in an ambivalent attitude toward the marketplace, coupled with a paternalistic and elitist conception of the commonwealth. It reflects an older, precommercial attitude that accepts a substantially hierarchical society as part of the ordered nature of things, authorizing and expecting those at the top of the social structure to take a special and dominant role in government. Like its moralistic counterpart, the traditionalistic political culture accepts government as an actor with a positive role in the community, but it tries to limit that role to securing the continued maintenance of the existing social order. To do so, it functions to confine real political power to a relatively small and self-perpetuating group drawn from an established elite that often inherits its right to govern through family ties or social position. Social and family ties are even more important in a traditionalistic political culture than personal ties in the individualistic, where, after all is said and done, one's first responsibility is to oneself. At the same time, those who do not have a definite role to play in politics are not expected to be even minimally active as citizens. In many cases they are not even expected to vote. As in the individualistic political culture, those active in politics are expected to benefit personally from their activity, although not necessarily by direct pecuniary gain.

As befitting its sectional position, Oklahoma's political culture is a synthesis of traditionalistic and individualistic elements. Its white and black populations derive their original political culture from their southern origins, whereas its Indian populations derive theirs more directly from traditional societies and fit nicely into the underlying traditionalistic base of the state's political culture. On the other hand, the western influence has sharpened the individualistic dimensions for all three groups, not to speak of those in-migrants from the middle states who came out of individualistic environments.

The result of this synthesis in Oklahoma is a kind of populism with traditionalistic overtones in which the average citizen holds political participation to be reasonably important and valuable while accepting the "right" of certain families to play leading roles in the political process. As in other states with strong traditionalistic dimensions, Oklahoma's public services tend to be underfunded and its politics conservative. The individualistic strain has also added a fair measure of endemic corruption. The almost one-party-like character of the state for many years, plus the strength of the Baptist church and its traditionalistic approach to issues of personal morality, stand out as part of the state's political culture.

SUMMING UP

Oklahoma's image is compounded of Indians, land rushes, oil booms, the Dust Bowl, and "Oklahoma"—that all-time most popular American musical. All of these celebrate the old Oklahoma. Yet today Oklahoma is changing far beyond what its image suggests. At the fringes of the sunbelt (once again Oklahoma is marginal), Oklahoma has benefited from the economic growth, industrialization, and in-migration characteristic of sunbelt states.

Its traditional links to the Democratic party and the Baptist church have been greatly undermined. While remaining Democratic in its counties and in the less visible state offices, in presidential, gubernatorial, and senatorial elections Oklahoma has been more Republican than the rest of the country. Moreover, in the past two decades the state has abandoned the traditional public morality of the Baptist church to become more individualistic and wide open in its public policy, whether with regard to liquor or gambling or any of the other conventional "sins."

What is consistent about Oklahoma is its populism and overall agrarian orientation. Despite its peoples' conservatism in other areas, it has continually rejected the enactment of "right-to-work" legislation, and though two-thirds of its population today is urban or metropolitan, a high percentage of people live in rural areas and a general agrarian outlook prevails in the state's ethos. This agrometropolitanism is ideally suited to the rurban frontier, and Oklahoma may very well come into its own as the new frontier envelops it.

Authors' Preface

The American states display considerable variation in historical development, socioeconomic characteristics, and political orientations. Thus, although together the fifty states define the American republic, individually
they are diverse political societies and laboratories. Unity with diversity is,
of course, one of the principle features of our federal system.

This book is about the forty-sixth state to join the Union, in 1907—Oklahoma. Our purpose is to provide a reasonably comprehensive overview of
the people, politics, and policies of the state. Surprisingly, such a book on
Oklahoma government does not already exist. Thus *Oklahoma Politics and
Policies* fills a gap in the literature.

The book was written for three audiences. First, the general citizenry
should find the volume helpful in gaining a better understanding of Oklahoma political traditions, institutions, and practices. Second, political scientists should find the book useful both as a teaching aid and as a general source
of information. The book is more than another brief descriptive account of
the government and politics of Oklahoma. In the first chapter we establish
general themes, using Daniel J. Elazar's well-known theory of state political
cultures as a foundation, and then proceed to build on these themes in an in-
tegrated fashion. Finally, students should find the book readable, informa-
tive, and, we hope, even enjoyable.

Debts are incurred in any endeavor of this type. We would like to thank
the following people for their participation and assistance. Professor Danny
Adkison of the political science department at Oklahoma State University,
wrote chapter 5. James J. Lawler and Robert L. Spurrier, Jr., contributed
chapter 8; both are professors of political science at Oklahoma State Univer-

sity. Fred E. Schnarre assisted in drafting chapter 13. Fred recently completed his master's degree in political science at Oklahoma State University. Frosty Troy, founder and general editor of the *Oklahoma Observer,* generously granted us permission to quote freely from articles in this paper. Attorney General Robert Henry, a student of Oklahoma politics and history and himself an example of the type of political leader who has helped improve the state's political system, offered us the benefit of his criticisms of the draft manuscript and agreed to write a foreword.

Special thanks go to John Kincaid, general editor, and Daniel J. Elazar, founding editor of the Politics and Governments of the American States series, for their comments and suggestions on drafts of the manuscript which improved the quality of the final book. We furthermore want to recognize Kathy Hoffman at Oklahoma State University for her efforts in making our last changes in the final draft. Of course, we assume full responsibility for any mistakes or omissions.

PART I

The State as a Polity

CHAPTER ONE

The Character of the State

Oklahoma remains a paradox—a state struggling with its sense of identity, a place where the old and the new vie for the attention and allegiance of its people. In some ways it is still backward and traditional; in other ways, quite modern and up-to-date. This clash between traditional and modern values is captured well by two unrelated events that occurred in the late 1980s.

In early 1987 Oral Roberts, dean of the television evangelists, who claims to heal illnesses with the laying on of hands, made a startling announcement. Speaking from the Tulsa campus of the university that bears his name, Roberts proclaimed that God was going to "call him home" if he did not raise some $8 million to save his faltering ministry. Donations poured in as believers responded to his plea. In the meantime, Johnny Carson loved it all. Repeated references to Roberts and his talks with God from his campus prayer tower elicited guffaws at the expense of the presumably unsophisticated Okies who responded to Roberts' call for contributions. The city of Tulsa, the self-proclaimed oil capital of the world, saw itself held up to ridicule. Many Oklahomans squirmed uncomfortably; once again the state was embarrassed by the antics of someone depicted by the national media as representing the redneck, backward, unenlightened image the state has fought so hard to escape.

A little more than a year later the front-page headline of the state's largest newspaper, the *Daily Oklahoman,* trumpeted, "Remington Park Enjoys Gala Debut."[1] Below the headlines was a color picture of the horses breaking from the gate for the first race at the new, ultramodern racetrack built by Ohio billionaire Edward DeBartolo, whose family owns several professional sports franchises and large shopping centers around the country. Oklahoma governor Henry Bellmon was there, pictured alongside the paper's publisher, Edward L. Gaylord. Over the months preceding the track's opening the public was treated to descriptions of the elegant luxury suites equipped with well-stocked bars and the latest electronic gadgets. The Oklahoma City paper rarely failed to mention the wonderful economic benefits the $93 million track would bring to the oil-depressed state. All this coverage came from one of the most conservative newspapers in the country—a paper that for years refused to carry any liquor ads, that rejected ads for the controversial movie "The Last Temptation of Christ," and that constantly sermonizes about welfare cheats and boondoggling politicians. In the name of economic development, however, gambling—in the form of pari-mutuel betting—gets front-page support.

Perhaps more than most other states, Oklahoma struggles to reconcile its traditional rural past with the demands of a postindustrial service economy. Partly for this reason the state's image is not well defined. To some, from the East Coast perhaps, Oklahoma might call to mind a land of open spaces, where cowboys ride the range and Indians live in tepees. Although that is no longer an accurate picture, the state still bears the marks of an early frontier area given over to American Indian tribes in the first part of the nineteenth century. But the Oklahoma of today is far different from the Oklahoma at statehood in 1907. The state has undergone a significant metamorphosis, a change made more noticeable because of the relative newness of Oklahoma's statehood. This change has not come easily. In fact, the underlying theme of this book is Oklahoma's transitional character and the tension and conflicts that have come with the struggle to emerge from a traditional rural background into a more modern progressive state.

Comparatively speaking, Oklahoma is a young state; in 1907 it became the forty-sixth state to join the Union. Unlike most other states, Oklahoma has had only limited time to mature, develop, and assimilate into today's global environment; it has had a lot of catching up to do. The changes brought by this compressed developmental process have been particularly hard to achieve because of the state's dominant traditionalistic political culture. Such a political value system is especially resistant to change; it places a premium on "business as usual."

One of the state's most prominent contemporary figures,[2] Edward L. Gaylord, publisher of Oklahoma City's *Daily Oklahoman,* exemplifies the paradox that is modern Oklahoma. The richest and arguably the most powerful person in the state, billionaire Gaylord has been an extraordinarily shrewd and successful business leader. Owner of a chain of radio and television stations around the country, the Grand Ole Opry and Opryland in Nashville, Tennessee, and one of Colorado's most prestigious grand hotels, the Broadmoor, he also holds one-third of the Texas Rangers American League baseball team.

Despite his obvious achievements in the world of communication and commerce, Gaylord is probably the most controversial person in Oklahoma. Part of the contention surrounding the publisher, born in 1919, stems from his ultraconservative political views and his eagerness to skewer his political foes with blistering front-page editorials. Generally opposed to tax increases at any level of government, Gaylord repeatedly assailed members of the Oklahoma legislature for raising taxes to maintain state services during the economic downturn of the early and mid-1980s. The sizable amount of "pork-barrel" spending by the legislature at the end of the 1988 session especially drew his ire. In front-page editorials calling lawmakers crooks and clowns, he urged readers to defeat incumbent legislators. The most scathing criticism of all was aimed at the house Democratic leadership. In a Sunday front-page blast he called the Speaker of the house, Muskogee's Jim Barker, an "arrogant, small-minded, petty demagogue." "Barker and his cronies are a disgrace," he complained.

Notwithstanding his extraordinary business success, in other ways Gaylord symbolizes traditional Oklahoma. His roots lie deep in the history of the Sooner State. His father, E. K. Gaylord, published the *Daily Oklahoman* for more than sixty years until his death in 1974 at the age of 101. E. K. was every bit as conservative and powerful as his son, who labored in his father's shadow for decades. The Gaylords have dominated Oklahoma City. In recent years, however, younger business leaders have challenged Gaylord's preeminence. For example, in 1987 some members of the Oklahoma City Chamber of Commerce broke with Gaylord over the need for tax increases. In addition, the chamber has not always endorsed the publisher's general opposition to increased funding for common and higher education in Oklahoma.

Nonetheless, Gaylord actively pushes economic development in the state. For years he has headed the Oklahoma Industries Authority (OIA), a county public trust that issues bonds to finance various public and private development projects. Even his stewardship of that agency has been controversial. Frosty Troy, the editor of the *Oklahoma Observer* and Gaylord's most outspoken media critic, periodically accuses Gaylord of using OIA to further his own economic interests and to reward his wealthy associates. Yet when proposals appear on the ballot to create new mechanisms to promote the state's economy, they usually draw Gaylord's support. In the very issue of the paper in which he lambasted Speaker Barker, Gaylord endorsed two state referendum measures designed to further economic growth. Both were authored by the Speaker and supported by the Democratic leadership in both houses of the legislature.

Perhaps the most curious and paradoxical side of Gaylord appears in his continuous and prominent support for Oklahoma Christian College (occ), a small, conservative, four-year school north of Oklahoma City. Affiliated with the fundamentalist Church of Christ, occ has a long history of promoting various events to foster citizenship, promote patriotism, and boost the capitalist economic system. The college's two most visible appendages are Enterprise Square, a museum devoted to extolling the virtues of large-scale capitalism, and the American Citizenship Center, sponsor of an annual Oklahoma Youth Freedom Forum at which various conservative political and military leaders speak.

The institution owes an enormous debt of gratitude to Gaylord. For example, in September 1988 a $7 million engineering center was dedicated at occ. The guest speaker at a luncheon ceremony held at the Gaylord College Activity Center was Laurence C. Seifert, vice-president of AT&T. Funding for the engineering center came from occ's $50 million fundraising campaign headed by Gaylord himself. Donors to the center included the AT&T Foundation, the Kresge Foundation, and three of the largest foundations in Oklahoma—the Mabee Foundation of Tulsa, the Merrick Foundation of Ardmore, and the Samuel Robert Noble Foundation of Ardmore. All of them have given to other private and public institutions of higher education in Oklahoma. But one cannot help wondering how much support these foundations otherwise might give to a small, undistinguished, fundamentalist college without Gaylord leading the way. But this highly successful business tycoon has chosen Oklahoma Christian College, an institution vigorously clinging to traditionalistic religious beliefs and conservative economic values, over the University of Oklahoma or Oklahoma State University, the state's two public, comprehensive universities, which are struggling to upgrade their research facilities at a time when the state's economy is very tight.

COMPETING IMAGES

Some people contend that Oklahoma is "one of those states without any intense sense of place in national thinking."[3] It is a state of competing images. Consider, for example, various regional designations. The U.S. Bureau of the Census classifies the state as southern. Oklahoma's social, economic, and political characteristics are indeed similar to those found in the southern states to its east. Oklahoma is sometimes referred to as a "border state," partly because of its geographical proximity to the Deep South, but also because Oklahoma Indian tribes split their loyalties between the North and South during the Civil War. Civil rights scholars often label Oklahoma as a border state because it was not a part of the Confederacy, although Indian Territory was represented in the Confederate Congress. Like southern states, however, Oklahoma did adopt laws that discriminated against blacks (e.g., separate schools for black and white children). For others, Oklahoma is part of "Middle America," a plains state inhabited by a people who epitomize the traditional American virtues of family, church, and independence.[4] Finally, Kirkpatrick Sale[5] and others (see below) contend that Oklahoma is in transition. Sale, for instance, includes Oklahoma as part of the contemporary "power shift" from the eastern establishment to the newly emerging economically and politically powerful sunbelt.

Other competing images of the land, people, and politics of the state are readily available.[6] A small sample of images might include (1) the oil-rich state that lies north of "the" state of Texas; (2) an underdeveloped, capital-poor, almost backward state that has not yet fully emerged from the rugged individualism of the cowboy and Indian era and "Okie" out-migration of the Dust Bowl; (3) a state of rural scenic beauty blessed with abundant resources strategically located and "ripe" for extensive economic development; (4) a state that seems afflicted by a "boom and bust" economy; (5) a state noted for its friendly but backward people; and (6) a state where political corruption is all too often evident, where politics is conservative, and where public services are poorly funded. Individually, a factual base supports all these images; each represents a "slice" of Oklahoma's past, present, and future. Collectively, the images underscore two major themes that help define the character of the state—traditionalism and transition.

THE CHARACTER OF THE STATE: A TRADITIONAL VIEW

Historical, social, economic, and demographic characteristics of a state help shape its political outlook and behavior. Daniel Elazar, one of the nation's foremost authorities on state politics, asserts that such factors help explain the presence of "political subcultures" among the states.[7] Political culture may be defined as "the collective orientation of people toward the basic elements in their political system."[8] According to Elazar, Oklahoma's political culture is primarily "traditionalistic" but with a strong "individualistic" strain.

The perspective of political culture assumes that the habits, attitudes, and values of the people play a major part in shaping the scope and behavior of public institutions. A state's political culture thus helps to define (1) the structure and functioning of government institutions, (2) the orientations and behavior of political leaders, and (3) public policies made in the name of the people. Clearly, a warning is in order. Elazar's typology of state political cultures is intended to facilitate explanation. As with any theory or generalization, anomalies can be found. With this caveat in mind, we now turn to a discussion of Oklahoma's prevailing political culture.

Characteristics of Oklahoma's Political Culture

As Elazar explains, the traditionalistic political culture, which is generally characteristic of the South, "retains some of the organic characteristics of the preindustrial social order." From such a perspective, "good government" involves "the maintenance and encouragement of traditional patterns and, if necessary, their adjustment to changing conditions with the least possible change. . . . Political leaders play conservative and custodial rather than initiatory roles unless they are pressed strongly from the outside."[9] A single political party usually dominates state politics, but party unity is weak, politics are personal and factional, and politicians often become celebrities.

Although it is not dominant, Elazar suggests that a strong strain of the individualistic political culture typifies Oklahoma, a political orientation generally characteristic of the middle states. This cultural variation, most noticeable in the northwest section of the state, places a premium on limiting government intervention in the marketplace, tolerates a fair amount of political corruption, and manifests an ambivalence about the place of bureaucracy in the political order. "The individualistic political culture holds politics to be just another means by which individuals may improve themselves socially and economically." In short, politics is viewed as a business, and political parties serve as "business corporations." Because the party system is competitive, party unity is more important than in the traditionalistic political culture. Nevertheless, "politicians are interested in office as a means of controlling the distribution of the favors or rewards of government rather than as a means of exercising governmental power for programmatic ends"[10] (e.g., pork-barrel and patronage politics).

No doubt, Oklahoma reflects much of the traditionalistic and individualistic political cultures. Few would disagree, for example, that (1) Oklahoma's organic roots are still quite conspicuous; (2) institutional change comes slowly and usually only after much debate, political conflict, or pressure from the federal government; (3) politics in the state is characteristic of a "southern-style" conservatism; (4) governments, particularly local units, often perform caretaker roles; (5) one party has dominated the halls of the state capitol since 1907; (6) historically, party unity has been less important to legislators than taking care of the needs of constituents back home; (7) the state has experienced its share of political corruption throughout its history; and (8) funding for many public services and the salaries paid to public servants fall below national averages—indicators of both fiscal conservatism as well as an ambivalence about the role of bureaucracy in state affairs. In brief, Elazar's classification of Oklahoma's political culture seems appropriate. Four questions remain unanswered, however. What influences helped shape the political culture of the state? What are the social, economic, and political consequences of traditionalism? Is traditional Oklahoma changing? What happens when folkways collide with the forces of change?

Influences Affecting Oklahoma's Political Culture

Two key and related influences have helped shape the state's political culture and have affected the public's perceptions about the proper role of government: the land and spatial living patterns.

The Land. The first and perhaps the most salient influence that helps define the traditionalistic political culture in Oklahoma is the state's organic roots—that is, the land. As H. Wayne Morgan and Anne Hodges Morgan aptly remind us, "The importance of land, man's hunger for it, his attitudes toward it, his use and abuse of it, [have] dominated Oklahoma history [and politics]."[11] Here we might note that Oklahoma's land size is often underestimated because the state is dwarfed by Texas to the south. In fact, Oklahoma is the eighteenth largest state, larger than any state east of the Mississippi River and larger than all of New England.

Oklahoma can be viewed as a geographic transition zone. Geographers have variously labeled it "as the most northerly of the southern states; as the most southerly of the northern states; as a part of the southwest; as a middle western state; and as a border state."[12] Although noted Oklahoma historian Arrell M. Gibson agrees that all of these designations apply to some degree, he argues that a more appropriate way of classifying the geography and climate of the state is as a "zone of transition."[13]

As an inland state, Oklahoma is bounded by six other states: Kansas and Colorado on the north, Missouri and Arkansas on the east, Texas on the south and west, and New Mexico on the west. The elevation of the state ranges from 5,000 feet above sea level at Black Mesa, in the extreme northwestern corner of the Panhandle, to 325 feet in the southeastern corner of the state, on the Red River.

Oklahoma is famous for abrupt climatic changes. Or, as the saying goes, if you don't like Oklahoma's weather, wait a minute and it will change. As a result of its location, warm and cold air masses collide in Oklahoma to spawn sudden and often dramatic temperature changes, violent thunderstorms, and life-threatening tornadoes. Horizontal and vertical climatic zone designations for the state include a humid belt in the south and east and a colder north and dry west. The northwestern section of Oklahoma is particularly arid and often bitterly cold in the winter. As part of the Great Plains, western Oklahoma receives a steady airflow primarily from the south. Nevertheless, a day without wind is rare anywhere in the state.

For those who have not visited or traveled the state, Oklahoma's image is probably that of a plains state where the land is flat and barren, the weather is dry and hot, and flora and fauna are sparse and uninteresting. This image is incorrect. As the eastern forests of Oklahoma blend into the grassy prairies and plains of central and western Oklahoma, one can find more than 130 different varieties of native trees, a number of types of grasses, "every species of bird found in the area extending from the Mississippi Valley to the Rocky Mountains," and wildlife (even alligators) and fish enough to make Oklahoma a haven for any naturalist. Moreover, an abundance of rivers and lakes, along with low mountain ranges, dispels the image that the Sooner State is dry and flat. In short, images often do not coincide with realities. Oklahoma is best viewed as a transition zone; it is a unique microcosm of those landforms, climatic conditions, and plants and animals found in surrounding states.[14]

Eastern and especially southern parts of Oklahoma were settled primarily by people from the southern states. These settlers brought with them the attitudes and values associated with the traditional agrarian political culture of the South. However, the topography, lack of rich topsoil, and shortage of capital hampered the development of an agricultural economy based on the plantation model. Instead, small homesteads became the norm. Little money was to be made, and times were often hard. So the economic conditions associated with subsistence farming tended to reinforce the Democratic political leaning these people brought with them from their native southern states. Even today the southeastern portion of the state, often called "Little Dixie," remains heavily Democratic in its voting behavior.

The land did hold other resources that would prove essential to the economic development of the state. Beneath the surface were valuable minerals—in particular, coal, oil, and natural gas. In fact, ever since the drilling of Number One Nellie Johnstone in the Bartlesville field in 1897, petroleum-related production has been a mainstay of Oklahoma's economy. On top of the surface was water. After World War II, Robert S. Kerr, Oklahoma's twelfth governor and a U.S. senator, would use water resources to help provide for future economic development and ensure the long-term stability of the agricultural economy.[15]

Finally, the land has served as the springboard for other events that have affected state politics. Shortly after the turn of the century, for instance, ties to the land by poor Oklahoma farmers served as the basis for one of the strongest state Socialist movements in the history of the United States. Drought, erosion, and misuse of the land resulted in the Dust Bowl of the 1930s and a mass exodus of Oklahomans. Although the Socialist movement in Oklahoma was short-lived and now long forgotten by most Sooners, the impact of the Dust Bowl and the denigrating "Okie" label given to state migrants are still very much a part of Oklahoma's image.

Spatial Living Patterns. A second major influence that helps explain Oklahoma's political culture, spatial living patterns, is basically a product of the state's agrarian origin. Oklahoma retains many of its original ties to the land; the state's rural, frontier, preindustrial character is still very much evident. The landscape is dotted with small family-owned farms and with communities centered around and heavily reliant on agribusiness. As a percentage of the total population, the state's farm population ranks fourteenth nationally.[16] Even today, much of Oklahoma might be viewed as a collectivity of pre-urban, agriculturally based communities. The state contains only two large cities: Oklahoma City (with about 446,000 people) and Tulsa (population about 375,000). Of the remaining 579 municipalities, only fourteen have 25,000 or more residents.

Ties to the land plus dispersed, low-density settlement patterns helped to create a social, economic, and political environment that has had a lasting impact on the state. Clarence Stone and his associates use the phrase "village politics" to capture the essence of this environment.[17] Small communities in Oklahoma, much like the general population itself, tend to be homogeneous and stable. Diversity and conflict are avoided as much as possible, and politics is a matter of trying to achieve consensus. The towns are socially conservative, with moral behavior regulated through the church and the school system. Political and social relationships are personal, and because everyone knows everyone else (and their personal affairs), social/moral regulation is not hard to enforce. Government is limited to caretaker duties. Fiscal conservatism, both private and public, follows naturally. Tax burdens are low; as a result, public facilities are modest and public services are minimal.

Before moving beyond the discussion of political culture, let us discuss briefly one other cultural feature of the state, one that appears in various forms—populism. In some ways, populism, defined here as a commitment to enlarging the economic and political power of ordinary people as opposed to the wealthy, represents the flip side of traditionalism. Both have strong southern ties. Near the end of the nineteenth century, economic hardship among many of the nation's small farmers led to a series of agrarian protests, out of which the populist movement emerged. For more than twenty years, populism played a significant part in the politics of many midwestern and southern states. By the early part of this century, however, southern populists had come under the influence of several redneck demagogues, such as Tom Watson and Pitchfork Ben Tillman, who helped turn the movement away from its more egalitarian roots to a preoccupation with "keeping blacks in their place." Still, suspicions of eastern banks, large corporations, railroads, and high-tariff Republicans hardly abated. A prominent anti-intellectual strain ran through much populist thinking as well.

As settlers from the southern states moved westward to occupy the Oklahoma and Indian territories, they brought their populist sentiments with them. The state's constitution stands as the most obvious early manifestation of populist influence in Oklahoma politics. It is a lengthy document replete with restrictions on railroads and large corporations, whose avaricious practices were thought to be a continuing threat to the economic well-being of common folks. The state's populist heritage appears in other ways, as the following example from higher education suggests.

Over the years, the Sooner State struggled to ensure that the sons and daughters of ordinary people—oil-field workers and farmhands—had access to higher education. Today, with twenty-six state institutions of higher education within its borders, Oklahoma manifests a continuing commitment to the populist ideal of making a college education available to its citizenry, and at bargain-basement prices—tuition at state colleges and universities remains relatively low compared to that of similar institutions around the country. Yet the state still does not have a first-class research university. The trade-off, at least implicitly, is obvious: quantity over quality. The lack of interest in creating top-notch universities is more than historical, however; it also stems from the economic lessons of the oil patch. "The commitment to academic life is basically not part of our culture," concedes Paul Sharp, former president of the University of Oklahoma. "You didn't have to have an education in Oklahoma to stick a hole in the ground and make a fortune. Prosperity was never associated with education."[18]

At least since 1982, when the bottom fell out of the oil market, Oklahomans have started to rethink their priorities. As state government specialist Alan Ehrenhalt put it, "In the past five years, Oklahoma has been wooing businesses worldwide, and has found them less interested in the university's football team than in the quality of its physics department."[19] In 1988 the state regents for higher education announced a change in the formula for higher education funding, to deemphasize enrollment. Under the new system, each school would be compared with similar institutions around the country. New funds would then be distributed to help any campus that fared poorly in this peer comparison. The first year's clear winners were the University of Oklahoma and Oklahoma State University, the only comprehensive state institutions. Such a change in funding arrangements predictably upset the leadership both of the junior colleges and of the other four year schools, along with their state legislators. As a result, the following year the regents' staff introduced a new group of peer institutions for each category of school. The outcome: 1989 funding for higher education looked much like the old division of funds among institutional types. Leaders of the noncomprehensive schools announced they were pleased with the outcome. In such a battle between the elites and the populists, history, of course, is on the side of the populists. Yet the changing economic character of the state may give those who want high-quality major universities a fighting chance. As the old cliché goes, only time will tell.

What does all of this discussion of political culture mean for understanding Oklahoma government and politics? To answer this question, we first examine the social and economic implications associated with traditional Oklahoma and then provide some examples to illustrate the intersection of politics and political culture.

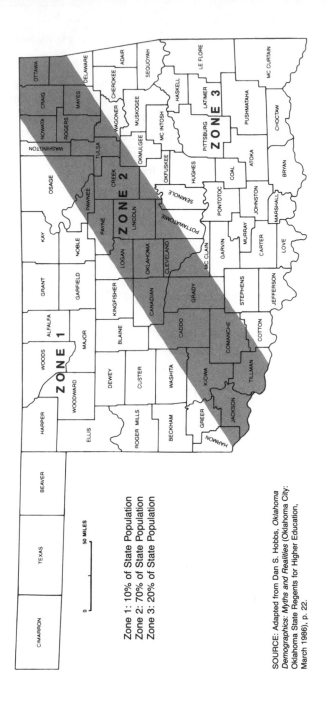

Zone 1: 10% of State Population
Zone 2: 70% of State Population
Zone 3: 20% of State Population

SOURCE: Adapted from Dan S. Hobbs, *Oklahoma Demographics: Myths and Realities* (Oklahoma City: Oklahoma State Regents for Higher Education, March 1986), p. 22.

Map 1. Oklahoma's Predominant Urban Population Corridor

Implications of Oklahoma's Political Culture

Social and Economic Implications. Historical ties to the land and spatial living arrangements carry with them long-lasting social and economic consequences. For example, Oklahoma ranks twenty-eighth among the states in total population (approximately 3.2 million residents) and twenty-sixth in percentage of population living in rural areas (33%).[20] In land area Oklahoma remains primarily a rural state. About 70 percent of the population lives in a diagonal corridor about thirty miles wide extending from Miami in the northeast to Lawton in the southwest (map 1).

Racial, ethnic, and religious differences in the state are minimal, compared to those in many other states. Thus, few demographic forces challenge the homogeneity and social conservatism of village politics. About 86 percent of the population is white (6.7% black, 1.9% Hispanic). Oklahoma does contain, however, the second largest number of Native Americans of any state in the nation, 5.6 percent of the state's population and 11.9 percent of the nation's Indian population.[21] A census of religious affiliations taken in 1971 documents one source of Oklahoma's social conservatism. About 33 percent of the state's population can be classified as Protestant fundamentalist, one of the highest percentages of any state in the Union.[22]

Given its agrarian base and few big cities, Oklahoma is not heavily industrialized, highly unionized, or wealthy. Only about 13 percent of the non-agricultural labor force is employed in manufacturing, and only about 13 percent belong to a union (37th in the nation).[23] In addition, the underdeveloped economic base of the state, combined with a low percentage of high-school graduates (72.6%; 30th rank nationally), a high percentage of persons aged sixty-five years or older (12.8%; 19th rank nationally), and an agricultural economy in which the annual value of products sold by about 60 percent of the farms is less than ten thousand dollars,[24] has not produced a prosperous citizenry. Despite the relatively large number of wealthy individuals created by the oil and gas industry, Oklahoma ranks thirty-eighth among the states in per capita personal income, and only twelve states have a higher percentage of persons living in poverty.[25] Also, like states in the deep South where the traditionalistic political culture prevails, personal income in Oklahoma is maldistributed. In 1970, the most recent year for which data are available, Oklahoma ranked ninth in the nation in income concentration or inequality among its populace.[26]

In sum, the long-term legacy of traditionalism, coupled with the state's socioeconomic base, produces a lack of heterogeneity, urbanization, industrialization, and wealth.

Political Implications. If Oklahoma's political culture contributes to social conservatism, there should be a connection between religion and politics. Research by David Morgan and Kenneth Meier suggests such a link.[27] They sought to assess the impact of religion on the passage of five state questions on moral issues occurring between 1959 and 1976: repeal of Prohibition, Sunday closing, two liquor-by-the-drink measures, and pari-mutuel betting. On the three liquor issues and the horse-betting vote, the higher the percentage of fundamentalist and "other Protestant" residents in the county, the more likely the county voted dry and against pari-mutuel betting. Moreover, only the Prohibition repeal passed, and that occurred in a special statewide election. After some years the other issues passed, the implications of which we turn to later.

Historically, one political party—the Democrats—and rural interests controlled Oklahoma's statehouse. As a result, according to political historian Stephen Jones, "Oklahoma is a state in which the influence of pressure politics and local issues is greater than party cohesion or national issues."[28] For many years powerful interest groups such as agriculture, oil, and the Baptist church played a prominent role in state affairs. Because interparty competition was weak, legislators could concentrate on delivering the "pork" back home. Given the subsistence nature of much of the state's agricultural economy and the depressed character of many of the communities dependent on agriculture, state assistance programs required stability and generosity. This legacy of legislative responsiveness to the needs of rural constituents in the state remains conspicuous today. At the time the federal Supplemental Security Income program replaced state-operated old-age assistance, Oklahoma ranked second in the nation in average monthly payments for old-age assistance.[29] And until 1987, two cents of the state sales tax (now four and one-half cents) was earmarked for the state's welfare agency.

Finally, another way to show the impact of the traditionalistic political culture and its accompanying fiscal conservatism is to look at state and local funding of public services and salaries paid to civil servants. Compared to other states, Oklahoma ranks thirty-ninth in 1988 state and local expenditures per capita, forty-fourth in 1988 expenditures for public elementary and secondary schools per pupil, thirty-ninth in 1988 per capita state and local spending on police protection, and thirty-second in 1988 per capita state and local spending on highways.[30] In 1987 the average wages paid to full-time state employees and local employees in Oklahoma ranked forty-third nationally. Average salaries of public school teachers in 1988 ranked forty-fourth among the states.[31]

A traditionalistic political culture has left Oklahoma with serious problems. But political culture is not immutable. As popular preferences, attitudes, and values change, so do the state's political culture and the people's expectations of government. Ample evidence suggests that Oklahoma is in a period of social, economic, and political transition.

THE CHARACTER OF THE STATE: A TRANSITIONAL PERSPECTIVE

After tracing the history of the state's development, historian Jerome Steffen concluded that like other states in the Southwest, "Oklahoma is on the verge of experiencing a major growth period."[32] The boom period of the early 1980s brought a large net migration to the state. When oil prices collapsed in 1983 and Oklahoma's economy floundered, however, that growth slowed considerably. Oklahoma's percentage of population increase from 1980 to 1988 was 7.2, slightly lower than the U.S. average. The Census Bureau projects only a 3 percent population growth for the state between 1990 and the year 2000 (32nd rank nationally).[33] Despite recent economic problems, the state's industrial base has expanded in the 1980s; in 1987 about 13 percent of nonagricultural employment was in manufacturing, compared to a figure of around 10 percent in 1950.[34] The economic downturn associated with the drop in energy prices along with the sluggish agricultural economy of the 1980s has created a renewed sense of urgency among state leaders regarding the need for economic diversification.

Historian Douglas Hale's message is similar to Steffen's: transitional Oklahoma is much different from traditional Oklahoma. After highlighting three previous phases of development, Hale contends that the state is now in an "age of resurgence." This era began in the 1950s, following the turmoil years of the Dust Bowl and "Okie" out-migration. According to Hale:

> The primary thrust for this expansion was provided by the long delayed emergence of a substantial manufacturing industry and the increasing influence of the governmental sector of the economy. By 1980 manufacturing contributed more to the gross state product than any other enterprise. In the process of growth it [Oklahoma] diversified. No longer concentrated in the processing of primary products like food and petroleum, the state has shifted into the high-income production of machinery, electronic equipment, and fabricated metals.[35]

In addition to the increased importance of the manufacturing and government sectors, other parts of the state's economy have been growing. Services, for example, accounted for 12 percent of earnings in 1960; by the late 1980s, services generated about 20 percent of state earnings.[36]

Hale maintains that the state has changed in other ways, too. The development of the state's lakes for leisure activities has boosted the economy, made Oklahoma a popular recreation site, and drawn people to the state for retirement. Disparities in income among sections of the state have decreased, particularly between those living in the northwest (the haves) and those living in the east (the have-nots). Oklahoma's blacks and American Indians have achieved notable gains in recent years. In comparison to most states in the South, for example, schools in Oklahoma were desegregated with relative calm. Finally, the state's educational system has made significant strides forward.[37] This list of changes is not exhaustive; nevertheless, the message should be clear—Oklahoma has changed and still is changing.

A CLASH OF VALUES

In recent decades population migration into Oklahoma, urbanization, and changing economic patterns have brought a new heterogeneity to a once primarily agrarian state. Associated with heterogeneity, of course, is diversity of opinion. What happens when traditional Oklahoma collides with the forces of change? The answer is obvious—conflict. Consider the events that transpired in Catoosa a few years back.[38]

Catoosa is a community of about thirty-six hundred people located northeast of Tulsa. In late 1982 the city was embroiled in a bitter fight over whether to change from the strong-mayor to the council-manager form of city government and whether to reduce Mayor Curtis Conley, a garage mechanic, to the status of council member. Reporters Linda Martin and Rob Kerby, of the *Tulsa World,* viewed the battle from a different perspective. The title of their article was "Old-Timers vs. Newcomers." As they explain, "on most issues, the council is divided along clear lines: longtime high school-educated Catoosans who live in small homes and work at blue-collar jobs versus college-educated newcomers who live in high-dollar homes and work in white-collar professions. Two of the newcomers own large, prestigious businesses." The newcomers advocated the change to a more professionalized city manager to run city affairs. They claimed that Conley "was not qualified to set the $1 million-plus budget." The "Old Guard" faction of the city noted, however, "that nobody knows what's better for Catoosans than Catoosans, who they said needed no help from outsiders to administer the city's money."

The political controversy spread to other issues, which also illustrate characteristics of village politics and Oklahoma's traditionalistic political culture. For example, half the town wanted to deannex itself to avoid paying higher taxes. Opinions differed over whether the city should use hundreds of thousands of dollars of surplus city funds to renovate the decaying and over-loaded sewer system and repair local streets. Finally, debate raged over the issue of spending $180,000 raised over ten years to buy an impressive, aerial snorkel fire truck.

Although the "newcomers" lost their drive to change the form of city government (in a special election), controversy continued. The "oldtimers are fond of saying the newcomers are 'educated idiots' who are dedicatedly destroying a once placid community."

CONCLUSION

Russell L. Hanson concludes that migration into sunbelt states "could trans-form their political institutions and policies."[39] The past few decades have indeed brought many social, economic, and demographic changes to Okla-homa. In the chapters to follow, we examine the links between these changes and politics in the Sooner State. Two related themes underlie these chapters: (1) transitional Oklahoma is much different from traditional Oklahoma, and (2) the politics, political institutions, and socioeconomic base of the state are in the process of transformation. Whether this transformation carries with it positive or negative connotations depends on one's value system. Regard-less of one's perspective, however, socioeconomic and political conflict is inevitable, as traditionalism collides with change and as new images of Oklahoma emerge.

CHAPTER TWO

Oklahoma in the Federal System

Although collectively the American states and the District of Columbia define the United States, individually each of the fifty states is a polity. Every state, for example, has well-defined boundaries (i.e., territory), people, and sovereignty—essential features of a polity. Each state has its own unique history and development, constitution, political institutions and processes, and customs and mores, which, as we argued in the previous chapter, are shaped by prevailing political subcultures. In reality, however, the American states are not free to pursue any and all actions or policies they desire; they are only semi-sovereign polities. Why? Because each state is part of the larger republic and must operate within the boundaries of the U.S. federal system.

THE NATURE AND MEANING OF FEDERALISM

With a federal system we have diversity; without diversity, there is no choice; without choice, there is no freedom . . . the great glory of the federal system is that some damn fool at the top can't ruin it.[1]

This quotation by Frank Bane, former chairman of the U.S. Advisory Commission on Intergovernmental Relations (ACIR),[2] captures well the essence of a federal system of government. Unlike a unitary system (such as Great Britain), in which subnational jurisdictions, if they even exist, possess only those powers granted by the national government, American federalism provides for one general, or national, government and many state governments. Both are sovereign in their own spheres of authority. As further explained in chapter 12, state governments in turn are responsible for creating units of local government (e.g., towns, municipalities, counties, special districts).

Thus, federalism ensures diversity in types of governmental units, provides some measure of independence (i.e., freedom to make choices) among governmental units, and gives life to the state as a polity.

As Daniel Elazar aptly reminds us, however, federalism is not without associated costs; diversity, freedom, and choice produce conflicts. One tension is between state sovereignty and national supremacy. The concept of state sovereignty is tied to the Tenth Amendment to the U.S. Constitution. It states, "The powers not delegated to the United States by the Constitution, nor prohibited by it to the States, are reserved to the States respectively, or to the people." As Elazar notes, state sovereignty thus assumes that "in a proper federal system, authority and power over most domestic affairs should be in the hands of the states." In contrast, national supremacy assumes that "the federal government has a significant role to play in domestic matters affecting the national interest." The concept of national supremacy is also constitutionally based. Article VI states, in part, "This Constitution, and the laws of the United States which shall be made in Pursuance thereof; and all Treaties made, or which shall be made, under the Authority of the United States, shall be the supreme Law of the Land; and the Judges in every State be bound thereby, any Thing in the Constitution or Laws of any State to the Contrary notwithstanding." Historically, when state sovereignty and national supremacy have collided, the judicial system has played the role of umpire. Another perennial federalism-related tension, according to Elazar, is between dual federalism and cooperative federalism. Dual federalism is the "idea that a federal system functions best when the federal government and the states function as separately as possible, each in its own sphere." The notion of dual federalism, of course, closely parallels the concept of state sovereignty. Cooperative federalism is the "view that federalism works best when the federal government and the states, while preserving their own institutions, cooperate closely on the implementation of joint or shared programs" (see p. xviii).

The idea of cooperative federalism applies to interstate and state-local relations as well. The dynamics of federalism have evolved in the United States in such a manner that we often speak of intergovernmental relations (IGR) when referring to federalism as a process. IGR can be defined as "an important body of activities or interactions occurring between governmental units of all types and levels within the [United States] federal system."[3] With more than eighty-two thousand governmental jurisdictions in the United States and about eighteen hundred units in Oklahoma alone, the range of activities and interactions involving federal, state, and local governments is quite broad, diverse, and often complex. Moreover, as intimated above and as the Oklahoma-related IGR examples below illustrate, intergovernmental relations can be either cooperative or conflictual in nature.

IGR as Cooperation

Oklahoma governor Henry Bellmon and Texas governor Bill Clements meet atop Lake Texoma Dam to sign a contract for the construction of a new bridge over the Red River. The cost of the bridge that links Oklahoma and Texas will be split between the two states.[4]

On July 1, 1987, Oklahoma joins forty-three other states in the Non-Resident Violator Compact (NRVC). This interstate compact facilitates the collection of monies owed state and local governments for misdemeanor violations of traffic laws. Violators may sign their traffic citations and be released without cash bond on the promise to appear as provided for on the citation. If violators fail to respond to the citations, their driver's licenses are suspended in the NRVC state until the citations are acted on.[5]

IGR as Conflict

Arkansas senator Dale Bumpers persuades the Senate Appropriations Committee not to approve the $11.8 million the Navy requested to build facilities at Oklahoma's Tinker Air Force Base for a fleet of communication aircraft. Reportedly, John Lehmann, Jr., former secretary of the Navy, and Donald Regan, former White House chief-of-staff, had intervened on behalf of Oklahoma Republican congressman Mickey Edwards to ensure that the Navy contract went to Oklahoma. Among other finalists for the project, however, were Little Rock Air Force Base and Blytheville Air Force Base in Arkansas. According to an aide of Bumpers, "This doesn't mean that the mission will go to Arkansas, but it certainly makes our chances better."[6]

Oklahoma attorney general Robert Henry says he will appeal, to the U.S. Supreme Court if necessary, a 1988 decision in which state officials lost their bid to stop the city of Fayetteville, Arkansas, from receiving a permit to dump sewage into tributaries of the Illinois River in northeastern Oklahoma. Governor Henry Bellmon says he supports Henry's efforts since the Illinois River flows into Lake Tenkiller, one of the clearest lakes in Oklahoma.[7]

In sum, as a concept, federalism involves both structure and process. Structurally, our federal system constitutionally provides for a national government and state governments. Local governments derive their existence and powers from state governments. As a process, federalism requires a delicate balance between states' rights and national supremacy. At times the process has been quite conflictual as states have bickered with each other and the national government over a myriad of issues. At other times state governments have engaged in cooperative intergovernmental relations with their legal offspring (i.e., local governments), each other, and the federal government to solve problems and implement programs.

FEDERALISM IN OKLAHOMA: BEFORE STATEHOOD

1803–90

The federal government's involvement in the affairs of what is today Oklahoma has been more direct and extensive than in perhaps any other state in the Union. Oklahoma was a "ward" of the federal government longer than it has been a sovereign, independent state. H. Wayne Morgan and Anne Hodges Morgan view this situation as an irony, because expectations were that Oklahoma would be among the first of the new states carved from the Louisiana Purchase of 1803; instead it was the last.[8]

Rather than conferring statehood, federal officials decided that Oklahoma would serve the nation (and satisfy the desires of whites for Indian lands) as a resettlement zone first primarily for the eastern-based Five Civilized Tribes (Cherokees, Choctaws, Seminoles, Chickasaws, and Creeks) and after the Civil War for other Indian nations as well. In the 1820s Congress set Oklahoma aside for tribal resettlement, and between 1820 and 1889 more than sixty Indian tribes were relocated there.[9]

Chapter 3 discusses the special place of Native Americans in Oklahoma history. For now we note that U.S. Indian policy "followed the British system in dealing with Indian tribes by treating each as an independent community."[10] Each tribe was self-governing, and members were subject to tribal laws, not U.S. law, and were citizens of the tribe, not of the United States. The Five Civilized Tribes, which had extensive political structures before their removal to Oklahoma, organized themselves quickly into sovereign states. Each established a written constitution modeled on those of various U.S. states but with significant modifications to accommodate tribal traditions. These separate Indian governments then entered into relations with the United States. Treaties between the federal government and tribes were negotiated in the name of the president of the United States by federal government representatives and were ratified by the U.S. Senate.

As a penalty for alliances between some Indian tribes and the Confederacy, during Reconstruction treaties between the federal government and Indian nations were declared void. The Five Civilized Tribes, which from the early 1800s to 1861 had occupied most of Oklahoma, were required to give up the western half of Indian Territory to the U.S. government. Plains tribes and other Indian groups were in turn relocated to this land. Spurred by the desire of whites for Indian lands and aided by the lobbying efforts of commercial interests and the railroads, in 1889 a small portion of land in central Indian Territory was opened to homesteaders. In 1890 Congress passed the Oklahoma Organic Act, creating Oklahoma Territory.

1890– 1907

The Organic Act stipulated that when Indian lands in western Indian Territory were opened for settlement, they automatically became part of Oklahoma Territory. The act also named Guthrie as the territorial capital and attached "No Man's Land" (the Oklahoma Panhandle) to Oklahoma Territory. About 1.5 million acres, called Greer County, located in the extreme southwestern corner of present-day Oklahoma were added to Oklahoma Territory under a decision by the U.S. Supreme Court in 1896. The Court ruled against the state of Texas by declaring that the South Fork of the Red River, not the North Fork, was the true boundary between Texas and Indian Territory.[11]

With respect to federalism, perhaps the most important event that occurred in Oklahoma Territory before statehood was the work of the Jerome Commission. The three-member commission, named after its chairman David H. Jerome, former governor of Michigan, was appointed by President Benjamin Harrison to open the rest of the western half of today's Oklahoma for homesteading. The process authorized under the Dawes Allotment Act of 1887 required the termination of common tribal ownership of land and the assignment of individual tracts of lands to Indians. Surplus reservation lands were then purchased from the tribes by the federal government and opened to homesteading. By 1906 the process was largely completed, and the western half of present Oklahoma constituted Oklahoma Territory.[12]

Beginning in 1893 the U.S. Congress took steps to ensure the demise of Indian Territory. In that year Congress rescinded the exemption of the Five Civilized Tribes from the Dawes Allotment Act of 1887. As a result, the Dawes Commission set about the task of doing away with tribal own-ership of land among the Five Civilized Tribes in Indian Territory. By 1902, leaders of all of the tribes had signed allotment agreements with the commission. In order to eliminate the perceived problem of five separate Indian governments in Indian Territory, Congress passed the Curtis Act in 1889. Under the act, "all persons in Indian Territory, Indian and non-Indian alike, were thereafter subject to federal laws and the laws of Ar-kansas."[13] Tribal courts were abolished. As private landowners, Indians transferred citizenship from their tribes to the United States government. By 1906, tribal governments' political control in Indian Territory had come to an end and so had a long legacy of direct federal government con-trol over much of Oklahoma.

FEDERALISM IN OKLAHOMA: AFTER STATEHOOD

State Sovereignty versus National Supremacy:
The Case of School Desegregation

With statehood status Oklahoma entered into a new relationship with the federal government. As citizens of an independent sovereign state, state pol-icy makers turned to the process of providing meaning to their new Progres-sive-influenced, reform-oriented state constitution (see chapter 5). The first Oklahoma legislature did adopt policies, however, that in subsequent years led to the first major direct confrontation with the federal government—Jim Crow laws.

Senate Bill 1 contained the state's "Jim Crow Code." This code provided for *de jure* (by law) segregation of blacks in public transportation, public fa-cilities, and education. In 1910 the rights of black citizens were further re-stricted when state voters approved the use of literacy tests for voting regis-tration. This requirement disfranchised many blacks because election officials could make the test as difficult as they wished. White voters were exempted from the test by a "grandfather clause."[14]

That state lawmakers established segregation laws should come as little surprise. As noted in chapter 1, Oklahoma historically has had strong ties to the South. Some members of the Five Civilized Tribes in antebellum Okla-homa, for instance, owned slaves and built plantations that emulated those of their white counterparts in the South. After the opening of the state to white settlers, a predominant migration stream was from southern states. Southerners brought to Oklahoma their traditionalistic political culture and its associated emphasis on traditional patterns of relationships, which in turn stressed a subordinate role for blacks in society.

Although the "grandfather clause" amendment to the state constitution was nullified in 1915 in *Guinn v. United States,* the battle to end *de jure* segregation in education did not end until the late 1950s. Indeed, Oklahoma was the site of several historic legal battles involving school desegregation. Rulings by the U.S. Supreme Court in two separate cases, *Sipuel v. University of Oklahoma* (1948) and *McLaurin v. Oklahoma State Regents for Higher Education* (1950), forced the desegregation of higher education in Oklahoma.

Until 1949, black students could pursue their education in the state only to the baccalaureate level and only at Langston, the black college established in territorial times.[15] Students who wished to receive professional training were provided modest out-of-state tuition grants by the state. In 1946 Ada Lois Sipuel-Fisher applied to the University of Oklahoma Law School. She was denied admission because of state statutes requiring "separate but equal" education for blacks. The U.S. Supreme Court ruled that Oklahoma either had to admit her to OU or establish a separate but equal law school for her to attend. The latter option was chosen. The state created a law school for blacks at Langston, classes were scheduled at the state capitol, and three attorneys were hired as the faculty. Sipuel-Fisher refused to enter the less-than-equal law school and again applied for admission to OU. Her admission was denied.

The battle to desegregate higher education intensified in January 1948 after the University of Oklahoma Graduate School denied admission to six blacks. In September, George W. McLaurin, one of those blacks who had been denied admission, reapplied and was once again rejected. Shortly thereafter the Federal District Court for Western Oklahoma ordered him admitted. University officials complied with the mandate, but McLaurin, who was seeking a doctorate in education, was still the victim of segregative treatment at OU. He was assigned to a special table in the cafeteria and library. In the classroom he was separated from the rest of his classmates by a wooden railing.

In the summer of 1949 the OU Graduate School admitted twenty-six more blacks. The OU Law School also accepted Sipuel-Fisher. Black and white students were still segregated, however, by classroom railings. McLaurin meanwhile took his case to the U.S. Supreme Court to protest the in-school segregation. He declared that such treatment impeded his ability to learn. In the summer of 1950 the Court ruled in favor of McLaurin; any form of segregation in *graduate study* in higher education was forbidden.

Four years later the Supreme Court, in its now historic *Brown v. Board of Education of Topeka* decision, declared separate but equal common schools to be unconstitutional. In the summer of 1955 all of higher education in Oklahoma was desegregated. Governor Raymond Gary responded positively to the Supreme Court's 1955 ruling in *Brown II* that common schools be desegregated with "all deliberate speed." He informed school district officials that state aid to their schools would be denied if federal orders to desegregate were defied. Unlike many other southern and border states with *de jure* segregation, the desegregation of public schools in Oklahoma, for the most part, proceeded with relative calm and ease. Desegregation in Oklahoma City and Tulsa, where blacks constituted a sizable proportion of the population, proceeded much more slowly. Despite these problems, Oklahoma as a whole did reasonably well in desegregating its public schools. In 1968, before the massive change in southern school desegregation, schools in the state were considered 48 percent segregated. This figure, used by federal officials in the Department of Health, Education, and Welfare, reflected the proportion of blacks attending 95 to 100 percent minority schools (including all nonwhites). By 1974, the segregation figure had dropped to about 3 percent.

In this major conflict between state sovereignty and national supremacy, Oklahoma's traditionalistic political culture finally yielded to the federal desegregation mandate. Slow in coming and incomplete in outcome, the confrontation did not, however, result in the bloodshed and open defiance of federal authority that occurred throughout much of the South.

Cooperative Federalism

Cooperative federalism has been present in Oklahoma since territorial days. In 1817, for example, at the request of settlers, the U.S. Army built its first fort in the Great Southwest   Fort Smith on the Oklahoma-Arkansas border. In 1824 Forts Gibson and Towson were constructed in Indian Territory. Originally built to protect settlers from Indians, in later years the two forts protected Indian Territory from white interlopers. Following the Civil War, additional forts (e.g., Fort Sill, Fort Supply, Fort Reno) were built in western Oklahoma to keep the peace among the newly relocated plains tribes.

The 1930s, however, brought an intensive version of cooperative federalism to Oklahoma in the form of large-scale federal assistance. The Dust Bowl magnified the effects of the Great Depression on Oklahoma. "Factories and mines closed, the oil market was depressed, and unemployment was the highest in history, as hungry, poverty-stricken citizens formed long lines at public soup kitchens.'' In response, the federal government's emergency relief program started by President Franklin D. Roosevelt, provided benefits to some ninety-three thousand Oklahomans. A succession of governors soon joined with the federal government to combat these disastrous economic conditions. For example, in 1934 Ernest W. Marland was elected governor on a pledge to bring the New Deal to Oklahoma; he did. By the end of his administration, the Works Progress Administration employed nearly ninety thousand workers on some thirteen hundred projects. In the next decade Governor Robert S. Kerr found that intergovernmental aid could contribute significantly to the state's infrastructure. Elected in 1942, Kerr declared that "he would support the national government administration and asserted that a friendly attitude toward Washington was essential in order to bring dams, roads, and other projects to Oklahoma."[16]

The results of this early Oklahoma-Washington fiscal partnership are readily visible today. In 1936, for example, the Oklahoma Department of Public Welfare (now Department of Human Services) was constitutionally created to provide services to the poor and needy. Establishment of that department was a direct result of available federal assistance for social services. The largely federally financed interstate highway system crisscrosses the state. The Arkansas River Basin Project, completed in 1970, links Oklahoma with eight other states and extends some five hundred miles from the mouth of the Arkansas River to Catoosa, near Tulsa. The estimated federal-share cost of the project was $1.2 billion.[17]

More recently, in 1985 the federal share of total government employment in the state was 21 percent. Expressed another way, approximately one out of every five public servants in Oklahoma is a federal government employee.[18] In fiscal year 1986 Oklahoma ranked twelfth among the states in federal salaries and wages per capita. The national government spent an estimated $9.75 billion in the state during fiscal year 1986. Much of the money went directly to individuals (e.g., $2.47 billion for Social Security and $1.99 billion for wages and salaries; the state has three large federal employers: Tinker Air Force Base, Fort Sill, and the Federal Aviation Administration). In addition, approximately $1 billion was for procurement contracts. About another $1.2 billion represented payments to state government for federally funded programs (e.g., Medicaid, unemployment compensation, and highway construction).

Although Oklahoma has certainly been a beneficiary of federal largess, when compared to other states, revenues from the national government have been steadily declining. In 1970 Oklahoma ranked eighth in the nation in percentage of state and local general revenues from the federal government; in 1975 the state had slipped to sixteenth. In 1980 the state's ranking was twenty-eighth, and by fiscal year 1984–85 the state had dropped to forty-first.[19] In a recent report released by the Congressional Sunbelt Caucus, composed of national lawmakers from southern and southwestern states, one of the primary reasons cited for the attenuation of federal dollars was the "steady flow of federal procurement dollars to states outside of the Sunbelt."[20]

INTERSTATE RELATIONS

Interactions among state governments have always been an important part of federalism. Although conflict appears at times, as states bicker over boundaries, water rights, and the like, cooperation is prominent as well. As David Nice notes, "One of the most significant types of interstate cooperation is the interstate compact."[21] Interstate compacts can be viewed as formal agreements that legally bind participant states. Some compacts create interstate agencies, boards, or commissions to administer the compact on behalf of member states.

Interstate compacts are a relatively recent phenomenon in federalism. Between the years 1783 and 1920, for instance, the states established only 35 compacts. Overwhelmingly, they served the purpose of resolving boundary disputes between two states.[22] Since 1920, the scope and use of compacts have changed in several ways. First, compacts have been adopted to address a broad range of policy issues, including crime, corrections, social services, water, waste disposal, education, and mental health. Second, particularly since the end of World War II, the use of multistate compacts has increased. Instead of the traditional two-state agreement, many compacts today are regional or even national in scope. Third, the number of compacts has increased greatly. By 1983, 119 interstate compacts were in existence, and the typical state belonged to approximately 20.[23]

The Interstate Oil Compact, established in 1935, was one of the early interstate compacts. Regional in scope with a commission to direct the compact program, it was largely the work of two Oklahoma governors, William "Alfalfa Bill" Murray and Ernest W. Marland.[24]

Alfalfa Bill Murray, who became governor in 1931, had the onerous task of keeping the state fiscally afloat during the Great Depression. The major recession in the oil industry and declining oil prices made his job especially difficult. Because the gross production tax on oil was a principal source of state revenue, this sector of the economy had to be stabilized. Stabilization could be achieved through limiting oil production and marketing below capacity. But oilmen and companies such as Sinclair, Champlin, and Wilcox refused to limit production. Heavy production in the new fields in East Texas and in the new Seminole and Oklahoma City fields further glutted the market, and by mid-1931 oil had fallen to about 20 cents a barrel.

After attempts by the Oklahoma Corporation Commission to regulate production failed, in August 1931 Murray called out the National Guard and turned off the flow of oil in Oklahoma. Some three thousand martial law areas were created, fifty feet in diameter around each oil well in the state. In some instances guardsmen were forced to turn back defiant operators with bayonets. After production limits were established, fields were reopened. Governor Murray then announced that the National Guard would remain to supervise production until the price of oil reached $1 a barrel. The guardsmen stayed until 1933 and were paid by a tax levied on oil production.

Alfalfa Bill realized that the problem of limiting production went beyond the borders of Oklahoma; it was a regional issue. Overproduction of oil in Texas or Louisiana, for example, affected Oklahoma—it lowered prices. He called for a meeting of oil-producing states. In a series of conferences, representatives from Oklahoma, Texas, Kansas, and New Mexico discussed petroleum-related issues of mutual concern. These meetings laid the groundwork for the creation of the Interstate Oil Compact initiated by Governor Marland and approved by the Oklahoma legislature in 1935. Today thirty states and six associate member states belong to the compact, with headquarters in Oklahoma City. The duty of the compact is "to make inquiry and ascertain from time to time such methods, practices, circumstances and conditions as may be disclosed from bringing about conservation and the prevention of physical waste of oil and gas and at such intervals as the Commission deems beneficial. It shall report its findings and recommendation to the several states for adoption."[25]

In addition to founding the Interstate Oil Compact, Oklahoma has joined some other national and regional compacts. These range from such nationwide agreements as the Interstate Compact for the Placement of Children to more regionally focused compacts, such as the Kansas-Oklahoma Arkansas River Compact.[26]

Interstate compacts are not the only way states practice cooperation. Constitutionally, for instance, states must grant citizens those "privileges and immunities" (e.g., civil rights) entitled to them among the states and extend "full faith and credit" to the public acts, records, and judicial proceedings of other states. Also, states cooperate through the extradition of fugitives from one state to another, most of the time.

CONCLUSION

As noted in chapter 1, Oklahoma's traditionalistic political culture places more emphasis on local concerns than national issues. Federal-state and interstate relations, however, have forced Oklahoma to turn outward in its politics; the state has been inexorably drawn into modern intergovernmental relations. Indeed, many of the programs, services, and facilities that Oklahomans enjoy today would not be possible without the cooperative efforts of state, local, and federal officials.

The driving force for intergovernmental cooperation, of course, is the growing interdependence that characterizes our complex society. Government today is pervasive, and public policies have spillover effects that can be addressed only through cooperative efforts. The general growth of interstate compacts reflects the recognition that states must collaborate to deal with the host of problems that are no longer confined to one region or the boundaries of individual states.

That cooperation among governmental units today is the rule rather than the exception does not mean that the tensions underlying federalism identified at the beginning of this chapter have disappeared. The issues of state sovereignty versus national supremacy and dual versus cooperative federalism arise today just as they did in earlier times. For example, currently in Oklahoma a major battle is raging over Indian sovereignty. At issue is the power of state and local officials to enforce state laws on Indian lands. The Indian Gaming Regulatory Act, passed by the U.S. Congress in 1988, places Indian gambling operations (bingo and a proposed pari-mutuel horse racetrack on Comanche tribal lands) under the purview of a federal commission and not the state of Oklahoma. Although Oklahoma has laws controlling bingo operations, those laws will not be applied to bingo operations on Indian lands. This matter has now been settled by the federal courts. Moreover, the federal statute requires that state officials begin "good faith" negotiations with the Comanche tribe concerning the proposed race track within 180 days or face a federal court lawsuit.[27]

In June 1990 the tribe agreed with Governor Bellmon on a compact establishing the responsibilities of state and tribal governments in regulating the proposed pari-mutuel racetrack near Lawton. In preparation for the track, the Comanche tribe enacted its own horse-racing laws and created a racing commission that is independent of the Oklahoma Horse Racing Commission. Although the tribe will not apply for a state racing license or be subject to state taxes, it will give the state authority to enforce civil and criminal laws related to the track. The compact was approved by a joint committee on state-tribal relations of the Oklahoma legislature and now requires only approval from the U.S. Secretary of the Interior. There are, however, limits to state-tribal agreements. Following the negotiated agreement with the Comanches, Attorney General Robert Henry advised the governor that the state could not become a party to any agreement with the various Oklahoma tribes for offtrack betting facilities.

Perhaps it is only fitting that the most salient federalism-related issue in Oklahoma today concerns Native Americans. We have come full circle. Oklahoma's history in federalism began with federal-Indian relations. The legacy of this interaction is one of the darkest periods in American history. Now the federal government is the protectorate of Indian rights at the expense of state sovereignty. Indeed, federalism is a dynamic process.

PART II

History and Culture

CHAPTER THREE

Territorial History: Indian Republics through the Twin Territories

Oklahoma means "land of the red people" in the Choctaw language. The first European contact with Oklahoma dates back to the Spanish explorer Francisco de Coronado's 1541 expedition through western and central Oklahoma. Inspired by Indian legends of a kingdom of great wealth, he and thirty of his soldiers traveled through Oklahoma and as far north as present-day Wichita, Kansas, on the Arkansas River. There he encountered a Wichita Indian village before returning to his base in Mexico. Although Coronado did not find any treasures of gold, his expedition marks the beginning of the recorded history of Oklahoma.

Coronado's and other Spanish expeditions to Oklahoma established Spain's claim to the area. Between 1541 and the U.S. acquisition of the Louisiana Territory in 1803, control of Oklahoma passed back and forth between the French and the Spanish. European exploitation of the area was slow, despite a relatively valuable fur trade in eastern Oklahoma.[1] Real control in Oklahoma remained in the hands of native Indian tribes. In fact, relatively speaking, the history of Oklahoma is to a large extent a story of Native Americans, their cultures, and their interactions first with Europeans and later with the United States government. Although much of this history reflects the numerous accomplishments of various Indian groups and their reverence for the land, it has a dark side because of the many broken promises of the whites.

AMERICAN ACQUISITION OF OKLAHOMA

Soon after the Louisiana Purchase, many Americans thought statehood for the area of today's Oklahoma would follow in a few years. The valuable fur trade, rich agricultural land, and advantageous geographical location for access to Santa Fe made the area attractive for settlement. Despite these advantages, as noted in chapter 2, Oklahoma was the last state carved out of the vast territory secured from France.

Congress initially placed the entire Louisiana Purchase under the administration of the governor of Indiana Territory, with the capital at Saint Louis. In 1812 Oklahoma became part of Missouri Territory and, from 1819 to 1829, part of Arkansas Territory. Oklahoma's development during the years after the Louisiana Purchase followed the normal pattern of frontier progress. Behind the explorers came the military, followed by trappers and traders, farmers, and town builders. How far in the future lay statehood? The Missouri and Arkansas territories lying north and east of Oklahoma were being rapidly settled and preparing for statehood. The drive toward statehood for Oklahoma, however, would be interrupted in a most decisive manner.

INDIAN RELOCATION

As the frontier pushed across the Mississippi River, the demand for cheap land and the expansionist desires of the young nation led to a reexamination of the federal government's Indian policy. The major interest was in tribal lands held by the Cherokees, Choctaws, Seminoles, Chickasaws, and Creeks in southeastern states, such as Mississippi, Georgia, and Alabama. Historians call these tribes the "Five Civilized Tribes" in recognition of their social and political development. President Thomas Jefferson encouraged the tribes to consider relocation in the West. Among the tribes, some members believed that it was in their best interest to move west beyond the interference of white civilization. Between 1807 and 1819, for example, several thousand Cherokees left the East to settle first in Arkansas and later in Oklahoma.

American policy toward Indian tribes east of the Mississippi River had been based on "civilizing" them and forcing them to relinquish their land held in common. With the Five Civilized Tribes of the southeastern states, this strategy appeared to work, but with an unanticipated result. As Native Americans adapted to white culture and even started to see merits in individual land possession, they became determined to hold onto those lands. As one historian notes, regarding the failure of pre-Jacksonian Indian policy, "Thus the federal government found itself pursuing two goals simultaneously, with success in achieving one likely to impair fulfillment of the other."[2]

During the 1820s white violence against the Five Civilized Tribes began to grow. White settlers who coveted Indian lands capitalized on the demand for revenge against the tribes following the great violence on the frontier caused by Tecumseh, the powerful Shawnee-Creek leader, whose "Red Sticks" were British allies during the War of 1812. Following Tecumseh's defeat, politicians in southeastern states increased pressure for a solution to the Indian question. The election of Andrew Jackson as president in 1828 provided the opportunity for decision.

By 1830 Congress was ready to adopt President Jackson's Indian policy, which called for the complete removal of the Five Civilized Tribes to the West. Jackson's solution to the southeastern states' "Indian problem" should come as little surprise, given his life on the frontier and experiences as an Indian fighter. As one historian explains:

> So obsessed was the president with driving the Indian tribes to the far frontiers of the United States that he gave his personal attention to the matter. It is significant that most of the Indian removals [to Oklahoma] took place during his administration and that those not completed before he left office had been set in motion. The fulfillment of the Jackson removal program, with its ruthless uprooting and prodigal waste of Indian life and property to satisfy the president's desires and the demands of his constituency, has been aptly described as the "Trail of Tears."[3]

Jackson was not an Indian hater. He was critical, however, of earlier American policy on the Indian and was determined to base his policy on removing the sovereign tribes from the various states. He believed that Indian removal would encourage national growth and improve the nation's security. Jackson's policy was strongly opposed both by the tribes and their friends and by his political enemies. The removal bill passed by narrow margins in each house of Congress, and Jackson signed it into law on May 28, 1830. Following passage of the Removal Act, efforts to thwart Jackson's policy were directed at the federal courts. At first, it appeared that the Indians would prevail. In a U.S. Supreme Court case (*Worcester v. Georgia*) brought by a missionary to protest a Georgia law extending jurisdiction over the Cherokees, the Court ruled against the state of Georgia. But the Court had no way of enforcing its decision, in effect leaving Jackson's policy intact.

Jackson's Indian plan encouraged local efforts in southeastern states to apply more legal and extralegal pressure on tribes to relinquish control over their land. In fact, such harassment caused a small faction of the Cherokees to support a westward move. However, removal was bitterly opposed by most tribal members. Taking advantage of these strong differences, the federal government pushed ahead with plans for removal, and on December 29, 1835, the Treaty of New Echota was signed by the mixed-blood "removal faction" of the Cherokee tribe. The federal government agreed to pay for the expense of removal, and the move was expected to be completed within two years. Only two thousand Cherokees departed voluntarily; the remainder had to be removed forcibly by federal and state militia. This forced removal, the "Cherokee Trail of Tears," was one of the darkest episodes in American history. Under the watch of white militia, lawless whites drove the Cherokees off their land like cattle. Of the estimated eighteen thousand Cherokees who were forced to leave their land, approximately four thousand died in stockades or on the trail to Oklahoma.[4] Oklahoma historians H. Wayne Morgan and Anne Hodges Morgan say of the psychological impact of removal on the tribe: "no set of memories ever remained more vivid, or with more compelling reason, than did the tragedies of this march among the Cherokees."[5] Nor was the reunification process in Oklahoma smooth. Strong emotions, which on several occasions erupted in violence, continued to divide factions within the tribe.

THE GOLDEN YEARS OF THE INDIAN REPUBLICS

Except for the more militant Seminoles and members of other tribes who managed to avoid removal, relocation of the Five Civilized Tribes to Oklahoma was largely completed by 1840. For the most part, the white settlers there were forced to leave their land, and Arkansas Territory's jurisdiction over Oklahoma ended. The federal government signed separate treaties with each of the tribes and divided Oklahoma among them.[6] Within the area now called Indian Territory, military forts were established to maintain peace among the tribes and to protect them both from hostile Osage Indians who controlled much of the area and from white trespassers.

Between relocation and the Civil War, the Five Civilized Tribes embarked on a truly remarkable experiment in Indian self-government. To maintain independence and self-determination, each of the tribes created republican forms of government, including written constitutions and legal codes. The Choctaws wrote the first constitution in 1834. It was based on the tribe's previous constitution adopted in 1826 and, like other Indian constitutions, was a mixture of Anglo-Saxon political doctrine and Indian practice. The constitution, for instance, provided for the separation of powers and checks and balances between legislative and executive powers. The executive function was granted to hereditary chiefs. The National Council met two weeks each year as a legislative body, and the chiefs held the veto power over its actions. Over the years, the constitution was revised numerous times to provide for a bicameral legislative body, additional courts, and a sophisticated electoral system.[7]

Despite the extraordinary physical and psychological consequences of the Trail of Tears, the Five Civilized Tribes demonstrated remarkable organizational skills and social resilience. In fact, historians call the period between relocation and the Civil War the "golden years" of the Five Civilized Tribes. With the assistance of Christian missionaries, school systems and institutions of higher learning were established in the territory. Newspapers were founded, and books in English and native languages were translated and published. Towns were built and became centers of commercial and political activity. Indian farmers cleared large areas of land for agricultural production and the raising of livestock. The plantation system that the tribes had employed in the East reappeared in Oklahoma; many members of the tribes continued to own slaves. By the Civil War an estimated seven thousand black slaves lived in Indian Territory.[8]

Despite tribal efforts to limit it, there was substantial contact with whites in antebellum Indian Territory. Tribes maintained representatives in Washington, D.C., to lobby for issues of concern to them. More army posts were constructed. A degree of white settlement on Indian lands was permitted, particularly if the settlers were skilled artisans. Some of the white settlers married into the tribe and gained tribal rights, swelling the mixed blood influence on tribal politics. Commercial contact with whites inside and outside the territory was also important. Using the territory's navigable rivers, particularly the Arkansas and Red rivers, the tribes traded furs and other cargo for guns, ammunition, and other finished products. Steamboats navigated the major rivers before the Civil War and became an important part of the area's economy. In addition, some major roads were constructed through Indian Territory, several of which led to Santa Fe. Thousands of people used the California Road on their way to the California Gold Rush during the late 1840s. In 1858 the Butterfield Stage Line crossed the southeastern corner of the territory; there were twelve stage stations in the Indian republics.[9]

Tribal contact with the white world encouraged whites to pursue unsuccessfully schemes involving Indian Territory, most of which called for white settlement of the richest Indian land. In 1857, for example, the territorial governor of Kansas urged the removal of the Five Civilized Tribes from their homes in eastern Indian Territory to the more desolate, western portion of the territory. William H. Seward's 1860 presidential platform

called for the complete removal of Indians from the territory to allow for
white homesteading.[10] Once again, the whites' desire for new land threatened Indian life. It was Indian participation in the Civil War that ultimately provided whites with a justification to rob Indians of their land
once more.

THE CIVIL WAR IN INDIAN TERRITORY

The Five Civilized Tribes initially pursued a policy of neutrality with respect
to the Civil War. Neutrality was soon abandoned, however, when Union
troops vacated territorial forts, leaving the Confederate influence to predom-
inate in the early stages of the conflict. Within the tribes, conflicts developed
regarding which side should receive Indian support. Tribes whose land bor-
dered southern states tended to support the Confederacy. The fact that the
tribes permitted slavery also led some to sympathize with the South. Given
the history of broken promises by the U.S. government, it is rather surprising that Indian support for the southern cause was not stronger. Cherokee
Chief John Ross and a large number of full-blood Creeks, Cherokees, and
Seminoles strongly argued for neutrality and the honoring of treaties with
Washington.[11] Nevertheless, Confederate agents signed a series of treaties
with the tribes in 1861, and Indian regiments were assembled to defend Indian Territory against Union invasion. In return, the Confederacy promised
material and military support to the tribes and allowed them to send delegates to the Confederate Congress.

Indian Territory, like the border states, was soon consumed by internal
civil war. This strife brought an end to the spectacular development of Indian
Territory by the Five Civilized Tribes. At first, those Indians remaining loyal
to the Union, under the leadership of Creek warrior Opothle Yahola, suffered
great losses of life and property. At the mercy of Confederate forces, including Indian regiments, the loyalists were driven from their homes. By 1863,
the North had regained the military advantage in Indian Territory despite the
brilliant guerrilla tactics of Brigadier General Stand Watie's Indian forces,
which caused great destruction to Union supply trains and lines of communication throughout the war. No major battles were fought in Indian
Territory, but the war was nevertheless costly to the tribes. An estimated
nineteen thousand Indian refugees were created. Throughout the Indian
republics, vast acres of farmland were abandoned or torched. From Kansas, white irregulars raided Indian Territory, wreaking great havoc and
driving off Indian livestock. By war's end, the tribes were economically

and politically weakened. They were left vulnerable to new forces demanding that they relinquish control of Indian Territory.

RECONSTRUCTION IN INDIAN TERRITORY

Union Reconstruction plans included harsh punishment of the Five Civilized Tribes for their alliances with the Confederate states. Although the tribes had divided their loyalties during the war, the framers of Reconstruction policy considered tribal treaties with the South an abridgment of earlier agreements with Washington and therefore treasonous.

In September 1865, federal negotiators met with tribal delegates from the Five Civilized Tribes, along with spokesmen for the Osages, Wichitas, Caddoes, Senecas, Shawnees, Quawpaws, Wyandots, and Comanches, at Fort Smith, Arkansas. The Indian delegates were treated as representatives of defeated nations and asked to accept dictated terms that required the tribes to (1) abolish slavery and accept their freedmen into the tribes as full citizens, and (2) surrender a large portion of Indian Territory for the removal of the Kansas tribes. The Indian delegations were shocked and dismayed by the harsh demands of the government. The Fort Smith Council ended with little accomplished, and final negotiations were held in Washington the next year, when tribal representatives were forced to accept the terms.

Under the new treaties, the Five Civilized Tribes lost their land in central and western Oklahoma, and the federal government began the relocation of Indian tribes from other states to Indian Territory. Reconstruction treaties marked the end of the experiment in independent Indian republics. The Five Civilized Tribes lost their ability to maintain political control over the Indians in the territory. Within a short period the Five Civilized Tribes were joined by the Caddoes, Delawares, Shawnees, Kickapoos, Poncas, Osages, Modocs, and numerous other tribes, making Indian Territory a "kaleidoscope of tribal cultures."[12] Friction among the tribes required a stronger military presence in Indian Territory. At the same time, the federal government was being pressed to make land in the territory available for white homesteading.

White penetration into Indian Territory increased during Reconstruction. The "silent migration" of whites into tribal lands continued, and there were new white influences as well. The Texas cattle industry gained a major foothold in Indian Territory by using Cherokee lands for grazing. Texas ranchers ultimately persuaded the Cherokees to lease them a large area of land in west-central Oklahoma. Moreover, several railroads, under the Reconstruction treaties, were permitted to build in Indian Territory.

FORMATION OF THE TWIN TERRITORIES

By the 1880s, the forces that supported white control of Indian Territory were ready to converge and reshape Indian policy once more. The railroads with lines in the territory employed lobbyists in Washington to encourage passage of legislation that would open Indian Territory for homesteading. Acting alone, the railroads failed to make much progress. They later switched tactics and effectively capitalized on the tremendous postwar demand for cheap land. Working against the tribes were the fact that they were already leasing large tracts of land to big cattle owners and the growing general belief that the Indian system of communal landownership was inherently evil.

Popular support for white settlement in Indian Territory swelled and was further intensified by the so-called Boomer movement. This movement is often associated with David L. Payne, who led several expeditions into Indian Territory before his death in 1884. Although the U.S. Army repeatedly arrested Payne and repelled his followers, the Boomers had captured national attention. On March 3, 1889, Illinois congressman William Springer added a rider to an Indian appropriation bill permitting the opening of the "unassigned lands" in central Oklahoma. President Benjamin Harrison later proclaimed that the land run would begin at noon on April 22, 1889.

The Great Land Rush was actually the first of a series of land openings in Oklahoma between 1889 and 1906. The 1889 run involved more than two million acres, including today's Oklahoma City, Kingfisher, Guthrie, and Norman. Eligible persons gathered under the close watch of the cavalry to claim a valuable 160-acre section of land or a strategic place in a proposed townsite. To many, townsites were considered more desirable than homesteads. As many as fifty thousand people participated in the Great Land Rush; towns such as Guthrie and Oklahoma City, which had been small railroad stops the day before, were bustling cities of ten thousand by nightfall. Some people chose their lots before the official starting time. These "Sooners," many of them well organized, took some of the best sites, despite the cavalry's determined effort to prevent early entry. The courts were later forced to judge many cases involving the Sooners, whose name became the state's nickname and is also used by the athletic teams of the University of Oklahoma.[13]

No government for the settlers existed until Congress passed the Organic Act on May 2, 1890. This act established the political system that governed Oklahoma Territory until statehood in 1907 (map 2 shows the division between Oklahoma and Indian territories). The act included presidential ap-

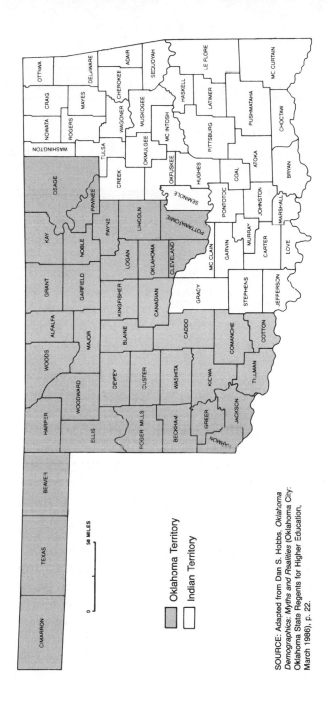

SOURCE: Adapted from Dan S. Hobbs, *Oklahoma Demographics: Myths and Realities* (Oklahoma City: Oklahoma State Regents for Higher Education, March 1986), p. 22.

Map 2. Oklahoma and Indian Territories, 1906

pointment of a territorial governor and supreme court justices, and the popular election of a bicameral legislature of twenty-six house and thirteen council members. The new territory was permitted to send a delegate to
Congress. The Organic Act also provided the means for the territory's future
growth; new lands would be opened to homesteaders. The Oklahoma Panhandle, or what was then called "No-Man's Land," was also attached to the
territory, and Guthrie was designated as the territorial capital.

Events of the 1890s moved the territory closer to statehood. Additional
land openings expanded the population and tax base of Oklahoma Territory.
At the same time, the territorial legislature created governmental and educational institutions, including a university at Norman, an agricultural and me-
chanical college at Stillwater, and a normal school for the training of public
school teachers at Edmond. Other towns campaigned vigorously to secure
the eventual state capital. The question of single or dual statehood for the
twin territories was the most vital issue that remained undecided.

Support for dual statehood was strongest in Indian Territory, although
many residents of the Oklahoma Territory were growing impatient with
Washington's slow deliberations on statehood. For the Indian tribes, single
statehood would mean the loss of their political clout and the eclipse of their
way of life. Their most obvious concern had to do with their system of communal landownership, which likely would not survive in a unified state. Political support for communal landownership, even among those who considered themselves friends of the tribes, was small. The tribes' ideas about land
and private property conflicted with Anglo-Saxon laws and customs. White
society generally considered communal ownership to be an impediment to
the ultimate advancement of the Indian.

Tribes in Indian Territory were slow to accept their fate. They lobbied
Washington for the status quo and passed bills in their own legislatures to
stem the "silent migration" of whites into their territory. These actions did
not deter Congress from passing legislation in 1893 authorizing the creation
of a three-member commission to negotiate for the allotment of tribal lands
to individual tribal members. The Dawes Commission, which took its name
from the retired U.S. senator who chaired the commission, worked over the
next decade to end the system of communal land tenure that had been so central to the tribal way of life. Given the complexity of the issue, the enormity
of the land area involved, the reluctance of the Indians to cooperate, and the
opportunities for corruption in the task, the Dawes Commission deserves
commendation for its honesty and efficiency, despite the human suffering
that came from the division of Indian lands to tribal members.[14] With the

Dawes Commission and individual allotment began the long process of Indian land theft, which the great historian Angie Debo so powerfully describes in her book *And Still the Water Runs*.[15] Many full-bloods refused to accept their allotment rights in the belief that Washington would eventually realize that allotment of tribal land violated treaties with the tribes. Efforts to protect the rights and interests of Indians ultimately fell short; white land grafters gained control of vast areas of tribal lands, leaving thousands of full-bloods landless and impoverished.

Still, Indian leaders continued to oppose single statehood. The major manifestation of this resistance was the 1905 Sequoyah Convention, named after the legendary Cherokee creator of the Cherokee alphabet. Several of the principal chiefs of the Five Civilized Tribes called for a constitutional convention to meet in Muskogee on August 21, 1905. Creek Chief Pleasant Porter was nominated convention president, and the other four tribes were allowed vice-presidents. Among them were two white members of the tribes who would later serve the state as governors: Charles N. Haskell, representing the Creeks, and William H. Murray, representing the Chickasaws. The Sequoyah Convention asked Congress to admit Indian Territory as the state of Sequoyah and produced a well-written constitution that had been approved by a large majority of the territory's electorate. Convention leaders knew this was their last effort for twin statehood, for Congress was nearing final deliberations on an Oklahoma statehood bill based on the unification of the twin territories. On June 16, 1906, President Theodore Roosevelt signed into law the Hamilton Statehood Bill, more popularly known in Oklahoma history as the Oklahoma Statehood Act. The act provided for unification of the Oklahoma and Indian territories and a referendum on unification of the New Mexico and Arizona territories. Although the Sequoyah Convention did not realize its goal of separate statehood for Indian Territory, the experience gained at the convention proved to be very valuable for certain eastern Oklahoma leaders who would play major roles at the statehood convention in 1906–7.

The statehood bill signed by Roosevelt authorized the calling of a constitutional convention with 112 delegates. The two territories were each allotted 55 delegates; the Osage nation was awarded the other 2. The act required the state constitution to provide for a republican form of government; ensure religious freedom; guarantee the right to vote without regard to race, color, or past servitude; ban liquor in Indian Territory for twenty-one years; and continue recognition of Guthrie as the capital until 1913. Oklahoma's only constitutional convention are described in some detail in chapter 5; for now let it suffice to say that in the election of constitutional delegates, the drafting and ratification of the constitution, and the first state elections, the Democratic party was overwhelmingly victorious over the Republican party.

The Democrats' victory was based largely on exploiting the emerging Progressive agenda in Oklahoma, which was an outgrowth of the larger national movement. Progressive ideas had gained great influence in Oklahoma on the eve of statehood (in large part because of a series of business scandals) and occupied much of the attention of the delegates at the constitutional convention. Antibusiness sentiments gained greater credibility before the convention because of the collapse of a railroad bridge over the Cimarron River, caused by the negligence of the company. Nearly one hundred persons were killed. Gruesome stories of businesses selling contaminated food products added further proof that big business was an evil that required tight regulation in order to protect the interests of the general public.[16] The work of the delegates was overwhelmingly approved by state voters in September 1907, and at 10:16 A.M. on November 16, 1907, the forty-sixth star added to the American flag represented Oklahoma.

Lost in the joyous celebration among white settlers was the fact that the independent Indian commonwealths had ceased to exist. The Five Civilized Tribes' political influence, except over tribal land, had been replaced by the new state government in Guthrie. Oklahoma historian Rennard Strickland assesses the economic cost of this loss for the Five Civilized Tribes. Before the Dawes Commission the tribes controlled twenty million acres of land. Now almost all of that has been lost, including control of the mineral wealth beneath those lands. Strickland adds that the extensive poverty among Oklahoma's Native Americans today stands in sharp contrast to the rare pauperism of the territorial period.[17]

In just a few years much of the heritage and culture that the Five Civilized Tribes and other Indian nations brought to Oklahoma was conveniently forgotten. For the most part, white males would embark on the journey of establishing a government for white citizens of the state. After all, Indians were wards of the federal government. Nevertheless, Oklahoma's Indian heritage can never be forgotten. Murals hang at the State Capitol of the great Cherokee Sequoyah; Oklahoma's most famous athlete, Jim Thorpe, a Sac and Fox Indian; Will Rogers, the state's most well-known political figure and humorist; and historian Angie Debo, whose histories on Oklahoma Indians were the subject of great controversy at the time she wrote them. All testify to the importance of Native American influence on Oklahoma. Finally, all one has to do is read the state constitution's description of the Great Seal of the State to be reminded of Oklahoma's Indian legacy:

In the center shall be a five pointed star, with one ray directed upward. The center of the star shall contain the central device of the seal of the Territory of Oklahoma, including the words, "Labor Omnia Vincit." The upper left hand ray shall contain the symbol of the ancient seal of the Cherokee Nation, namely: A seven pointed star partially surrounded by a wreath of oak leaves. The ray directed upward shall contain the symbol of the ancient seal of the Chickasaw Nation, namely: An Indian warrior standing upright with bow and shield. The lower left hand ray shall contain the symbol of the ancient seal of the Creek Nation, namely: A sheaf of wheat and a plow. The upper right hand ray shall contain the symbol of the ancient seal of the Choctaw Nation, namely: A tomahawk, bow, and three crossed arrows. The lower right hand ray shall contain the symbol of the ancient seal of the Seminole Nation, namely: A village with houses and a factory beside a lake upon which an Indian is paddling a canoe. Surrounding the central star and grouped between its rays shall be forty-five small stars, divided into five clusters of nine stars each, representing the forty-five states of the Union, to which the forty-sixth is now added. In a circular band surrounding the whole device shall be inserted, "Great Seal of the State of Oklahoma, 1907." [18]

CHAPTER FOUR

From Frontier Oklahoma to a Global Economy

STATEHOOD TO WORLD WAR I (1907–18)

Democrats, particularly those who supported the Progressive agenda, fared quite well in the first state elections. Charles N. Haskell was elected governor; voters selected labor leader Peter Hanraty for mining inspector; Robert L. Williams was chosen as a supreme court justice; and William H. Murray was elected to the state house of representatives and became its first Speaker. Although women were denied the right to vote, the electorate chose Kate Barnard as commissioner of charities and corrections, a position she would use to protest the unfair treatment of Oklahoma's Indians and other disadvantaged groups. Too much, however, can be made of the Democrats' sweep of this and other elections before World War I. As historian Danney Goble argues, Oklahoma has been incorrectly labeled a one-party state, for at statehood and during the decade following, "the Democrats' electoral supremacy was tenuous."[1] In the next two gubernatorial races, for instance, Democratic governors Lee Cruce in 1910 and Robert L. Williams in 1914 failed to receive a majority of votes cast. Williams won with less than 40 percent of the popular vote.

The Democratic party was in trouble. Its strength was being drained by the remarkable growth of the Socialist party in the state and by a split in the Progressive coalition. Demands for further social reforms by farm and labor groups on the left wing of the Democratic party alienated party conservatives. As a result, the Progressive movement divided into two camps: one wishing social change within the framework of orderly economic progress and the second seeking more radical change to benefit those groups being left behind. The stage was set for a decade of social conflict of often explosive proportions. The conflict had an urban-rural dimension that pitted "on one side, a smalltown merchant-banker-lawyer-landlord element; on the other, a landless and/or debt-ridden farming class."[2]

The economically distressed citizens of Oklahoma were attracted to the Socialist party. In 1914 the party received nearly 20 percent of the vote in the gubernatorial election; a half-dozen state legislators and scores of local officials who ran on the party's ticket were elected. There were more registered Socialists in Oklahoma than in the state of New York. Thus a state that generally is viewed today as conservative registered the largest vote for a Socialist presidential candidate of any state in American history. Socialist gains came at the expense of the Democrats, weakening the reformist wing of the Democratic party and providing the state with a third party nearly equal to the Republican party in voter strength. Clearly, the Socialist party had inherited the Progressive agenda as it attempted to appeal to the most disadvantaged groups and their hatred of the "parasites of the electric-light towns."[3]

Before the start of World War I, Socialists were blacklisted in many counties. Repression intensified during the war as conservatives reacted to what they believed was an unpatriotic and alien ideology. Consider, for example, the so-called Green Corn Rebellion. A group of tenant farmers from central Oklahoma protesting conscription and America's entry into the war decided to march on Washington to force the government to withdraw. Rebellion members said they would survive by eating the green corn in the fields during the march. The protest was poorly organized and failed to enlist support along the way. Instead, it was broken up by authorities nearly as quickly as it was formed. But the short-lived rebellion began a period of political reaction aimed at the destruction of the radical movement in Oklahoma. Local defense councils, created to bolster wartime patriotism and led by conservative community leaders, sometimes became mobs intent on destroying the Socialist movement as well as labor and farmer unions. Unfortunately, these local councils also became the training grounds for the Ku Klux Klan, whose activities intensified in the 1920s.[4]

Historian John Thompson asserts that the Green Corn Rebellion and the repression that followed were instrumental in terminating the relatively open attitude many Oklahomans had displayed to radical ideas in the early statehood period. He concludes that "local leaders and ambitious farmers and workers feared that Oklahoma's reputation for turbulence would discourage outside investment and thus prevent the state from outgrowing its 'colonial status.' "[5]

The rapidly changing economy perhaps touched Oklahomans more directly than any other development before the war. Specifically, the fast growth in the petroleum industry had a most profound effect on the future of the state. Mining had been important in Oklahoma for several decades, particularly for coal and zinc in eastern Oklahoma. But the state attracted national attention with the opening of great oil fields, such as Glenn Pool (1905), Cushing (1912), and Healdton (1913). Oil strikes made fortunes for some, gave rise to numerous boom towns, and established the state's reputation as an oil state. The spectacular growth of Tulsa was largely a product of the oil boom. Oklahoma was the largest oil-producing state in the Union from statehood to 1928, and it has remained among the top four oil states ever since.

The oil patch had additional effects on the state's development. Future political leaders, including governors E. W. Marland and Robert S. Kerr, were oilmen. Fortunes made in oil also were partly responsible for the sharp disparity in incomes of Oklahomans, between the few who had great wealth and the many who were on the verge of destitution. The psychological impact of the oil industry, however, helped Sooners to accept inequalities in wealth. Angie Debo, in her portrait of the Sooner character, writes:

> The hard-pressed farmer struggling through a bad year hopes that Santa Claus in the form of a lease man will bring that dollar an acre to pay the interest on the mortgage. Any trapped individual turns instinctively to "If I could only sell some royalty—." And almost everyone has moments of letting his imagination range over "If I were rich—." Why not? It has happened to his own friends and relatives. And this has increased the already restless and adventurous spirit of a frontier population.[6]

THE ROARING TWENTIES

The political history of Oklahoma from the end of World War I to 1930 has been called the state's "most interesting and distinctive."[7] In the 1920 elections Democrats lost a U.S. Senate seat, three congressional seats, control of the state house of representatives, and more than half of the open seats in the state senate. For the first time, and what would prove to be a short time, Democrats lost dominant control of state politics. James Scales and Danney Goble conclude that "the 1920 elections ushered in an unprecedented period of impassioned strife, rather than a calm [postwar] return to 'normalcy.' "[8] Indeed, the elections commenced nearly a decade of state politics marked by

a series of pitched battles that shocked the nation and stymied progress. The legislature of 1921, for instance, was a partisan body in which Republicans, arriving in the landslide election of President Harding, used their control of the house to impeach elected Democrats, including Governor J. B. A. Robertson. The impeachment proceedings ultimately failed as the senate, by a straight party vote, refused to sustain the charges.[9] Although Robertson completed his term, he earned the hatred of labor for his use of the state militia to break strikes.

The early 1920s also brought significant racial and social tensions to Oklahoma. Racial strife resulted in the bloody Tulsa riot of 1921, which left at least thirty-six blacks dead and scores homeless because of arson.[10] Racial and social unrest also encouraged the growth of the Ku Klux Klan on the right and the Farmer-Labor Reconstruction League on the left as political forces to be reckoned with. The latter group tried to recapture the radical spirit of the Progressive period. The league's program asked for government ownership of railroads, public utilities, banks, warehouses, and insurance; it was also outspoken in its opposition to militarism.

The interaction among the Ku Klux Klan, the Farmer-Labor Reconstruction League, and state politics produced a series of events that rivals any Roaring Twenties story.[11] At the center was John C. "Our Jack" Walton, the state's fifth governor, who took office on January 8, 1923. Walton's ascendancy to the governorship was in large part a result of disunity among old-line Democrats and the support from the Farmer-Labor Reconstruction League, which included Socialists Oscar Ameringer, Patrick Nagel, and J. Luther Langston. After a vigorous campaign in which Walton "revealed himself as a master of rough-and-tumble politics matched by few—if any—in the state's history," he won both the Democratic party primary and the general election. Walton's tenure as governor was short-lived, however; less than a year. Soon after his historic inauguration his "diverse coalition . . . began to come apart." The events that followed can only be viewed as a tragicomedy. For example, Walton appointed George Wilson, a former Socialist and president of the Farmer-Labor Reconstruction League, president of Oklahoma A&M College and had him installed under military guard, only to concede soon after to public opinion and cancel the appointment.

With talk of impeachment threatening his administration in the summer of 1923, Walton "launched a grand diversionary maneuver" by declaring war on the Ku Klux Klan. Because of Klan violence, he imposed martial law on Okmulgee County in June and July and in Tulsa County in September. In Tulsa, military officers imposed a sundown curfew, suspended the powers of

the city police and county sheriff departments, and suspended the right to a writ of habeas corpus (the last action being in direct violation of the state constitution). Later in September, Walton extended martial law to the entire state and "imposed absolute martial law on Oklahoma County, where a grand jury was scheduled to convene to investigate the governor." About six thousand guardsmen were called up by Walton. Some of them "trained machine guns on the doors of the county courthouse to prevent the grand jury from assembling."

On September 26, members of the legislature were turned away from the state capitol by military forces under Walton's orders. In a meeting at a hotel in Oklahoma City, displaced lawmakers decided to add to an upcoming special election scheduled for October 2 a constitutional amendment authorizing the state legislature to call itself into special session. Walton secured a court order barring the State Election Board from placing the question on the ballot. It was immediately overturned by the state supreme court. Walton then fired the members of the election board and appointed a new board, which in turn ordered county officials to prevent the election. Once again this ruling was overturned by the courts, and Walton ordered the national guard and local police to stop the election. The election was held, however, and the constitutional amendment was approved overwhelmingly.

On October 10 the legislature called itself into a special session. The house gathered evidence and considered twenty-two charges of impeachment. Based on the rumor that "Walton was prepared to empty the state prison by a blanket pardon," twenty-two articles were adopted and sent to the senate on October 23, 1923. Walton was suspended from office, and Lieutenant Governor Martin E. Trapp assumed the governorship. Eleven of the impeachment charges were subsequently sustained by the senate. As for the Klan, Trapp pushed through the state legislature the nation's first anti-mask law.

After Walton's removal, Scales and Goble argue, "in the countryside, the old indignation that had fueled the nation's strongest grass-roots radical movement began to give way to resignation and fatalism."[12] The state's frontier acceptance of nonconformity had come to an end. Thompson goes so far as to assert that after Walton, "no political party espoused a significant ideology, and politics was reduced to a noisy method of distributing patronage."[13] A new set of economic and social issues was placed on the political agenda. For example, the collapse of the cotton economy had a disastrous effect on already depressed state farmers. By 1930, more than three-fourths of the land engaged in agricultural production was in a state of

accelerated erosion, and about 61 percent of the farmers were tenants, a figure exceeded only by six of the Deep South states.[14] Even before the Great Depression, farm foreclosures were frequent in eastern Oklahoma.[15] Also, blacks in Oklahoma were clearly second-class citizens under Jim Crow laws. During early statehood, blacks were victims of mob violence and lynch law. Although violence against blacks declined after the Tulsa riot, white supremacy laws prevented blacks from enjoying full citizenship rights. Jimmie L. Franklin blames the lawlessness toward blacks on white leaders who accepted a system of race relations common to the South:

> One cannot escape or ignore the relationship between mob violence and the existing political system that maintained and reinforced the social order of the times. The political system made assumed racial inferiority and racial separation a central question in the lives of white Oklahomans and that in itself, subtle though it may have been, granted a degree of license to those who callously chose to disregard the rights and the humanity of black persons. The point is this: white mobs in Oklahoma often did what respectable white men would not do.[16]

As detailed in chapter 2, advancement of black civil rights was not realized until the 1950s.

THE GREAT DEPRESSION AND DUST BOWL (1930S)

The Great Depression years were hardest for Oklahoma's two most important economic sectors: oil and agriculture. The oil patch suffered from excess production caused by the opening of the lucrative oil fields of East Texas. This development, in fact, ended the Sooner State's supremacy in southwestern oil production. Farmers were no better off, as years of land abuse, drought, and floods devastated agribusiness. Erosion ruined thousands of acres of farmland. The freakish climatic conditions of the 1930s that affected Oklahoma and surrounding states will be forever known as the Dust Bowl Years. Morgan and Morgan write of the Dust Bowl: "These dust storms entered national folklore as examples of man at the mercy of nature. Awesome, majestic, frightening, they advanced on spectators as if they were rolling walls. Since the dust obscured sunlight, the storms added the terrors of darkness to those of suffocation." The gravity of the state's situation was related to its dependence on outside markets and its historic lack of capital. The Morgans accurately conclude that "with an unstable extractive economy and an immature political structure, the state was destined to be a major casualty in any national depression."[17]

A major issue in the historiography of Oklahoma is the explanation for the great out-migration from the state and the depopulation of the land during the Great Depression. All one-dimensional interpretations based on geography, technology, weather, natural disasters, or poverty have proven inadequate to explain what was unquestionably a major event in Oklahoma history.[18] Oklahoma was hit hard by the Dust Bowl, though no harder than several other states; other states were affected by population shifts during the Great Depression, but none like Oklahoma. Between 1935 and 1940, Oklahoma had a loss of native-born whites of 284,000; 95,000 moved to California and 68,000 to Texas. This "Okie migration" had multiple effects on the state, including the breaking up of families, friends, and communities.

The migration left an indelible mark on the state and national consciousness through the photographs, folk culture, and literature that it fostered. Through national magazines, readers saw the faces of Oklahoma migrants and pictures of the Dust Bowl. Oklahoma's Woody Guthrie, a native of Okemah, became the nation's leading spokesman for the homeless and landless migrants fleeing the Dust Bowl and depressed Great Plains states. But it was John Steinbeck's 1939 masterpiece novel *The Grapes of Wrath* that was most responsible for "fixing" the "Okie" image in the national consciousness. That the term *Okie* has taken its place along with other pejorative terms describing groups of Americans was certainly not the author's aim. The main character of the book is an illiterate ex-convict, Tom Joad. Tom, his family, and the migrants they meet have a degree of humanity and integrity mostly lacking in the more sophisticated Californians they encounter. Unfortunately, all too often this part of the story is overlooked. Instead, as historian William Savage explains, for the most part readers find in *The Grapes of Wrath* a negative image of rural Oklahomans, and "in many quarters, 'Okie' is a pejorative, roughly synonymous with such terms as hick, yokel, and redneck."[19]

In any case, state historians and policy makers even today are forced to cope with and reply to this undeserved stereotype. Perhaps one fruitful explanation for the migration from Oklahoma is contained in an essay by Sheila Manes. She prefers to see the migrants not as driven by any single force from the land, but as representing the "last pioneers, attempting in some way to abandon their Oklahoma status quo to start over on the land."[20]

The politics of the depression years was highlighted in chapter 2. In brief, Governors Murray (1931–35) and Marland (1935–39) attempted to keep state government afloat. Marland is credited with bringing the New Deal to Oklahoma. His successor, however, Governor Leon Phillips (1939–43), was a foe of New Deal politics, just as was Murray. Phillips also bitterly opposed the construction of dams in the state. At one point, he called out the National Guard to stop construction of the Grand River Dam, but a federal injunction spoiled his plan. Perhaps Governor Phillips's greatest legacy was the call for and subsequent approval by the people in 1941 of a constitutional amendment for a balanced budget, which ended the irresponsible fiscal policies of the legislature during the Marland years.

THE TRANSITION PERIOD (1940–73)

By the Second World War, Oklahoma showed signs that it was prepared to enter the mainstream of national affairs. The war restored economic stability, in large part because the state fared well in securing its share of government contracts and military installations, such as Tinker Air Force Base in the Oklahoma City area. In contrast to the antifederal diatribe of the Phillips administration, Governor Robert S. Kerr (1943–47) courted the federal government and its projects, which he viewed as critical to developing the state's economy. A wealthy oilman and later influential U.S. senator, Kerr was the first of a line of pragmatic governors whose political tactics signaled a change in Sooner politics. Although somewhat reminiscent of Murray in his political style and appeal, Kerr, according to the Morgans, "sensed the need for a new frontier and realized that the old individualism was chaotic and dangerous." Kerr deserves considerable credit for bringing order and confidence to state politics and ending the long period of "Wild West" government. The Morgans conclude that he "consciously helped restore Oklahomans' sense of pride and place, and he gave them a feeling of involvement in large national affairs."[21] In essence, he launched Oklahoma into the modern era.

The new governor's political style matched the growing maturity of Oklahoma's political culture. Changes in the state's economy had undermined the rural character of state politics that had helped elect Alfalfa Bill Murray governor. The Oklahoma of the post–Second World War period looked for a businesslike political style from its governors. Governor Kerr and most subsequent governors built their political support on a philosophy of government modernization and economic development which appealed to an electorate increasingly removed from its ties with the frontier experience and values of early Oklahoma.[22]

The changing nature of the state's political system and populace was vividly illustrated in race relations. As discussed in chapter 2, school desegregation came to Oklahoma in the 1950s. Without a doubt, the end of the Jim Crow era was a difficult one for white Oklahomans; after all, the change ran counter to the state's traditionalistic political culture. The political tone under which desegregation took place was set by the state's political leaders, who chose to obey rather than defy U.S. Supreme Court decisions. Governor Raymond Gary (1955–59), who spearheaded the attack on segregated schools, exemplifies the pragmatic approach of postwar politics. He also added his religious beliefs to the school desegregation controversy by noting: "'I grew up in "Little Dixie" . . . , [but as] an active Baptist and believer in the Scriptures . . . I have never understood how persons can call themselves Christians and believe that God made them superior because they were born with white skin.'"[23] Although state compliance with federal desegregation orders was not immediate, it was impressive because Oklahoma broke ranks with the Deep South states that chose the massive resistance.

Postwar governors, elected on campaigns pledging no new taxes, continued to set a conservative tone regarding the funding of state programs and services. Nevertheless, they worked closely with congressional delegations in Washington to secure the state's share of federal projects available during the 1950s and 1960s. As federal aid increased, state politicians responded to the demands for more public services without boosting state taxes. Voters were interested in pocketbook issues; they were unsympathetic to the posturing against federal intervention in state affairs which had hurt the state's interest in dealing with Washington during earlier administrations. All this helped to quiet collisions between governors and legislatures during legislative sessions. For the most part, Oklahoma governors followed the example of Kerr, assumed the leadership style of corporate executives, and focused their efforts on budgetary concerns or on attracting new industry. "Under those circumstances," writes Goble, "most legislative assemblies were altogether boring affairs."[24]

Governors were wise to avoid direct confrontations with the legislature, which, along with its allies at the county courthouses, comprised what is frequently termed the "Old Guard" in Oklahoma politics. Although the state had changed a great deal socially and economically since statehood, its political structure remained remarkably the same. Despite tremendous growth in urban areas over the years, rural interests continued to dominate the state capitol. The number of rural lawmakers represented a much larger percentage in both legislative chambers than for the population as a whole. In spite of urban complaints about underrepresentation, the legislature resisted reapportionment for decades. The reapportionment issue was not unique to Oklahoma, but its legislature was considered among the most poorly apportioned in the U.S. Through their control of the legislature, rural lawmakers had a significant say on government jobs and projects, and few governors were willing to challenge this control directly. Eventually, however, urban population growth and interests collided with Old Guard politics and provided the basis for a major confrontation during J. Howard Edmondson's administration (1959–63).

Edmondson's campaign and his administration departed from those of other postwar governors by breaking with their pragmatic political style and confronting the Old Guard. Only thirty-two years old when he took office, Edmondson campaigned on the promise of reform. He won office largely on the overwhelming support he received from urban areas. During his first legislative session, he capitalized on his popular support to secure passage of legislation implementing a merit system for hiring state employees and central purchasing by state agencies. Both measures were viewed as sharp defeats for the Old Guard, particularly the merit system bill, which removed many state jobs from the patronage control of legislators and county officials.

Edmondson followed with a successful campaign to end the state's anachronistic Prohibition law. The Old Guard quickly rallied, however, to defeat the governor's other reform efforts in a series of state questions in 1960, including legislative reapportionment and greater state control of road spending. The failure of the Democratic party to support these reforms ultimately worked to the advantage of the Republican party. Under the capable leadership of party chairman and later governor Henry Bellmon (1963–67), the Republicans undertook a major effort aimed at infusing the party with new vitality by drawing on the urban support that the Democrats were unable to sustain, and in 1962 Oklahoma elected Bellmon its first Republican governor. He was followed by another Republican, Dewey Bartlett (1967–71). The Old Guard suffered perhaps an even greater setback when the 1964 *Baker v. Carr* U.S. Supreme Court decision finally forced Oklahoma, along with all other state legislatures, to reapportion on the basis of "one man, one vote." Reapportionment weakened the rural influence at the state capitol and prepared the way for other reforms.

Following World War II, the state's economy also entered a period of transition. Themes that united Oklahomans were economic development and diversification. For a state ravaged by the Great Depression and the Dust Bowl and dependent on mineral production and agriculture, the road to future prosperity was thought to be better planning, commitment to industrial recruitment and development, and establishment of a favorable business climate. As it had since the 1920s, the state continued to lose population in the immediate postwar period. During the 1950s, for example, more than two hundred thousand people left the Sooner State. Population decline stopped, however, during the 1960s as the state's economy improved.

Leading the economic recovery were several new sectors other than the traditional mainstays of agriculture and petroleum. The government sector nearly doubled its role in the Oklahoma economy between 1950 and 1968 and accounted for 220,000 jobs, one-fifth of the Oklahoma work force. Federal government employment in defense installations, such as those at Tinker Air Force Base near Oklahoma City and Fort Sill in Lawton, accounted for much of the growth during this period. It was the expansion of the manufacturing sector, however, that was the most dramatic development in the state's economic diversification. Oklahoma's historic dependence on mineral extraction and agriculture, though still important, had begun to lessen. Manufacturing, wholesale and retail trade, services, and government emerged as the primary growth sectors.[25]

With a more expansive economy, the postwar years marked the beginning of a period of "good feeling" in Oklahoma. The negative impressions left by the Great Depression, the Dust Bowl, and the tumultuous politics of previous decades were now largely history. In the postwar "age of resurgence," Douglas Hale asserts, the state was engaged in a "process of convergence, whereby it . . . [was] becoming less distinctive and more like the rest of the country."[26] There were numerous manifestations of the newfound Oklahoma pride, not the least of which were the high-flying University of Oklahoma football teams coached by Bud Wilkinson. Oklahoma's governors, from Robert S. Kerr to Dewey Bartlett, aggressively marketed the state to industrial leaders throughout the nation to attract new business. The 1970 census statistics provided Sooners with more tangible evidence that hard times were over, for the state's population actually increased— slightly.

THE BOOM, THE BUST, AND THE FUTURE (1970–PRESENT)

Quality-of-life studies showed that Oklahomans felt positive about the state and the future during the 1970s. More than three-fourths of state residents reported that their quality of life was excellent, that they were hopeful for the future, and that they were satisfied with their jobs. One national survey ranked the state's quality of life as thirty-third in the nation—better than

Missouri, Arkansas, and Texas, but worse than Colorado, Kansas, and New Mexico. Other studies of the nation's largest cities designated Oklahoma City as an "excellent" place to live and Tulsa as "outstanding."[27] Clearly, Oklahoma had changed, or had it? We answer in the affirmative. But for about a decade, state policy leaders and ordinary Sooners forgot the lessons of history. The frontier mentality of "boom or bust" replaced the pragmatic politics of the postwar era as the state became a major benefactor of historical circumstances caused by a national panic over energy dependence and the Arab oil embargo of 1973. The result was a boom of such magnitude that Oklahoma became a haven for speculators and fortune seekers in the mid-1970s and early 1980s. During this period the "era of good feeling" peaked as Sooner bumper stickers such as "Oil Field Trash," "Don't Tell My Folks I'm Working in the Oil Patch. They Think I Play Piano in a Whorehouse," and "Turn Up Your Thermostat and Freeze a Yankee" displayed the state's arrogant attitude toward much of the rest of the nation's economic plight—almost a reverse "grapes of wrath." In his study of the Penn Square Bank failure that marked the beginning of the end of the boom, Mark Singer described this sense of self-satisfaction as "Okiesmo."[28]

As the price of oil passed the threshold of $30 per barrel with optimistic projections that it would soar to between $70 and $100 before the end of the century, the state's oil and gas industry once again was in the driver's seat. From the slumping industrial states of the Northeast and Midwest, tens of thousands of people migrated to the state's oil patch in search of jobs and fortune. Western Oklahoma, particularly the Anadarko Basin area, was the center of the most vigorous activity. Wages grew dramatically, as did housing prices, and landowners made substantial fortunes for their surface and mineral rights. From 1972 to 1982 the value of crude oil produced in Oklahoma increased 633 percent (from $709 million to $5.2 billion). Production declined, however, from 208 million barrels to approximately 159 million. Natural gas production was the most significant commodity fueling the Oklahoma boom. During the same ten-year period the value of natural gas production grew from $294 million to almost $5.4 billion, a 1,729 percent increase with only a slight increase in production volume.[29] On the strength of this tremendous boom in the energy sector, Oklahoma ignored the national recession. For the first time since statehood, the average income of Oklahomans almost reached the national average. Although national unemployment percentage figures approached double-digit, the state's employment picture was rosy. State tax coffers swelled from the taxes levied on oil and natural gas production. Revenue surpluses enabled policy makers to trim the tax base and provide substantial increases in salaries to educators and public employees, salaries that had lagged behind national averages during the 1950s and 1960s.

In 1982 the boom came to a crashing end. The Arab nations' petroleum cartel came apart, oil prices fell precipitously (to under $15 a barrel), and natural gas production from the Anadarko basin became unprofitable. In a 1987 article in *The Economist,* one analyst wrote of the boom: "Oil made the oil patch rich; it also made it reckless, lazy, and conceited. Oil was a commodity that came out of the ground more or less unbidden. It allowed country boys with no education to stroll into jobs and make fortunes; it allowed state governments to coast along on a seemingly infinite roll of money. Thanks to oil, regions that were intrinsically poor and backward, scrub or swamp, could become self-indulgent."[30] Most Sooners would take exception to this harsh indictment. Nevertheless, two facts remain. First, while much of the nation was adjusting to changing economic realities (e.g., fiscal stress, the movement from a national to an international marketplace, the decline of manufacturing, and the rise of the service and high-tech sectors) and reforming political structures and practices (e.g., government reorganization, alternative service delivery systems, productivity improvement), Oklahoma during the 1970s was exporting a substantial portion of its tax burden to other states via the gross production tax on petroleum products. Oil producers added the tax to their cost of production and passed it on to other states, primarily in the Northeast. Second, to a large extent, the resurgence in the oil patch threw Oklahoma off its course toward economic diversification and modernization, a direction the state had followed with success since the 1950s.

The "bust" that followed the boom has had a tremendous impact on the politics and the people of Oklahoma. A depressed petroleum industry coupled with a sagging agricultural sector brought scores of bank failures along with hundreds of business and individual bankruptcies. Much of the newly created income from oil and gas had not been invested wisely. Oklahoma City banker Dale Mitchell told journalists Neal Peirce and Jerry Hagstrom that instead of investing in stable "asset-building" firms, too much money went to fly-by-night companies that spent too heavily on "promotion, office buildings, inflated salaries, and even jewelry."[31] Beginning in 1982, state government entered a period of fiscal retrenchment. Oil-based gains in funding for education and the state's infrastructure quickly evaporated. The "era of good feeling" seemed to be over as many of the negative feelings about the state associated with *The Grapes of Wrath* were raised again.

Despite this rather gloomy picture of Oklahoma in the 1980s, many residents believe the state has now turned the corner. Economic indicators suggest that Oklahoma in 1990 is on the road to recovery; the Sooner spirit has endured. Oklahoma has come a long way in the past century—literally from the preindustrial economy of the Indian Territory to the recent quest by state leaders to make the state a prominent participant in the national and global economies. The effort at economic diversification has picked up steam. In spite of intense opposition from the state's largest newspaper, the legislature raised taxes three times during the tough years of the mid-1980s in hopes of preventing irreparable damage to public services. Yes, Oklahoma has changed, and for the better, most would agree. But the story isn't over, of course. The days that lie ahead are critical. To compete effectively for knowledge-intensive industries, a state must offer a high quality of life and make a substantial commitment to education. How will Oklahoma respond? Chapter 11 provides a more extended discussion of contemporary policy concerns and how state leaders and the people of Oklahoma are addressing issues that are critical for the future of the state.

PART III

The Constitutional and Institutional Framework

CHAPTER FIVE

The Oklahoma Constitution

Danny Adkison

In many respects the most solemn and important political act a group of people can perform is to write a constitution. A constitution reflects what is most important to individuals; it contains the basic values of a polity. The Oklahoma Constitution, for example, discloses those issues that were of the greatest concern to the people living in the twin territories at the turn of the century. In addition, and just as important, the election of delegates to the constitutional convention and the document those delegates produced played a large role in establishing the partisan leanings of the state for years to come. Before examining events leading up to the convention, the forces that help explain the document drafted by the delegates, and the fruit of the delegates' labor, we look at the issue of partisanship in Oklahoma on the eve of statehood.

POLITICAL IMPLICATIONS

Before the first elections in the twin territories, considerable doubt existed as to how the state as a whole would align itself with respect to partisanship. Oklahoma Territory was dominated by Republicans. But was this domination a reflection of "true" partisan feelings of the population or was it the result of more circumstantial factors? In territorial days the governor was an appointee of the president of the United States. The governor, in turn, used his patronage powers to appoint other officers holding political positions in Oklahoma Territory.

President Benjamin Harrison, a Republican, formally opened the territory of Oklahoma to settlement. From the passage of the Organic Act in 1890 until statehood in 1907, the nation elected three Republican presidents and one Democrat. Thus, during the seventeen years of territorial status, for only four years was a Democratic territorial governor (William C. Renfrow, 1893–97) in charge of making political appointments. As a result, partisan proclivities were unclear. Were residents of Oklahoma Territory truly sympathetic to the Republican party, or was the strength of the party tied to the feeling that one had to be a Republican to get ahead politically? The question of which political party dominated Indian Territory was even more difficult to answer because each of the Five Civilized Tribes had its own system of governance, and political parties were hardly relevant until the years immediately before statehood.

As statehood approached, it was generally assumed that the Republican party had more followers in Oklahoma Territory and that Democrats constituted the majority party in Indian Territory. What would happen when the territories were joined? This question was in the minds of many as the call went out for the election of delegates to the constitutional convention. Parenthetically, we might also note that this question was a major issue during the entire "single versus dual" statehood debate. Perhaps William Murray, who was one of the principal spokesmen for Indian Territory statehood at the Sequoyah Convention, captured the essence of the question by stating: "all foresaw that the party which wrote the Constitution would have a strong hold on the future State government."[1]

ANTECEDENTS TO THE CONSTITUTIONAL CONVENTION

Before the convention convened in Guthrie, three important events transpired that would have a significant effect on the proceedings: (1) the Sequoyah Convention, (2) a meeting of Democrats from both territories, and (3) formation of a joint legislative board representing farm and labor interests.

As mentioned in chapter 3, the Sequoyah Convention was Indian Territory's last attempt to seek separate statehood. Although many of the Indians living in the territory knew their proposed constitution and request for separate statehood would go unheeded by Congress, they believed that the Atoka agreement (the end product of negotiations between the Dawes Commission and the Five Civilized Tribes concerning the allotment of Indian land) entitled them to separate statehood. Several of the Sequoyah delegates, including William Murray and Charles Haskell, played an active part in producing the constitution the convention offered to Congress—a constitution that was heavily influenced by the Progressive movement and that would serve as a forerunner to the state's constitution.

Two other events were also important for establishing the issues the delegates at the Guthrie convention would feel obligated to address. As at the Sequoyah Convention, the meeting of the twin-territory Democrats resulted in a platform that supported the Progressive movement. In August 1906 the Farmers' Union, the Twin Federation of Labor, and the railroad brotherhoods held simultaneous meetings in Shawnee to authorize the formation of a joint board that would issue the so-called Shawnee Demands in September. The Shawnee Demands included a list of Progressive reforms, such as the initiative and referendum, recall of public officials, the eight-hour work day, political control of public utilities, and strong worker-safety legislation. Danney Goble explains that the real meaning of the Shawnee platform was that "organized workers and farmers were set to make the government answerable for economic and social questions."[2]

Pursuant to guidelines contained in the Enabling Act, on November 20, 1906, the men selected as delegates to Oklahoma's only constitutional convention assembled in Guthrie. One-hundred and twelve delegates had been elected, 55 from each territory and 2 from the Osage Nation. Among the delegates were 99 Democrats, 12 Republicans, and 1 independent (who aligned at the convention with the Democrats). With the help of delegates who had also participated in the Sequoyah Convention, William H. Murray defeated labor leader Peter Hanraty for convention president. Displeased with the composition of the group, President Theodore Roosevelt, a Republican, called the delegates assembled a "zoological garden of cranks."[3] In reality, the delegates represented numerous professions, including 38 farmers and ranchers, 29 lawyers, 14 merchants, and 8 ministers.

CONSTITUTIONAL ANTECEDENTS

The exact determination of the forces responsible for the type of constitution written at Guthrie is difficult to discern. Any explanation that relies on a single influence is probably incorrect. Nevertheless, three factors contributed to its substance: (1) the U.S. Constitution of 1787, (2) the state constitutions of the forty-five states that comprised the Union before Oklahoma's statehood, and (3) the Progressive movement, which was sweeping the United States at the time of Oklahoma's convention.

THE U.S. CONSTITUTION

The Oklahoma Constitution incorporates several features of the U.S. Constitution; however, this statement can be misleading. It is misleading because the framers, when writing the U.S. Constitution, borrowed what they considered to be the "best" provisions of the thirteen state constitutions then in existence.[4] So, to find something in Oklahoma's constitution that resembles or is copied exactly from the U.S. Constitution might mean that it originated first in the early state constitutions. A good example is the two-house, or bicameral, legislature.

Still, that does not mean the U.S. Constitution had no effect on Oklahoma's constitution. The U.S. Constitution did affect those state constitutions written after 1787. One example of this influence is the separation of powers. In the early state constitutions reference was often made to a separation of powers, but most powers resided in the legislature in most states. In that sense the provisions were mere lip service. The contribution made by the U.S. Constitution was in taking the concept of separation of powers seriously. The U.S. Constitution created a rather strong chief executive (president) independent of Congress. In contrast, most of the the states had rather feeble governors. This difference can be clearly seen in the example of the veto: in 1788 only two states gave the governor the power to veto bills, but the U.S. Constitution gave the president a veto. By 1906 all states, except two, had granted the veto to the governor. That is the kind of indirect influence the U.S. Constitution had on state constitutions. Areas of similar influence are in the method of selecting the governor, the lack of executive councils, constitutional revision, and the term of office for members of the legislature.[5] Thus, the U.S. Constitution did have some effect on state constitutions, and early state constitutions also influenced later state constitutions. Such was the case in Oklahoma.

PREVIOUS STATES' CONSTITUTIONS

The constitutions of the forty-five states that entered the Union before Oklahoma proved to be invaluable for the delegates in Guthrie. In addition, several students of Oklahoma's constitution note the resemblance it bears to the constitution written at the Sequoyah Convention.[6] In fact, the committee that drafted the Sequoyah Constitution obtained copies of all other state constitutions, from which they copied freely.[7] A comparison of the similarities and differences of Oklahoma's constitution with those of states that preceded it should be useful.

Length

One major difference between Oklahoma's constitution and other state documents is its length. State constitutions up to 1907 had an average length of
fifteen thousand words.[8] This average length fails to reveal that, following
the Civil War and particularly after 1900, state constitutions in general tended to be much longer. Thus, the length of Oklahoma's constitution fits the
pattern of the time. The longer state constitutions were probably the result of
either a response to the "complexity of modern life" or a distrust (prevalent
in southern states) of state legislatures.[9] Oklahoma's was approximately fifty
thousand words long. Like most states, however, Oklahoma followed the
typical constitution in the wording of its preamble, the placing of a bill of
rights and a suffrage article at the beginning of the constitution, and in the
arrangement of the three branches of the government.[10]

The Calling of a Constitutional Convention

Nearly three-fourths of preceding state documents permitted the calling of a
constitutional convention for purposes of revising or amending their constitutions; so does Oklahoma's. The legislature may call for such a convention
following a vote of the people approving such action (Article XXIV, Section
2). Perhaps as an endorsement of Thomas Jefferson's statement that every
constitution should be revised at least once every twenty years, this section
also mandates that a proposal for a constitutional convention "shall be submitted to the people at least once in every twenty years."

Amending the Constitution

As with most states, Oklahoma's constitution provides alternative ways for
amending the document. The legislature may propose a change through the referendum process, which must be approved by the voters. But Oklahoma became only the second state (Oregon was the first) to permit the people through
the initiative process to propose constitutional amendments, which also must be
approved by the voters. Until amended in 1974, the constitution required all
proposed amendments initiated by the people to receive the approval of "a majority of all the electors voting at such election."[11] This arrangement allowed a
constitutional initiative to be killed by what was called the "silent vote." In general, people tend to cast more votes for the glamour offices—president or governor—than for secondary offices and proposals placed on the ballot by initia-

tive or referendum (these matters are often technical, difficult to understand, and receive little media attention). As a result, it was not uncommon for an amendment proposed by initiative (the silent vote did not apply to those proposals referred by the legislature) to go down to defeat even though it received over 50 percent of the vote on the measure itself. To pass, it had to receive a majority of all votes cast at the election. That unusual feature was finally eliminated by a 1974 amendment submitted to the people by the legislature.

The Bill of Rights and Suffrage

The second article of the Oklahoma Constitution is the Bill of Rights. The Maryland Constitution lists the most rights, and Kansas's document specifies the fewest. Typically, states list twenty to thirty; Oklahoma's constitution enumerates thirty-three rights.[12] Many of these rights, such as freedom of religion and the rights of assembly and petition, closely resemble federal constitutional guarantees. Others depart from the national document, such as the provision regarding the right to bear arms, which allows the Oklahoma legislature to regulate the carrying of weapons. Other rights appear to arise out of the antitrust mood of the period in which the constitution was written. These include the state's right to inspect corporate books and to engage in any business for public purposes, except agriculture.

Under Article III, the right to vote was originally restricted to males (except in school board elections) who were over the age of twenty-one and met residency requirements. These standards were quite typical of most state constitutions of the time. Unlike fourteen other states, however, Oklahoma's constitution did not contain any education or property requirements for voting, with the exception of voting in city and town indebtedness elections (Article X, Section 27).[13] Although many speeches were given at the convention for and against giving women the vote, the issue was overshadowed by race. "The delegates from counties that had no Negroes were nearly all in favor of women suffrage, while the delegates from those counties having a great number of Negroes were almost unanimously opposed to it."[14] Apparently, the delegates from counties containing a high proportion of blacks feared that high turnouts of black voters would dilute the white vote (perhaps even changing the election's outcome). Denying women the vote was, first of all, one means of guaranteeing that at least one-half of the blacks (black women) would not affect the outcome of any election and, second, might further dilute the influence of the black male voter. Thus, though the Fifteenth Amendment to the U.S. Constitution prohibits denying individuals the right to vote on the basis of race, the Oklahoma Constitution was amended in 1910 so as to effectively disfranchise the black voter by use of a grandfather clause. The U.S. Supreme Court invalidated the clause in 1915, but other means (e.g., residency requirements) were used to disfranchise blacks. In fact, considerable evidence suggests that blacks were intentionally left out of the Progressive reforms being debated by delegates at the convention. In 1918, however, Oklahoma's constitution was amended to grant women the right to vote (two years before the U.S. Constitution was changed).

The Branches of Government

The legislature is the first branch of government addressed in Oklahoma's constitution. The delegates followed the pattern found in most states by establishing a bicameral legislature, with house members serving two-year terms and senators four years (one-half of senate seats are contested every two years). In drafting this article, delegates continued a trend that had developed in the 1830s and was perpetuated by the populists and progressives—a great distrust of the legislature. This distrust, according to one contemporary observer, helps to explain the extraordinary length of Oklahoma's constitution: "every detailed command, prohibition, or regulation in a constitution, is in effect a usurpation of the statute-making power of legislatures, so that, in a sense, the length of a constitution roughly indicates the amount of limitation placed on legislatures."[15] The legislative article contained a vast number of restrictions, such as limiting the length of the session to sixty legislative days (to encourage short sessions), requiring that "no act shall take effect until 90 days after the adjournment of the session" (except those containing an emergency clause) to enable voters to challenge the bill, and requiring that bills must be passed by an absolute majority of the membership rather than a majority of the quorum present.[16] Over the years some of the restrictions have been changed, such as in 1966 when the constitution was amended to require annual sessions of the legislature.

Under Oklahoma's constitution as written in 1907, only males aged at least thirty who are citizens of the U.S. and three years a resident of Oklahoma can be elected governor (Article VI, Section 3). Except for the requirement that the governor be male, these provisions were found in most other state constitutions. Unlike Oklahoma, however, fifteen states allowed their governors to be elected to two successive terms. Oklahoma's constitution gave the governor the power to veto bills passed by the legislature with the restriction that the legislature could override the veto with a two-thirds vote or three-fourths on bills with emergency clauses. Additionally, the governor was given the power to exercise an item veto over bills containing appropriations.[17]

The Guthrie delegates were in the mainstream of the trend for establishing departments, boards, and commissions, whose heads were elected by the voters to assist the governor in the execution of state laws and to ensure accountability to the voters. In addition to elective offices that could typically be found in other state constitutions (lieutenant governor, secretary of state, treasurer, auditor, attorney general, and superintendent of public instruction), Oklahoma's constitution included the elected positions of state examiner and inspector, chief mine inspector and three assistants, commissioner of labor, commissioner of charities and corrections, commissioner of insurance, state printer, president of the State Board of Agriculture, and the clerk of the supreme court (Article VI, Section 1). The delegates also provided for a Board of Agriculture (whose method of selection was left up to the legislature) and a Corporation Commission (whose three members were to be elected). This elected bureaucracy has been criticized often as inefficient and uncontrollable.[18] Reformers have repeatedly called for making many of these officers appointive under the control of the governor on the assumption that such centralization will enhance efficiency and gubernatorial power (see chapter 7).

Historically, one constitutional scholar has said of the state courts, "the judiciary is the department of our government which has undergone fewest changes and given most satisfaction."[19] Nonetheless, constitutional articles dealing with the courts began expanding just before the writing of Oklahoma's Constitution. Once again the reason was a disrespect or fear of the legislature, which in the absence of constitutional directives would be responsible for defining the judiciary. The Guthrie delegates preferred to follow the practice of other states and add detail to the judicial article. The constitution originally provided for the election of high court judges to six-year terms. Other judicial provisions that followed previous state guidelines were the staggering of elections for supreme court justices, giving the house of representatives the power to impeach judges, granting judges a higher salary than most officials, specifying a jury of fewer than twelve members in certain cases, and denying the governor the constitutional power to ask the courts for an advisory opinion.

THE INFLUENCE OF THE PROGRESSIVE MOVEMENT

Conventional wisdom suggests that delegates at Oklahoma's constitutional convention were embarking on new, uncharted territory when writing articles to regulate trusts or provide for direct democracy. True, not many state constitutions contained such provisions, but these arrangements were not entirely original. Instead, the delegates relied on the innovative sections of more recent state constitutions or statutes rather than turning, as they had when writing so many other portions of Oklahoma's constitution, to what was the norm in most other states.

Regulating Trusts

Why did the delegates see a need to place strict regulations on corporations? As noted in chapter 3, the Progressive movement and its critique of the ills of big business provided a tonic to Oklahoma's boomers, who believed that the evils of the trust-dominated national economy conflicted with the pioneer philosophy built on the virtues of individual effort. Territorial concerns about the unhealthy aspects of economic giants, however, were not only intellectual. People of the territories had witnessed tremendous inflation, at levels of 35 to more than 50 percent annually, which had "awakened a consumer consciousness."[20] Sharp increases in the cost of living were blamed on the trusts' manipulation of the economy in order to enhance corporate profits. Another concern was taxation; corporations simply were not paying their fair share of taxes. Small businessmen, along with farmers and laborers, naturally felt outraged by this state of affairs. And legislatures seemed unable to protect the people. As James R. Scales and Danney Goble comment:

> The power of business was pervasive in government. Mass frustration turned to mass rage as citizens saw the Standard Oil Company twice bribe the territorial legislature to emasculate any attempt to regulate the quality of its kerosene. The experience was repeated when the American Book Company—the "textbook trust"—successively bribed two territorial assemblies and innumerable local school boards to subject helpless parents to outrageous prices for textbooks.[21]

In studying Oklahoma's constitution, two law professors have concluded: "The task undertaken at Guthrie was not to 'get' corporations but rather to have a way of 'getting at' them if need be . . . the attitudes were not essentially anti-corporation but, rather, anti-trusts or against evil corporations and corporations acting in an evil and destructive manner." In reality, the importance of land, as mentioned in chapter 1, was the major concern in regulating corporations: "We can conclude that the number one concern motivating economic regulation at the Oklahoma Constitutional Convention was the protection of individual ownership of resources, especially of the preservation and encouragement of individually owned and operated family-style farms."[22]

In regard to taxes, Oklahoma's constitution required them to be uniform and to be the product of general legislation. Various types were authorized, including graduated income taxes. Limits were placed on state, county, city, and school district debt, and a State Board of Equalization was created to adjust and equalize the valuation of real and personal property in the counties. To prevent the legislature from succumbing to pressures at the end of a legislative session, the legislative article prohibited the passage of new taxes during the last five days.

Some of the major provisions of Oklahoma's constitution pertaining to labor were also "lifted" from other state constitutions. The constitution created a Board of Arbitration and Conciliation; established an eight-hour work day for state, county, and city employees; required that the legislature pass laws to protect the health and safety of employees in factories, in mines, and on railroads; prohibited the contracting of convict labor; and forbade young boys and all females from working in mines. All of these provisions appeared in earlier state constitutions and were part of the Progressive agenda.

Direct Democracy

Distrust of the legislature found its ultimate expression in the referendum and initiative. These two devices make the people legislators and appropriately were placed in Article V of the constitution—the Legislative Department.

With the initiative, 8 percent of the voters can propose any legislative matter or amendment to the constitution and have it placed on the ballot. Under the referendum, 5 percent of the voters or an absolute majority of the legislature may require that a bill passed by the legislature be submitted to the voters for approval. Only four other states allowed the initiative and referendum before the adoption of Oklahoma's constitution.[23] Now seventeen states permit the initiative as a method for amending their constitutions.[24]

Prohibition

The issue of liquor was a major concern of the day and found its way into the debates of the Guthrie delegates.[25] Congress itself had ensured that the matter would be placed on the convention's agenda. In the Enabling Act, Con-

gress directed that Prohibition should be extended to that part of the state formerly part of Indian Territory for a period of twenty-one years. The "drys,"
led by the Anti-Saloon League, lobbied to extend Prohibition throughout the
Oklahoma Territory. The convention generally supported the dry position.
Nonetheless, the framers decided to place the question on the ballot as a separate issue for fear that its inclusion with the rest of the constitution might
jeopardize approval of the entire document. Campaigning over Prohibition
by both sides was intense. When the ballots were counted, the Prohibition
amendment carried by a comfortable margin, although it received nearly
fifty thousand fewer votes than did the constitution. Thus on the eve of statehood Oklahoma citizens celebrated both the creation of the forty-sixth state
and the beginning of nearly a half-century of legal Prohibition.

RATIFICATION

The people voted on approval of the Oklahoma Constitution on September
17, 1907. On the same day, they also voted for candidates for those offices
established by it. Since Republicans generally opposed the document, this
situation placed them in a dilemma. As Scales and Goble put it: "The Republicans were trapped. . . . On the Constitution, the Republicans pledged
a fervent opposition, which, if successful, would have meant no statehood at
all. In the next order of business, the party nonetheless named candidates for
the offices whose very existence they had just chosen to oppose."[26]

The partisan battle over the proposed constitution was heightened by the
visit of two distinguished politicians to the state just before the election: Republican Secretary of War William Howard Taft and two-time Democratic
presidential candidate William Jennings Bryan. In a packed convention hall
in Oklahoma City on August 24, 1907, Secretary Taft, in reference to the
proposed constitution, urged Oklahomans to "vote it down" because "it
was no constitution at all." He was referring to its length. Hoping to cast an
unfavorable light on the document, he relied on guilt by disassociation. In
logic that would make today's advocates of original intent cringe, he argued,
"Compare it with the Constitution of the United States, a model of comprehensive diction and brevity; and yet that instrument has lasted for 130 years
and has adapted itself to the enormous changes in our condition that have
come far beyond the dream of any of the founders of the government and the
men who constructed that wonderful instrument."[27]

Concluding a two-day whirlwind tour across the state, Bryan spoke to an
estimated ten thousand people in Oklahoma City on September 5. Like Taft,

Bryan invoked the memory of the authors of the United States Constitution. He referred to Oklahoma's proposed constitution as "the best constitution in the United States today" and spoke highly of the initiative and referendum as well as other Progressive provisions of the document.[28]

The outcome of the vote was an overwhelming show of support both for the constitution and for the Democratic candidates. The constitution carried in every county with a 71 percent statewide approval.[29] Given the document's implicit faith in the people to govern themselves, it was ironic, although prophetic of voter participation in mechanisms of direct democracy, that only 19 percent of the eligible voters voted on the constitution.[30] The Democrats won every elective position in the executive branch, all statewide judicial elections, overwhelming control of both houses of the legislature, and four of the five congressional seats.[31] The location of the state capital was addressed three years later when, in 1910, voters approved its relocation to Oklahoma City. Although most assumed that the change would take place after 1913 as Congress intended, Governor Haskell decided to move the seat of state government immediately. The legally dubious nature of the move was settled when the U.S. Supreme Court ruled in *Coyle v. Smith* (1911) that relocation of the state capital was a legitimate exercise in state sovereignty.[32]

The Best Constitution in the United States?

We have already argued that very little of Oklahoma's constitution is original. Rather, it is an amalgamation of provisions found in the U.S. Constitution, previous state constitutions, and Progressive ideas of the day. Perhaps the most serious criticism that can be made is the document's extraordinary length. It was partly the result of the delegates' great distrust of the legislature and, in a sense, all politicians. The initiative and referendum provisions clearly indicate this distrust, as does the decision of the delegates to create administrative commissions and boards whose officials were elected rather than appointed. As one astute student of state constitutions predicted, such requirements may result in officials who are more familiar with running for office than with competent administration: the state superintendent of public instruction may know "politics better than pedagogy."[33] Distrust of the legislature and politicians, although understandable at that time, became an obsession, and its effects can be seen throughout the constitution. It explains to a great degree why the document includes so much that is statutory in nature.

The Guthrie convention produced a paradox. As products of the Progressive era, responding to excesses of corporate power and greed, the delegates were eager to protect the land, small farmers, and ordinary working folks from unscrupulous politicians who might gain control of state government. Elect as many officials as possible and give the people ready access to the ballot box to keep the legislature honest: that was the basic idea. But detailed constitutional restrictions requiring frequent amendment coupled with the election of executive officials offer some veto points and clog the machinery of government. The state government loses flexibility and the capacity for rapid response to pressing problems. Such a governmental arrangement also becomes more vulnerable to influence by entrenched and powerful minority interests. In many ways Progressive and populist ideals were inspiring, but they required an active, well-informed electorate that would be constantly vigilant in supporting only those measures for the common good. Even in the early days of statehood that might have been too much to expect.

CONSTITUTIONAL CHANGES

From 1908 through the general election of 1986, 264 amendments have been proposed to the constitution; 129 (49%) have been approved. This figure stands in stark contrast to the 26 amendments to the U.S. Constitution in a two-hundred-year period.

What kinds of changes have been made? Many of the amendments deal with revenue matters.[34] Several pertain to suffrage: the grandfather clause disfranchising blacks (1910), the female vote (1918), and the eighteen-year-old-vote (1971). Others repeal deadwood, although in some cases it took several votes to do so: repeal of provisions relating to segregated schools (1966), repeal of the definition of "colored race" (1978), repeal of the obsolete prohibitions of girls and young boys working in underground mines and granting women equal rights to work in such mines (1986), and repeal of the poll tax (1986).

Other amendments remedy flaws or modernize the operation of the government. Examples include requiring a balanced budget (1941), creation of a court on the judiciary (1966), allowing the governor to be elected to two successive terms (1966), providing for annual legislative sessions (1966), consolidation of certain state offices, and giving the governor the power to appoint certain previously elected state officers (1975).

On three occasions (1926, 1950, and 1970) Oklahomans have rejected the idea of holding another constitutional convention. In no case was the vote close. In 1947 the legislature requested that a study be conducted concerning the need for a constitutional convention. A Constitution Survey Committee was formed, and after much study, it advised the legislature to put the question of a constitutional convention before the voters. A vote was held in 1950. Perhaps because of the attention the Constitution Survey Committee brought to the issue, the measure came the closest it ever has to passing. Still, 68 percent voted against calling a convention.

A FINAL WORD

In 1987 a report by the Hudson Institute recommended so many changes in Oklahoma's constitution that some observers speculated there might be a call for another constitutional convention or at least another large-scale constitutional study. Governor Henry Bellmon recommended the creation of such a study commission in his first message to the legislature in 1987.[35] If the past is any guide, a complete revision seems highly unlikely. The procedures for replacing constitutions are cumbersome, and building consensus for major change is difficult. This may be even more true for a state like Oklahoma, where change has been viewed skeptically. Although the delegates in Guthrie made ample provisions for the constitution to be revised, amended, or scrapped for a new one, the people have seen fit to make only piecemeal, although sometimes significant, changes in the document. Even some who are considered progressive do not favor a constitutional convention. For example, Frosty Troy, editor of the *Oklahoma Observer,* worries about the inevitable political maneuvering of vested interests seeking to have their pet ideas incorporated into the state's basic law. "It scares me to death," he says.[36] He adds:

> Maybe if we could wish ourselves a model document it would be the right thing to do. But we cannot—and the complexity and power politics of a constitutional convention [con-con] is a frightening prospect. . . .
>
> But what happens if we try to write an entirely new document? Expect the biggest swarm of lobbyists and interest groups in America. I saw that happen when I attended the Maryland con-con. Everybody was jockeying for power—and their particular version of the Constitution. It could be a nightmare when you consider the power groups as diverse as county commissioners and religious fundamentalists.

In 1988 a commission to study constitutional revision, chaired by Attorney General Robert Henry, with Governor Henry Bellmon and Senator David Boren serving as honorary co-chairs, began holding public hearings around the state to solicit opinions on proposals for changing the constitution. The commission has made a large number of recommendations for updating the document. Governor Bellmon announced before the conclusion of the commission's work that he would not seek another term, in part so he could concentrate his efforts during the remainder of his term on implementing constitutional reforms. He announced that he would lead an effort to raise five hundred thousand dollars from private sources to promote passage of the various amended articles. Three of the more far-reaching and controversial changes include provisions to (1) strengthen the office of the governor, (2) create an independent state ethics commission, and (3) revise the article on corporations to remove "antibusiness" language. A citizen committee, which had succesfully worked for the passage of Governor Bellmon's proposal in 1989 to shorten legislative sessions, circulated petitions for these three new questions. Its efforts, however, were thwarted in June 1990 when the Oklahoma Supreme Court rejected the questions on executive branch reorganization and corporations because each included more than one subject. Bellmon was incensed by the decision, although the court did leave in place the question calling for the creation of a constitutional ethics commission. That question ultimately passed by a wide margin in the 1990 fall elections, providing Oklahoma with one of the nation's strongest watchdog agencies to monitor state officials.

At this time, it appears that the governor does not plan to support a constitutional convention as a means of achieving changes to other parts of the constitution, apparently in the hope that the legislature will refer them to a popular vote by a series of referenda. Although the constitution calls for a vote on such a convention every twenty years (the last vote was in 1970), the voters have decisively rejected past efforts to bring about such a gathering. Convention or not, major revisions will not come easily in Oklahoma with its conservative political heritage. Only with strong support from the governor and state leaders (both public and private) are fundamental changes in the state's constitution likely.

Finally, we need to remember that reformers almost always oversell the need for structural reform as a way of curing the ills of government. A new and modern state constitution might facilitate some desirable changes in Oklahoma government (it is likely to be the only way, for example, to further reduce the number of elected statewide executive officials). The question to be answered is, Would Oklahoma politics change significantly if large-scale institutional changes were made? The rules of the game do make a difference, most experts agree. It is equally clear, however, that the basic political culture of a state would be little affected by even major changes in the state's constitution. The next three chapters in this section examine in more detail the institutional framework of Oklahoma government and the transition to a more modern state.

CHAPTER SIX

The Oklahoma Legislature

Under our representative form of government, legislative bodies are law-making institutions above all. They do other things as well, of course: they represent the people in a variety of ways; they may investigate charges of wrongdoing among state agencies or departments; they serve as a forum for discussing important policies and programs; they may provide some oversight of the state's administration not only through hearings and investigations, but by conducting post-audits of program outcomes; and finally, they may serve in a judicial capacity if impeachment proceedings are initiated against a governor or other official subject to such proceedings. Legislators also represent their districts and constituents at the capitol, particularly to influence the bureaucracy on behalf of constituents. In short, legislatures, sometimes referred to as the first branch of government, play an indispensable role in shaping state policy and influencing a wide range of public and private activities.

Despite their vital role in lawmaking, legislative bodies are often criticized for raising taxes, spending the public's money foolishly, or otherwise passing laws some groups oppose. During the late 1960s the Citizens Conference on State Legislatures conducted the most comprehensive comparative study of state legislatures to date. In its 1971 report the conference pointed to a variety of problems plaguing state legislatures. The most important were (1) poor organization and lack of staff; (2) a weak, ill-defined public image; and (3) constitutional constraints that prevent legislatures from meeting in order to act on important issues. The Citizens Conference concluded that the states' assemblies were a "drag" on the nation's political system and in need of "thorough institutional reform." In fact, the conference labeled state legislatures as "a series of sometimes governments [whose] presence is rarely felt or missed."[1]

Such criticism has not been ignored. Most legislatures, including Oklahoma's, undertook significant institutional reforms in the 1970s and 1980s. The extent of the reform movement's impact on Oklahoma's legislature can be quickly sensed by briefly contrasting its operations during the 1960s with those of today. Before popular approval of a 1966 state question, legislators were restricted to one regular session every other year. Today the Oklahoma legislature meets annually from February through May. A 1980 state question amended the Oklahoma Constitution to enable the legislature, on approval of two-thirds of the members of both houses, to call itself into special session. This amendment gives state lawmakers an important tool to maintain their influence when the legislature is not in regular session.

Compensation and the composition of the legislature, issues of vital importance to reformers, have changed significantly as well. Before the passage of a state question creating the Legislative Compensation Board in 1968, lawmakers were paid $15 per day for a maximum of seventy-five legislative days during the biennial session and $100 per month for any additional months that they met. For 1989–90, the Legislative Compensation Board raised lawmakers' annual salaries from $20,000 to $32,000, eighth best in the nation.[2] In addition, legislators can qualify for state retirement benefits if they contribute to the plan. They also receive state insurance benefits, travel allowances, and per diem expenses for the performance of their jobs.

Perhaps no change has been more important than the reapportionment of the legislature. Reapportionment followed the U.S. Supreme Court's 1962 landmark decision in *Baker v. Carr,* which established the "one person, one vote" standard for state legislatures. In Oklahoma, which had one of the worst-apportioned assemblies, the legislature lost much of its rural domination as the more populated metropolitan areas gained seats in both houses.[3]

For several reasons, we argue that the Oklahoma legislature needs to be a more effective participant in policy making than it was a quarter of a century ago. First, recent trends in federal policy making indicate that Washington is not as likely to take the active leadership role that it has in previous decades. Under the "new federalism" and with fiscal policy focusing on deficit reduction, the federal government has preferred whenever possible to turn programs back to the states and to allow states to solve their own problems. Perhaps more important, economic competition among the states has made the activities of state policy makers a critical factor as states struggle to improve their business climates to ensure the future prosperity of their citizens. No longer can Oklahoma afford a legislature that is a "drag" on the state's political system. Even lawmakers have become sensitive to media and voter criticism of the legislature. Such criticism became a major driving force in the dramatic showdown at the end of the 1989 legislative session which resulted in the removal of the house Speaker.

The 1989 rebellion in the Oklahoma house of representatives against its veteran Speaker may represent a watershed in state politics.[4] The ouster of veteran, four-term Speaker Jim Barker (*D*-Muskogee) on May 17, 1989, took state capitol observers by surprise. Frosty Troy, veteran capitol newsman and publisher of the *Oklahoma Observer,* said of the move, "Nothing in 30 years of the legislature has been this exciting. This has been a traditionally redneck legislature with a small progressive wing. But this progressive wing is now strong enough to pull this off." Indeed, one of the notable features of the revolt was the exceptional cooperation between Democratic representatives from the Oklahoma City and Tulsa areas.

Barker was elected Speaker in 1983 after another veteran Speaker, Dan Draper, had been convicted of vote tampering (the charge was later overturned by a federal judge). The new Speaker won high marks after assuming control of a deeply divided body by restoring leadership over the often unruly house and then taking the lead in passing tax increases in 1984, 1985, and 1987. Although some complained about pressure on legislators for their votes from the leadership, the additional revenues were necessary to avoid deep and devastating cuts in the state budget.

By the 1988 legislative campaigns, however, Barker's critics had seized the initiative. Barker and his leadership were widely attacked from within the legislature and in the media for employing heavy-handed tactics and indulging themselves in pork-barrel politics. The Oklahoma City *Daily Oklahoman* and its publisher, Edward Gaylord, made the removal of Barker's allies the issue in state legislative races with front-page editorials and gloating accounts of the defeat of veteran lawmakers. Those incumbent house members who did hold onto their seats, particularly Democrats in urban areas, soon recognized that the Speaker was a political liability in their districts. New members promised their constituents not to be Barker rubberstamps.

Nonetheless, Barker was reelected easily to a fourth term as Speaker. The switch from secret ballot to a pledge-card system in 1986 made his task easier. The incumbent Speaker was difficult to deny when he approached members directly for their support. The 1989 session, however, proved rocky for the Barker leadership. First, twenty-one of the seventy house Democrats opposed majority leader Guy Davis when he allegedly threatened to hold the higher education appropriation hostage until a state regent apologized for sponsoring a full-page newspaper ad attacking the Speaker and his lieutenants for their pork-barrel politics in the previous session. The Speaker, who placed a high premium on loyalty, backed Davis by withholding appointments of the letter signers to the powerful General Conference Committee on Appropriations and allegedly threatening other committee assignments.

As resentment toward the house leadership intensified, the dissidents began to organize. Cal Hobson, a Democrat representing Cleveland county and one of the most progressive members of the legislature, became one of the ringleaders of the Barker opposition. Hobson was one of the "insiders" during the Draper speakership but never enjoyed a close relationship with the Barker leadership team, although he held responsible committee chairmanships. Matters grew much worse for Hobson during the 1989 session, starting with his defeat in the Speaker Pro Tempore race. He later joined with the twenty other Democrats who protested Davis's attack on the state regent. Finally, when the Speaker failed to appoint Hobson to the budget reconciliation conference committee on which he had customarily served, he became convinced of the need for a change in the house leadership. As with the other dissidents, his desire for change arose out of both personal dissatisfaction and a deep concern that a change in leadership had to occur in order for the legislature to enact programs that would be beneficial for the state.

The dissidents, later known as the "T-Bar Twelve" (named after a popular Oklahoma City restaurant where they met several times), assembled to plot their strategy. At first their meetings focused primarily on how to respond to immediate concerns. But when house members dealt the leadership a crushing defeat in late April on a procedural measure, the T-Bar Twelve began to think that changing Speakers was possible. They systematically and secretly classified their Democratic colleagues as to how they would vote on an ouster motion. Freshmen were given special attention. By mid-May, the conspirators had forty-five of seventy Democrats committed to the ouster in a floor fight. The attorneys among them were assigned to research the parliamentary script.

At 10:40 A.M. on May 17, Dwayne Steidley, a Claremore Democrat and chairman of the House Judiciary Committee, made the motion to remove the Speaker. The planning paid off; every move by Barker's allies to block the revolt was parried. Unlike the case of embattled U.S. House Speaker Jim

Wright, whose problems stemmed from specific ethical charges, the debate over Barker's removal focused on more nebulous issues of leadership style, public image, political loyalty, the institutional power of the lower chamber, and the state's future. There was, however, no doubt about the outcome, as Republicans joined with the forty-five Democrats for a 72–25 vote for the ouster motion. Only fifty-one votes were required.

In the Democratic caucus that followed, Shawnee representative Steve Lewis, the T-Bar Twelve's candidate, won the nomination for Speaker over two opponents. He was elected subsequently on a strictly party vote. For his part, the former Speaker conducted himself with great tact during and after the revolt. The entire house of representatives paid public tribute to him the next week. The new leadership quickly resurrected several political reforms during the last days of the 1989 session which the more rural Barker leadership appeared to have shelved.

POWERS OF THE OKLAHOMA LEGISLATURE

First and foremost, legislatures are lawmaking bodies. Lawmaking is a joint exercise, of course, involving in a formal way the legislature and the governor. In fact, in recent years governors have played an ever larger role in shaping legislation. The governor proposes the budget and often includes programs and priorities in the budgetary message and the state-of-the-state address. Beyond that, many departments of the executive branch get involved in the process in various ways—by preparing reports for the governor or legislature, by testifying before legislative committees, and by working with constituent groups that support specific policy proposals. Yet, ultimately, the legislature must act. It alone has the responsibility, through its extensive committee system, to put proposed legislation in final form. When the two houses disagree on the specifics of a bill, the two conflicting measures go to a conference committee that must hammer out the final version. Then the measure goes back to each legislative chamber for a final vote without amendment. All revenue-raising measures constitutionally must originate in the house of representatives.

The representative function of the legislature is perhaps less clearly apparent, although it is of fundamental importance. Representation is at the heart of the democratic political process. In a very basic way legislators stand for or speak for the people they represent. Elections are the mechanism for ensuring this accountability to the legislator's district in a single-member district system such as that in Oklahoma. In a practical sense the representative role may bring legislators into frequent contact with the people, organized groups, businesses, and institutions in their districts. Letters may be exchanged; personal meetings held; telephone calls made; and appearances arranged before local groups—all in the name of representation and accountability.

The Oklahoma legislature has other formal responsibilities. It reviews and disapproves state administrative rules and regulations, and the senate confirms the appointments of certain agency directors and almost all members of state boards and commissions. Through the work of individual members or legislative committees, the legislature focuses media and citizen attention on current issues. Lawmakers thus help to educate the public and to convince it that change may be necessary, usually by legislation.

Legislative power is limited in a variety of ways. The initiative and referendum permit the electorate to enact legislation directly. The governor's veto power represents at times a powerful constraint on legislative action. Finally, legislative influence over many state agencies, including the higher education system and the largest agency of all, the Department of Human Services, is diminished by the constitutional provisions that created them and provide for their duties and powers.

The creation of a merit system in 1959 reduced the informal powers of the legislature substantially, but not completely. Lawmakers still retain considerable influence over public jobs. Consider Senator Gene Stipe (D-McAlester), for example, who has served Little Dixie in the legislature for nearly forty years.[5] Stipe is one of the state's most respected and feared lawmakers. His seeming invincibility at reelection time is based at least in part on his ability to find jobs for his constituents. Every Saturday morning, he sees his constituents, most of whom look to him for assistance, at his McAlester law office. According to Stipe, "'Saturday mornings are something of a tradition around here. . . . Every Saturday morning, the people know they can see Gene Stipe in his office. I don't turn anyone away.'"

Stipe's 1988 Republican opponent Lois Edington of Hartshorne, tried to make the senator's patronage politics her major campaign issue: "'I want to break tradition. . . . I don't feel any elected official's office should be an employment office. . . . This is degrading, un-American and unacceptable.'" She blamed Stipe for the sluggish southeastern Oklahoma economy because new industry would bring jobs to the region he could not control. She lost in her second effort to unseat the dean of the state senate; Stipe won by a comfortable margin of 61 to 39 percent.

State senators, particularly Democrats, dispense a considerable number of jobs. Democratic senators control appointments to county election boards, for example, and in rural areas choose the local motor vehicle tag agencies. Both of these arrangements are valuable sources of local influence. Senators also control, through senatorial advice and consent, a large number of prestigious appointments to the governing boards of state agencies. Although most are only part-time, these positions can be powerful and highly sought after. It is almost inconceivable for the senate to confirm an appointment if the appointee's senator opposes it.

THE LEGISLATIVE ENVIRONMENT AND MEMBERSHIP CHARACTERISTICS

In its evaluation of legislatures the Citizens Conference on State Legislatures focused on how these bodies operate. The comparison, in other words, emphasized the legislatures as institutions, disregarding the decisions they make. This approach can be challenged for its failure to include output considerations, particularly the quality of legislation produced. The authors justified their study design as follows: unless a legislative assembly is adequately developed as an institution, its performance in making policy is likely to suffer. Its members will spend the majority of their time trying to compensate for the structural deficiencies in the legislative environment. Thus their more creative and innovative work will be stifled.

The Citizens Conference examined nine core areas of each legislature: members' compensation, professional and clerical staffing services for the members and committees, the ability of the legislatures to manage their time, committee structure and operations, physical facilities, the role of legislative leaders, legislative rules and procedures, the size of the legislature, and legislative ethics. From these categories, each legislature was then ranked on a series of five major characteristics, commonly called the FAIIR system. FAIIR stands for functionality, accountability, information handling, independence, and representativeness of the legislatures.[6]

How, then, did the Citizens Conference rank Oklahoma in comparison with other state legislatures? In fact, it was ranked quite high—fourteenth. Although the study noted the wide gap in the state's very high rankings in certain areas and its considerably lower rank on others, only New Mexico's eleventh ranking was higher than Oklahoma's among its neighboring states.[7] Arkansas ranked forty-sixth, Texas thirty-eighth, Missouri thirty-fifth, Colorado twenty-eighth, and Kansas twenty-third. Oklahoma's score was based on its relatively high marks in functionality (9th) and representativeness (8th); scores on accountability

(27th), information handling (24th), and independence (22nd) were significantly lower, but still better than most states.

The Oklahoma legislature has changed significantly since the Citizens Conference study as lawmakers have endeavored to improve their ability to shape state policy. The extent of the changes can be examined as we review the Oklahoma legislature using the FAIIR categories.

Functionality

Oklahoma's legislature received a very high rank (9th) in the functional category, largely on the basis of its ability to manage its workload. Time, staff, and procedures are the central issues that were studied to determine how well an assembly functions. Staff changes were of strong interest to the legislature in the 1980s. The 1981 legislature, for example, abolished the Oklahoma Legislative Council, a centralized staff supporting both houses. The house of representatives and senate now maintain separate professional staffs with only a centralized staff agency for copy services, bill processing, sharing computer technology, and periodic joint legislative projects.

These reforms have been somewhat controversial. From a national perspective, Oklahoma's legislative staff ranks in the middle in size, which is appropriate to the state's population. The Oklahoma legislature employs approximately 165 full-time staff and considerably more session-only employees. Nevertheless, a commission appointed by former governor George Nigh in 1984 to recommend state government reforms objected to the growing influence of the legislative staff. Terming it the "Washington syndrome," the Commission on Reform of Oklahoma State Government argued that legislators delegated too much responsibility to their staffs.[8]

The Citizens Conference raised some other issues that deserve mention. The size of the Oklahoma legislature, with 101 house and 48 senate members, is not excessive by conference standards. The number of legislative committees, however, has generally exceeded the recommended ten to fifteen for each house. For the 1987 legislature, the senate listed seventeen committees, while the house of representatives retained twenty-eight committees (four fewer than the previous session). One of the first changes of the new leadership following the 1989 overthrow of Speaker Jim Barker was to reduce the number of house committees to twenty-one. Concerns about the number of committees is important because an unwieldy committee system can blur committee jurisdictions and force members to serve on too many panels. In Oklahoma, representatives serve on four to six committees; many senators have five committee assignments.

Accountability

The Citizen Conference's assessment of the Oklahoma legislature's accountability (27th) listed many areas for improvement. The accountability of a legislative body is determined by three measures. First, is the legislative process understandable to the interested public? Second, is sufficient information available and accessible to allow the public to know what is going on in the legislature? Finally, does the legislature allow individual members the opportunity, "consistent with the need to get the work done," to influence decisions?[9]

Accountability is particularly important in the area of committee operations. Oklahoma's legislative rules governing committee operations are relatively brief, committees do not normally maintain detailed records on votes, and their records on debates and intent are virtually nonexistent. Although the standing committees generally comply with the intent of open meetings (senate rules include an open meeting provision), it is possible for bills to be signed out of a committee without a public meeting. Critical to making committee meetings more accessible to the public is the lack of advance meeting notices.

Conference committees are even more difficult to obtain access to than standing committees. Normally, conference committees have three members from each house appointed by the presiding officers; others, however, such as the General Conference Committee on Appropriations, which writes the state budget, are much larger. Frequently, these committees meet secretly, if at all, during the rushed final weeks of the legislative session. The activities of most conference committees are not easily traced because their required records are scant.

Public demand for accountability in the legislature has forced greater financial disclosure requirements by lawmakers. They must file financial disclosure statements and campaign finance reports with the Oklahoma Council on Campaign Compliance and Ethical Standards (formerly the Ethics Commission). Financial disclosure reports do not provide the public a complete report on legislators' personal wealth or income, but require only that members disclose their individual income by sources that exceed one thousand dollars annually.

One final issue relating to accountability is the ability of individual members to affect the activities of the legislature. This is a complex issue. As a body, the Oklahoma legislature has been dominated historically by the Dem-

Table 1. Republican Party Membership in the Oklahoma Legislature, 1959–89

	House			Senate		
	Total Members	Republicans	% of Total	Total Members	Republicans	% of Total
1959–60	119	9	7.6	48	7	14.6
1965–66	99	21	21.2	48	10	20.8
1969–70	99	23	23.2	48	9	18.8
1975–76	101	25	24.7	48	9	18.8
1979–80	101	26	25.7	48	11	22.9
1985–86	101	32	31.7	48	14	29.2
1987–88	101	31	30.7	48	17	35.4
1989–90	101	32	31.7	48	15	31.3

Source: Council of State Government, *Book of the States* (Lexington, Ky.: Council of State Government, various years), and Oklahoma Department of Libraries, *Who Is Who in the 41st Oklahoma Legislature* (Norman: University of Oklahoma Printing Services, 1987).

ocratic party, as indicated in Table 1, but that domination has been weakened to the point that the Republican party controls approximately one-third of the seats in both houses. This proportion is important for at least two reasons. First, by controlling one-third of the seats in either house, the Republicans have the opportunity to block passage of bills with emergency clauses, including budget and tax legislation. In addition, one-third of either house, by voting as a block, can prevent a legislative override of gubernatorial vetoes. By the strategic use of this power, the Republican caucus can force Democratic support for Republican issues, as the following case illustrates.[10]

In the 1987 legislative session an unusually large turnover among incumbent Democratic senators resulted in a 31–17 Democratic/Republican division in the state senate. The additional seats gained by the minority party provided it with the ability to block passage of emergency clauses on important appropriation and revenue measures and to prevent a legislative override of any vetoes issued by newly elected Republican governor Henry Bellmon.

Faced with a budget shortfall for the 1988 fiscal year exceeding $300 million, Governor Bellmon's first state budget message called on the legislature to act on a series of major government reforms, program reductions, and tax increases to balance the budget and stabilize essential government services. Democratic legislative leaders, who had taken the heat during previous years for tax increases to deal with similar budget shortfalls during earlier Democratic administrations, now expected Republican lawmakers to follow their party leader's call for a tax increase. Unaccustomed to that role and fresh from campaigns in which they had pledged opposition to a tax increase, the two Republican caucuses were reluctant to accept higher taxes. House Democrats finally were able to secure enough votes from their members along with the few Republicans willing to support the tax increase to pass the bill. But senate Republicans would go along only in return for significant reforms at the Oklahoma Tax Commission.

Senate Democrats had long controlled the tax agency, which was often criticized for lax enforcement and a patronage-laden staff. The compromise called for the appointment of a Republican chairman of the three-member commission and the creation of an administrator for the agency appointed by the new chairman. These changes were quickly confirmed by the senate; statutory changes to ensure a bipartisan commission were expected to follow. With the compromise, both houses passed the tax increase. The governor then signed the bill, despite the support of only six of the seventeen Republican senators and sixteen of thirty-one representatives—figures significantly smaller than Democratic leaders had expected. So senate Democrats refused to honor the agreement for reforms at the Oklahoma Tax Commission.

In a dramatic response Governor Bellmon vetoed the appropriations to the agency, a move that threatened to shut down the operations of state government and impair municipal services. To avoid that and to support the agreement made with senate Republicans, Bellmon called the legislature into special session in July. The charge was to act on tax commission reforms and to appropriate funds to the agency and for the state's application for the federal supercollider project that the governor wanted funded. When the special session convened, Democratic legislators politely listened to the governor's message and then adjourned without acting on any of Bellmon's requests. The governor issued a call for a second special session for the next day on the same issues. This session met with the same fate as the first.

A constitutional crisis appeared to be developing. The impasse was resolved, however, when the legislature agreed to return and take up Bellmon's agenda in the last days of the regular session. In an omnibus bill, legislators presented the governor with the statutory reforms he had demanded, including funds for the supercollider project and a host of Democratic measures he had previously vetoed, among them controversial changes in state retirement laws. The governor quickly signed the bill, ending one of the rockiest sessions in recent Oklahoma history.

Information Handling

The Citizens Conference on State Legislatures found that the Oklahoma legislature of the 1970s ranked only twenty-seventh among the states in its ability to acquire, assimilate, and act on information useful for legislative decision making. Staffing and the use of time are the critical issues here. Creativity and innovation in a legislature requires considerable staff resources and effective use of interims and sessions.

In recent years the Oklahoma legislature has made significant improvements in its information-gathering capabilities. Standing committees of both houses can now meet throughout the year and conduct in-depth studies during legislative interims. Budget reductions, however, have been partly responsible for the elimination of the legislative program evaluation function of the Oklahoma Legislative Council. The absence of systematic program evaluations or post-audits of state agency operations represents a significant gap in the legislature's information-gathering function; moreover, it reduces state agencies' accountability to lawmakers. On the other hand, the Oklahoma legislature, through its Joint Committee on Fiscal Operations, has recently contracted with respected research firms to conduct extensive studies on major state issues.

Independence

The Citizens Conference ranked Oklahoma twenty-second in the independence category. Subsequently, however, several major deficiencies, such as the inability of the legislature to call itself into special session, were removed. The 1989 constitutional provisions that shortened annual sessions to February through May and the abundance of constitutionally created state agencies and statewide elected officials remain as checks on the independence of the legislative branch.

On the whole, the reform movement has worked to the benefit of legislative independence in Oklahoma. The most obvious measure of legislative independence is in the stronger oversight and control of the executive branch through the budget process. In the 1970s the legislature's ability to determine the overall state budget was comparatively limited. Of the total state budget, the legislature appropriated only one-third directly. The remainder of the budget pie, which was divided equally between federal and "earmarked" state fees or taxes, escaped the annual appropriations process. For example, the Department of Human Services administered a vast array of public assistance programs under a constitutional board with little interference from or accountability to the legislature. The agency's earmarked source of support was the state's two-cents sales tax. In 1981 the legislature passed a measure requiring that state funds be directly appropriated to the Department of Human Services, and in 1987 the practice of earmarking sales taxes for the mammoth agency ended.

There are other important considerations in examining the legislature's independence. The constitutionally created Legislative Compensation Board enables legislative compensation to be changed without a vote of either the people or the legislature. And though the state's lieutenant governor has some legislative duties, including presiding over joint sessions and the power to cast tie-breaking votes in the senate, he or she does not actually preside in the senate as in some other states such as Texas. Furthermore, the legislature is responsible for its own apportionment, unless it fails to take action during the session after each decennial census.

Of critical concern to the independence of any legislature is the ethics provisions under which it operates. In Oklahoma, statutes regulate activities of lobbyists and require them to register with the Oklahoma Council on Campaign Compliance and Ethical Standards; other laws direct legislators to file financial disclosure statements and campaign finance and expenditure reports with the council as well. Legislators are prohibited from engaging in activities or having interests that conflict with their legislative duties. A constitutional provision requires members to disclose personal or private interests on measures before the legislature and not to vote on them. In recent years there has been considerable pressure within and without the legislature to give the Council on Campaign Compliance and Ethical Standards additional powers to discipline lawmakers, in the belief that the two houses will not do so on their own. A 1990 constitutional amendment to replace the council with a State Ethics Commission armed with stronger powers to initiate ethics provisions related to the legislature will likely set the stage for a series of stronger checks on legislators and lobbyists.

Representativeness

The Citizens Conference on State Legislatures, which studied Oklahoma after the reapportionment of the 1960s finally gave urban voters an equal voice

Table 2: Oklahoma Legislators' Occupations, 1989–90

	House		Senate	
	No.	%	No.	%
Law	15	15	13	27
Insurance	5	5	5	10
Farming/Ranching	15	15	9	19
Real estate	12	12	5	10
Education	11	11	1	2
Business	30	30	13	27
Other	26	26	8	17

Source: Data from Midwest Political Research, *On the Record: A Guide to Oklahoma Legislators and Districts* (Oklahoma City, 1989).

Note: The numbers add to more than the total membership because some legislators list more than one occupation.

at the state capitol, ranked the legislature quite high (8th) in representativeness, owing to the fairly liberal qualifications for election and the fact that the state employed single-member districts. Yet how "representative" is the legislature of the state's population? In his study of the Oklahoma legislature published in 1978, political scientist Samuel Kirkpatrick determined that lawmakers did not mirror accurately the social and demographic characteristics of Oklahoma,[11] a conclusion that still is true and can be drawn about virtually all state legislatures. In many ways Oklahoma's lawmakers, again as in all states, tend to be "elitist" on the basis of education and occupation (achieved characteristics), but more representative of the population in age, gender, race, and religion (ascribed characteristics). In certain major categories, however, the legislature is much less representative of the population, particularly in female and minority representation. The 1989–90 legislature had, for example, only six women senators (an all-time high, but only 12.5% of total) and seven female representatives (6.9% of total); there were two black senators (4.2% of total) and three black representatives (3.0%).[12] Both black senators and one black representative were also women. Black and female legislators held one key leadership post and two major committee chairs.

The occupational characteristics of lawmakers are further evidence of their differences from the general population. As Table 2 suggests, a large percentage of legislators are professional or business persons. They are also, with few exceptions, part-time or citizen lawmakers; that is, they are expected to have regular jobs of their own. That is certainly different from many large states, where the majority of lawmakers consider themselves full-time.

Despite the relatively large percentage of lawyers in both houses, the number of attorneys has declined over past assemblies, a trend consistent with legislatures throughout the nation. Of the two houses, attorneys are a much smaller minority in the state house (13%) than in the senate (27%). As a group, Oklahoma's lawmakers have much more education than the general public. Sixty-four percent of the members who served in the 1989–90 legislature were college graduates; another 27 percent had some college education.[13] For the state, only 15.1 percent of persons over twenty-five had four or more years of college, according to the 1980 census.[14]

LEGISLATIVE PERFORMANCE

The FAIIR system was designed to evaluate the technical capacities of legislatures to perform their tasks, not to measure the decisions they actually make. Earlier we noted that the Citizens Conference on State Legislatures ranked the Oklahoma legislature the fourteenth best in the nation on its institutional capacity. In Kirkpatrick's study of the Oklahoma legislature, he considered whether or not Sooner lawmakers deserve the high ranking they were given by the Citizens Conference.

Kirkpatrick's analysis primarily involved a comparison of the Oklahoma legislature's rank with some state policy indicators, including expenditure and tax effort. On most of these measures the state ranked well below its high legislative ranking. Based on these comparisons, Kirkpatrick raised the question as to whether Oklahoma "deviated" from the anticipated pattern of states with high legislative rankings also having high marks on policy issues. He also conceded, however, that without extensive study it is difficult to make definitive statements about the effectiveness of any legislature. Certainly a major influence that Kirkpatrick's comparisons fail to account for is that of the external political environment and its effect on legislative decisions.[15]

How well does the legislature serve as an agent for making the kind of changes required for the state to function in the economic and social environment of a global society? The question is itself difficult because so many possible policies have been proposed and debated in the name of economic development. The legislature has refused to enact several reform proposals, such as right-to-work, for example, despite strong business pressure for that measure. The legislative record on other reforms has been, when supported by a consensus of interested groups, much better. To promote economic diversification, the legislature has passed landmark legislation to mobilize funds for research at the major universities, to improve economic development planning, and to increase the availability of venture capital. To prevent erosion of the state's education system and vital government programs, lawmakers increased taxes three times during the 1980s and again in 1990. Although Oklahoma remains a low-tax state, legislators have adjusted to the reality that Oklahomans can no longer fund their government programs by exporting their taxes, namely, taxes paid out of state through the Oklahoma severance tax on oil and gas.

Clearly, problems remain for the legislature. Throughout this chapter, we have identified institutional weaknesses within the legislature that impair its operation. Lack of staff to do program evaluations, for example, limits the accountability of state agencies to lawmakers. A poor public image can restrict the legislature's ability to sell its programs to the voters and can undermine its leadership on important policy issues.[16] To some extent, the public image issue also contributes to one of the most common problems of all legislatures: turnover. For example, turnover for both houses was higher than usual for the 1986 and 1988 elections. Excessive turnover can affect political alignment and make continuity in policy making more difficult. It can also make it harder for state leaders to gather support for controversial votes by members who fear losing their seats.

THE ROLE OF A LEGISLATOR

In addition to making laws, the legislator plays another fundamental role— representing the people, especially the individuals, groups, and economic interests in his or her district. Some years ago, in a study of state legislators from California, New Jersey, Ohio, and Tennessee, the following questions were asked of these lawmakers: "How would you describe the job of being a legislator—what are the most important things you should do here? Are there any important differences between what you think this job is and the way your constituents see it?"[17] Responses to these questions yielded three classic role orientations—trustee, delegate, and politico. *Trustees* see themselves essentially as their own people, not necessarily under obligation to vote just the way their constituents want. After all, trustees might say, they have far better information than constituents do, and it is their duty to vote the way they think best or the way their consciences dictate. Of course, such legislators might hold views similar to those of their constituents, so this role orientation may not lead to a great deal of conflict or disagreement with their constituency.

Delegates, as the name implies, take just the opposite view. They tend to believe that above all it is their job to follow whatever their district wants regardless of their own views. As one legislator put it, "What the district wants me to do is my most important job. I carry out their decisions. I'll put any bill in the hopper they give me. If they wanted me to move this capitol, I'd break my neck to do it."[18]

The third role is that of *politico,* which describes the legislator who falls between the other two extremes. These lawmakers might take the position that in some cases, where the pressure from home is especially strong, it might be wise to follow the perceived views of the district. On the other hand, occasions may arise in which lawmakers decide to discount constituency interests—perhaps the facts are complicated, and the people are not likely to understand the matter; there may be considerable pressure to vote with the party or the leadership; or legislators may just feel very strongly on the issue as a matter of principle.

Kirkpatrick's mid-1970s study of Oklahoma legislators includes information on their role orientations. The most prevalent role was clearly that of trustee (table 3). Half of the Oklahoma house members saw themselves as trustees; almost 46 percent of the senators agreed. In summarizing the comments of trustees in the Oklahoma house, Kirkpatrick quoted one member: "I don't explain my vote to anybody. . . . What I do is my own decision. If they don't like it, then they don't have to send me back. . . . I am burned up about being misinformed by uninformed people. Quite often I vote my own conscience."[19] Perhaps surprisingly, few legislators opted for the purely delegate role. No doubt, most lawmakers try to stay in touch with their constituents, and in many cases they may feel that no conflict exists between the way they look at most issues and the views of those they represent.

A 1986 survey of most Oklahoma legislators provides more up-to-date information on lawmakers' perspectives of how they see their jobs. They were asked how they resolved conflicts in which they disagreed with the voters of their districts. In cases in which their positions conflicted with the opinions of their constituents, 56 percent of the lawmakers said they would vote their districts; only 26 percent said they would vote their consciences. If the conflict was between their political party and the voters, an overwhelming 80

Table 3. Role Orientation of Oklahoma Legislators
in the mid-1970s (in Percent)

Role	Senate	House
Trustee	45.8	50.0
Politico	41.7	40.0
Delegate	12.5	10.0

Source: Data from Samuel Kirkpatrick, *The Legislative Process in Oklahoma: Policy Making, People, and Politics* (Norman: University of Oklahoma Press, 1978), pp. 204–11.

percent again would vote their districts. Local influence also won, but by a closer margin (53%/36%), if the choice were between the state and the local district.[20]

These more recent answers suggest that legislators are concerned increasingly with taking care of their districts. This goal is often achieved by "bringing home the bacon"—inserting in appropriation bills projects that will benefit their districts. These projects can range from funds for rattlesnake hunts, to renovating old railroad stations, to construction of school facilities. Critics call it pork-barrel politics, and all legislatures, including the Congress, play the game. Minority party legislators often lose out, however, because the dominant party leaders control the agenda and have the votes to decide which projects will be funded and which legislators will get the pork. Moreover, the governor might get involved, especially if he or she is of the minority party, as happened in the 1988 legislative session in Oklahoma when the governor led the effort to cut pork-barrel spending.

CONCLUSION

The legislative reform movement of the 1960s and 1970s brought extensive changes to the Oklahoma legislature. Higher salaries, annual sessions, larger and better staffs, and more independence are a few tangible benefits of the efforts to upgrade the legislature's effectiveness. Despite the usual criticisms leveled against a state legislature, Oklahoma's legislative capacity has been ranked, at least by the most extensive study of state legislatures, as much better than most.

Nonetheless, frustrations with the Oklahoma legislature have grown in recent years. Several explanations come to mind: the series of tax increases required to save the state budget, four years of fights between Democratic legislative leaders and the Republican governor, and a hostile Republican metropolitan press that likes to blame the legislature for economic problems. Whatever explanation one chooses, dissatisfaction has contributed to the recent defeat of an unusually large number of incumbent lawmakers in both parties and to open discussions about a "breakdown" in the legislative process.

What does the future hold? Is Oklahoma's legislature joining those of a large number of states, including some of those that have been judged as the best, in "entering a period of decline"? Alan Rosenthal, one of the most respected students of state government, recently charged that legislatures are becoming more like the Congress—a development he does not see as positive. The causes of "congressionalization" are legislative careerism, greater politicization of the legislative process, and fragmentation of power within the legislature. According to Rosenthal, salaries of lawmakers are a key ingredient; higher legislative salaries lead lawmakers to devote their energies full-time to their political careers and to act in such a way to protect their seats.[21]

Despair over the Oklahoma legislature seems premature, however. Almost all Sooner lawmakers still see themselves as part-time, citizen legislators. Although salaries are much better than before, these increases were accompanied by a successful drive to shorten the session. Perhaps surprisingly, these apparently incongruous positions were both supported by Republican governor Henry Bellmon. Finally, careerism has been offset by the large number of incumbents who failed to win reelection.

Following the close of the 1988 legislative session, the Oklahoma League of Women Voters asked lawmakers what they believed would fix the problems of the legislature. One of the most thoughtful responses was that of retiring senator David Riggs, a Democrat from the Tulsa suburb of Sand Springs. Riggs, elected to the house in 1970 and narrowly defeated in his race for house Speaker in 1983, suggests, "The whole parliamentary system has broken down. It's become a rotten, rank spoils system caused by four main problems." They are (1) concentration of power in the legislature; (2) pork-barrel politics; (3) trading of votes, commonly called "logrolling"; and (4) weaknesses in the committee system.[22] Apparently, some legislators believe that conference committees sometimes make too many substantial changes to the bills reported out by the standing committees.

Criticism clearly has brought changes in the legislature, but it is not clear that recent problems forecast a decline in the Oklahoma legislature as a vital participant in the state's policy-making process. The challenges to the legislature in the 1990s are evident. STOP New Taxes, a group organized to overturn the 1990 tax increase and backed by the powerful publisher of the *Daily Oklahoman,* is circulating a petition to have voters act on a constitutional amendment that would almost certainly force future legislative tax increases to be approved by a vote of the people. Another question, passed in September 1990, led Oklahoma to become the first state to place limits on legislative incumbency. In the future, the state constitution will limit the tenure of lawmakers to a maximum of twelve years. Meanwhile, special interest groups have discovered that they can circumvent the legislature entirely through the initiative and referendum process. Furthermore, it is certain that partisanship in the legislature will be sharp. Both political parties are keenly aware of the high stakes in the 1990 legislative elections. That legislature will be expected to prepare the reapportionment plans for the state legislature and the Oklahoma congressional delegation. The drawing of legislative boundaries can have a significant influence on the balance of power between the parties and ultimately affect a wide range of policy outcomes in the years ahead.

CHAPTER SEVEN

The Governor and the Administration

Nearly everyone in Oklahoma knows the name of the governor. Surveys have shown that next to the president of the United States, more people know the name of their governor than of any other elected public officeholder.[1] According to a former governor of North Carolina, Terry Sanford, "The center of the state system, and its chief proponent in the eyes of the people, is the governor."[2] The Oklahoma Constitution confers on the governor the title of "Chief Magistrate" endowed with "supreme executive powers." The governor is made "conservator of peace" and "shall cause the laws of the state to be faithfully executed." Some power, right? Alas, there is less here than meets the eye, at least in Oklahoma, and in many other states, too. Some might logically compare the office of governor to that of the president. In some ways such a comparison makes sense, but in other important respects, the governor is a much less powerful officer, relatively speaking of course, than the nation's chief executive.

The enumeration of the governor's powers and responsibilities in the Oklahoma Constitution suggests a chief executive in fact as well as in name. But the governor of Oklahoma must share executive powers with other elected and appointed state officials, including such top-level elected officers as the lieutenant governor, attorney general, state treasurer, state auditor and inspector, and the superintendent of public instruction. These officials serve independently of the governor and are accountable only to the electorate. The secretary of state, once an elected official, also shares executive power with the elected officers. In addition to elected officials, an abundance of agencies established by statute and by the state constitution perform executive functions. In short, although the governor occupies the single most important position in state government, less power resides in the office than many people think. So we need to examine the nature, functions, and power of the state's chief executive and see how recent changes have strengthened and modernized that office in Oklahoma. Indeed, the office has grown more powerful, although as we will see, it still remains relatively weak compared to its counterparts in many other states.

THE NATURE OF THE OFFICE

The essential characteristics of the office of governor in Oklahoma include the following:

Qualifications: A qualified elector in Oklahoma at least ten years before election who is at least thirty-one years of age and a U.S. citizen.

Term: Four years, with the right of immediate succession for two consecutive terms.

Compensation: $70,128 per year with an additional $26,800 annual amount for maintenance of the governor's mansion (both amounts are set by act of the legislature).

If the governor resigns or is impeached by the legislature, the lieutenant governor takes over, although the two officers do not run as a team. In fact, the two may be of different parties, as is the case in 1987–91 with Republican governor Henry Bellmon and Democratic lieutenant governor Robert S. Kerr III. If for any reason the lieutenant governor cannot serve, the next in succession is the president pro tempore of the senate. Until the mid-1960s Oklahoma governors could not directly succeed themselves in office. That provision was changed by constitutional amendment in 1966. But the state's first gubernatorial reelection did not take place until 1982, when George Nigh, a former lieutenant governor, became the first governor to be reelected. Even though he had served once before (1963–67), governor Henry Bellmon (1987–91) was eligible to succeed himself in 1991 because the constitutional limitation restricts the incumbent to two *consecutive* terms (Bellmon, however, announced in the middle of the term that he would not seek reelection).

As indicated above, immense responsibilities reside with the governor. In addition to serving as the state's chief administrative officer, governors function as chief legislator, ceremonial head of the government, and leader of their party.[3] Research shows some of these responsibilities to be considerably more important (chief legislator) than others (party leader).[4] According to the governors themselves, the job of managing state affairs demands the most time of all.[5] As the National Governors' Association observes, "The governor is one of the largest employers in his state. Altogether, states employ many more people than the federal government."[6] About thirty-five thousand people work for state government in Oklahoma (excluding higher education), many more than work for Tinker Air Force Base, the state's next largest employer of civilians.[7] Moreover, according to the State Office of Personnel Management, the state has 110 "employing" agencies, apart from higher education.[8] Not all of these agencies report directly to the governor, but such numbers help convey the enormous task of managing state government in Oklahoma.

Serving as chief legislator actually represents part of a larger basic gubernatorial function—the formulation of policy. Since the legislature plays such a critical part in the lawmaking process, much of the discussion of the governor's policy role centers on legislative relations. The chief executive can influence legislative activities in several ways. All governors enter office with a "program" they hope the legislature will enact into law. Parts of the governor's program may stem from campaign promises. Or various ideas and commitments may come from the state-of-the-state message the Oklahoma governor delivers to the legislature at the beginning of the session. The governor also prepares the state's budget, a document that contains a series of specific programmatic recommendations. The budget message likely has more detailed program requests than the obligatory state-of-the-state message.

Except in North Carolina, all governors can veto bills. In Oklahoma a two-thirds vote of the members of each chamber of the legislature overrides the governor's veto. If lawmakers attach the emergency clause to a bill, the governor's veto must be overridden by a three-fourths majority vote of the legislature. During the session governors have five days in which to veto a bill; otherwise it becomes law without their signature.[9] After legislative adjournment, the governor may use a "pocket veto" to kill a bill by refusing to sign it within fifteen days.[10] Oklahoma governors also possess the line-item veto, permitting them to veto any part of an appropriations bill. The same override provisions apply to the item veto. By simply threatening to veto a measure, the governor often can induce legislators to seek a compromise solution.

Another vehicle available to the governor for influencing policy is the power to call special sessions of the legislature. At such "extraordinary," or special, sessions, the legislature may consider only those subjects presented to it by the chief executive.[11] Governor Bellmon, for example, called the legislature into special session four times during his most recent term in office. The most controversial special session (which ran August 1989 through April 1990) resulted in a major education reform and tax increase in funding for Oklahoma's elementary and high-school system.

Governors may shape state policy in other ways, too. Consider appointments, for example. The value of making top-level appointments, to head major state agencies such as the transportation or human services department, is obvious. The governor may name sympathetic administrators who presumably will serve as effective advocates of the governor's programs and priorities. Lower level appointments or those to various boards and commissions may also enhance the governor's policy powers. They may prove especially useful as patronage to secure legislative or interest-group support for the governor's policy initiatives. Finally, a crucial instrument for influencing policy is the governor's authority to prepare and submit the state budget to the legislature. Budgetary matters are considered further in chapter 10.

Policy leadership for what? one might ask. Today's governors are under pressure as perhaps never before to hammer out new solutions to critical problems. Political analyst David Osborne argues, for example, that given the forces transforming our economy, namely technological advances and global competition, the nation's future rests on the ability to innovate.[12] Government must help to create and nourish a climate in which innovation flourishes as an everyday process. And, Osborne contends, in the 1980s the states responded to these demands more readily and effectively than the national government. He identifies such governors as Mario Cuomo of New York, Michael Dukakis of Massachusetts, Bruce Babbitt of Arizona, and Richard Thornburgh of Pennsylvania as among those who provided critical and imaginative leadership in this process of economic transition. So even today, and especially for the years ahead, successful governors will be judged perhaps more than any other way by how effectively they provide the policy leadership to encourage creative and innovative responses to meet the demands of economic change.

We noted above that governors traditionally serve as party leaders. Nonetheless, most chief executives do not view party leadership as an important duty.[13] Consider Democratic governors in Oklahoma. Within the highly fragmented Democratic party, with its emphasis on personality-based politics, governors seldom become involved extensively in party affairs. Rather, they usually build on a personal following, often leaving the party organization playing a distinctly minor role in the operations of the chief executive.

As ceremonial head of state government, the governor engages in a public relations role. What the governor says and does is news, and the demand for public appearances is endless. Meeting with the press, the public, and various groups consumes vast amounts of the chief executive's time. Coleman Ransone, a long-time student of American governors, contends that public relations may be the most time-consuming of all gubernatorial responsibilities.[14] Although some of this PR activity may appear trivial, a governor can hardly avoid much of this public contact. Moreover, such activities can be quite useful for building and maintaining goodwill and support. Other things being equal, who can doubt that a popular governor should be a more effective political leader? If one reflects on the American presidency, for example, most of the nation's most powerful presidents were exceptionally skilled communicators who made effective use of their popularity to further their political objectives. No less is true for governors.

GUBERNATORIAL POWER

Students of gubernatorial affairs have long been fascinated by the power inherent in the governor's office. Two forms of power can be identified: formal and informal. Formal authority comes from the laws and constitution of the state. Informal powers depend heavily on the chief executive's governing style and leadership ability.

Over the years, governors have become more and more powerful. In the words of William H. Young, the story of the American governorship has been a progression from "detested minion of royal power, to stepson of legislative domination, to popular figurehead, to effective executive."[15] This transition has not been easy, nor has it occurred equally in all states. Most of the interest in the evolution of gubernatorial power concentrates on the formal powers of the office because they are more visible and easier to measure than the informal ones. Before comparing Oklahoma's governorship with others on an index of formal power, let us briefly discuss the informal nature of gubernatorial power.

Informal Power

Measuring political power is problematic. Yet most authorities agree that power, or the politics of leadership as it might also be called, involves persuasion more than command. Consider Richard Neustadt's well-known work on the presidency. In effect, Neustadt argues that Harry Truman was correct—the power of the president is the power to persuade. The status and authority inherent in the office reinforce persuasive power, of course, but persuasion above all requires negotiation, bargaining, and compromise.[16] Robert Dahl discusses bargaining by the chief executive in what he calls an "executive-centered coalition."[17] Within their states, governors become the center of a network—the dominant figures—and achieve their policy objectives largely by means of leadership skills and resources. The exercise of such leadership may require that governors carefully pick and choose their issues so as not to dissipate their effectiveness. Former Arizona governor Bruce Babbitt, considered one of the best, comments on how he used the informal powers of the office: "If you look at what I've done over the last ten years, you will find that in any given year I have selected one or two or three issues and used everything at my disposal—initiative, referendum, the bully pulpit, the press, browbeating, tradeoffs, threats, rewards—to get what I needed. My agenda is concentrated and aimed at overwhelming the opposition."[18]

In Oklahoma, although chief executive in name, governors must share administrative authority with ten other elected state officials.[19] Moreover, their attempts to influence critical functions of government, such as welfare and highways, must operate through governing boards that officially appoint agency directors and shape agency policy. With restricted appointment authority and limited power to reorganize the executive branch, a governor's success may depend largely on the ability to negotiate, bargain, and persuade.

The Governor's Formal Powers

Despite the ultimate importance of a governor's personal skills and resources, the formal or official powers of the office may either facilitate or impede the exercise of effective political leadership. If governors cannot succeed themselves in office, for example, even very successful political entrepreneurs may find their bargaining capacity considerably diminished as their terms draw to a close.

As we saw earlier, the framers of Oklahoma's constitution feared concentrated power; they wanted high-ranking public officeholders to be directly responsible to the people. As a result, the executive branch of Oklahoma state government consisted initially of seventeen officials elected statewide, including the three-member Corporation Commission. Over time the number of statewide elected officials has shrunk, so that more formal authority now abides in the office of the governor. In 1960 Oklahoma's governors ranked in the middle in a fifty-state comparison of formal powers (based on tenure capacity, appointment authority, veto power, and control over the budget).[20]

More changes in formal gubernatorial power have occurred since 1960, allowing the Oklahoma governor two consecutive terms of office, for example. Still, compared to other states, Oklahoma's chief executive office remains relatively weak. A 1983 nationwide assessment puts the Sooner State in a tie for fortieth place in formal powers of the governor.[21] Even so, Oklahoma's chief executive received the maximum score for veto powers and for budgetary control. The real weaknesses appear in appointment authority and the power to reorganize the executive branch of government. Indeed, the office of governor in Oklahoma received the minimum number of points possible on the power of reorganization, a component newly added to the original gubernatorial power index. The power-to-reorganize measure includes such items as whether the governor and lieutenant governor run as a team, the number of existing boards and commissions with appointment power, and the span of gubernatorial control (the number of officials reporting directly to the governor; the more limited the span of control the better, presumably).

As discussed further below, Oklahoma indeed continues to exhibit a highly fragmented executive branch, and the governor has very little formal authority to do anything about it. Before considering the executive branch of state government, we might profit from a brief historical account of how certain governors in Oklahoma have used their powers to advance or impede the more general drift toward state modernization.

Gubernatorial Power and Recent Efforts at Reform

Regardless of formal powers or their capacity for political leadership, Oklahoma governors have varied considerably in their commitment to change and modernization. Some have pushed hard for various reforms; others have been willing to accommodate the status quo. Thus we find that gubernatorial efforts to move the state away from its traditionalistic past have achieved only intermittent success. Several examples illustrate the sometimes enormous difficulty of breaking new ground.

The most reactionary governor of the past fifty years was Leon C. "Red" Phillips (1939–43). Chapter 4 discussed his anti–New Deal efforts. Here we might consider another of his actions to prevent any Progressive influences from penetrating the state's borders. Historians Scales and Goble call the following story one of the ugliest episodes of that administration.[22]

Allowing his negative views of liberalism full expression, in the late 1930s Governor Phillips joined forces with extreme conservative groups in an antiradical crusade. Just after his inauguration in 1939, Phillips charged the University of Oklahoma with harboring subversives on its faculty. Fire them, he demanded. That was not all, though. Determined to cut state spending, Phillips had his eye on the university's budget. According to Scales and Goble, "It was not an unpopular tactic; he was appealing to that segment of public opinion that is always suspicious of increased spending for higher education."[23] So the budgetary attacks were coupled with charges of Communists on campus. The legislature soon joined the fray, and in 1940, with Phillips's blessing, lawmakers cut the university's budget by more than 25 percent. Accompanied by favorable publicity in the *Daily Oklahoman,* a select senate committee then launched an investigation of certain alleged subversive faculty at o u, including a Dr. W. C. Randle in mathematics. The committee even decided to scrutinize Randle's scholarly publications. An interested house member, Claud Thompson, admitted, "This stuff may be mathematics, I wouldn't know. It doesn't look like anything I ever studied, but I only went to the third grade."[24]

In 1943 oilman Robert S. Kerr (1943–47) became chief executive, a man with a bold vision of economic modernization for the state. The next year, with Kerr's endorsement, voters approved constitutional amendments creating independent boards of regents for the University of Oklahoma and the A&M colleges (including, now, O S U). Kerr was also an early supporter of the right of eighteen-year-olds to vote.

But state modernization and the reduction of political influence by the Old Guard did not progress linearly. In 1955 a fourteen-year veteran of the senate, Raymond Gary (1955–59), became governor. From Madill, in the heart of Little Dixie, Gary was a staunch southern Baptist and a confirmed "dry." Because of his immense knowledge of state affairs and his intimate familiarity with legislative politics, the governor worked smoothly with lawmakers in pursuit of various state improvements. In particular, Gary achieved real success in highway construction. Of course, the governor deserves considerable credit for the smooth way in which the state desegregated its public schools. Despite these accomplishments, Gary was not considered a reformer. He stubbornly opposed reapportionment of the legislature and fought to keep the state dry. At one point, he supported a move to force a vote of the people on a county option for the sale of beer. Finally, Gary was a master in the use of political patronage and political road building. Political scholar Jean McDonald concludes that of all recent Oklahoma governors, Gary was the most adept at using political patronage to get his way with the legislature.[25] Above all, Gary used roads to secure legislative support for his programs. Martin Hauan, who was press secretary to the governor, tells how Gary operated. He would call recalcitrant lawmakers into his office one by one. "Raymond got out his road maps and said, 'We've got this road [planned] in your district and I guess we'll just have to cancel that.' . . . They all changed their minds."[26] As often happens, however, the politics of favoritism led to scandal. Such was the case during the Gary administration, when allegations emerged involving corruption in the building of the Tulsa bypass (Interstate 44), a vote scandal involving state officials in Wagoner County, and charges by the metropolitan press of blatant politics in road building.[27]

In 1958 a genuine reform candidate for governor appeared—J. Howard Edmondson (1959–63), Tulsa County prosecutor. In part reacting to the charges of political favoritism and patronage politics associated with Old Guard politics, Edmondson campaigned on a platform of almost pure reform. He promised a quick vote on repeal of Prohibition, he advocated a constitutional highway commission as a way of presumably minimizing political influence, he favored a merit system for state employees, and he supported legislative reapportionment. Running a sophisticated television campaign using the slogan of the "Big Red E" and the symbol of a prairie fire, Edmondson overwhelmed his Democratic challenger in the runoff primary and devastated his Republican opponent in the fall. He carried all seventy-seven counties and racked up more than 74 percent of the popular vote, the most one-sided gubernatorial election in state history.[28]

The governor acted quickly to fulfill one important campaign promise. By vigorous enforcement of existing liquor laws, Edmondson and his band of "crew cuts," as they were called, forced a vote on the repeal of Prohibition. On April 7, 1959, Oklahoma went wet, leaving Mississippi as the only dry state in the Union. The governor achieved other early successes against the Old Guard in his first legislature, including the creation of a central purchasing system and a merit system for state employees.

Buoyed by these accomplishments, Edmondson pushed on. But the rural-dominated legislature balked, and lawmakers buried the young governor's other reform proposals. He then decided to appeal directly to the people by initiative petition. Three questions went on the ballot in 1960: State Question 396 would create a constitutional highway commission, SQ 397 called for legislative reapportionment, and SQ 398 would transfer county road funds to the state highway department. It was too much. As historian Arrell Gibson reports: "Small towns, rural interests, most legislators, and county commissioners—the backbone of support for the Old Guard power structure—rallied . . . against the Edmondson proposals. Each proposition went down to smashing defeat."[29]

The governor's early support of John F. Kennedy for president further alienated many old-line politicians, who were decidedly unenthusiastic about the young Catholic senator from Massachusetts and preferred Lyndon B. Johnson of Texas. During his last few years in office, Edmondson lost control of the leadership in the legislature and control of his party, dooming all further efforts at reform. Edmondson resigned his office early so that Acting Governor George Nigh could appoint him to the vacant U.S. Senate seat created by the January 1, 1963, death of Robert S. Kerr. When Edmondson left office, many analysts regarded him as the most controversial chief executive since Alfalfa Bill Murray (1931–35).[30]

Much of what happens in the state obviously lies beyond the control of state government, much less the control of the governor. Yet more than any other person, certainly in the public arena, the governor can affect the course of events in the state. Whether that influence is used to promote or retard progress rests greatly on the governor's ideological orientation. The degree of success achieved, of course, depends more on the powers of persuasion than any formal powers to command. Because of inherent weaknesses in the office, Oklahoma's governors more than others must rely on the effective exercise of political leadership.

THE EXECUTIVE BRANCH IN OKLAHOMA

Voters in Oklahoma choose not only the governor but an additional ten administrative officials: the lieutenant governor, attorney general, state treasurer, superintendent of public instruction, insurance commissioner, labor commissioner, the state auditor and inspector, and three corporation commissioners. None of these officials reports to the governor, of course, whose only real control over them may be budgetary and by dint of persuasion.

Beyond this, a multitude of separate boards and commissions exercises administrative authority, again with little or no formal control from the governor. The chief executive appoints, usually with senate confirmation, the membership to virtually all of these separate boards. For the most part, the governor cannot remove these members without cause. Moreover, these appointed boards and commissions control some of the most basic functions of state government. Consider education, arguably the most vital of all state responsibilities. The district school boards exercise direct control of the public schools, of course, but the State Board of Education supervises and manages the overall public school system. Who controls that agency? Not the governor, but the elected superintendent of public instruction along with a State Board of Education appointed by the governor, for which the superintendent serves as president. For higher education, the state has a system of regents, with the constitutionally established Oklahoma State Regents for Higher Education at the top. The state also has created seventeen additional boards of regents, ranging from those governing the University of Oklahoma and Oklahoma State University to a series of junior college boards. Although the governor appoints the regents, higher education has been removed quite deliberately from gubernatorial control. The governor appoints an education cabinet secretary, but that office has little formal power because of the independence of the major education agencies.

The situation is only marginally better for highways, welfare, and health, all among the most critical of state services. Each of these agencies has its own board or commission with the power to appoint a chief administrative officer. The governor is not totally helpless, of course. The chief executive may exert considerable influence over some board-controlled agencies, especially where political benefits can be derived, as in the case of highways. By tradition, the governor for all practical purposes names the director of transportation. In other areas gubernatorial control appears less certain. Oklahoma governors take less interest in and exert less control over health, for example, because the commissioner of health must be a licensed physician. Health activities provide fewer opportunities for significant political rewards as well. In some instances, however, the governor can exercise some direction over major state agencies. In 1989, after three years of conflict, the governor finally gained control of the Mental Health Board and forced the resignation of its commissioner.

Apart from these boards for major functions, the state has spawned a host of relatively obscure boards and commissions. Some are more visible and important than others. For example, a separate Board of Mental Health and Substance Abuse operates a large program and dozens of institutions for treating the mentally ill and substance abusers. Literally hundreds of obscure boards flourish, ranging from the Oklahoma State Board of Public Accountancy to the Will Rogers Memorial Commission. Some have full-time paid directors; others do not. Among the more inconspicuous are the Santa Claus Commission (created to purchase Christmas gifts for orphans in state-supported homes), which lists both a treasurer and an executive secretary, and the J. M. Davis Memorial Commission in Claremore, which lists no administrative officers (it was created in 1965 to provide state control over the large private collection of guns and historical artifacts of J. M. Davis).

In all, Oklahoma has 31 constitutionally created executive branch agencies, boards, and commissions. In addition, about 230 separate boards, commissions, trusts, committees, and advisory councils (including higher education) can be identified, depending on what one counts.[31] The governor, sometimes with senate approval, appoints the membership of the vast majority. Still, it is no wonder various experts have long complained that the executive branch of Oklahoma government is a "many splintered thing."[32] For years various groups have offered proposals and recommendations to do something about this fragmentation, obviously with little success.

Before leaving the discussion of boards and commissions, let us discuss perhaps the most important commission of all, the Corporation Commission. The three members of this constitutionally created body are elected for six-year terms. The commission's basic responsibility is regulatory and judicial rather than strictly executive in nature; it regulates certain private businesses whose services the state considers to be essential for the public welfare. Regulating the railroads came first; now the commission devotes far more attention to public utilities (telephone, electricity, natural gas), oil and gas drilling, and motor carrier transportation (e.g., in-state trucking). It sets utility rates, periodically determines market demand for oil and natural gas, and authorizes routes and establishes rates for motor carriers operating entirely within the state. The Corporation Commission serves as both a judicial tribunal and an investigative agency, accomplishing its regulatory task through a combination of legislative, executive, and judicial powers. Its orders carry the weight of law, and appeals from its decisions go directly to the state supreme court. The governor has no direct control over this very powerful state agency, which touches many aspects of the Oklahoma economy.

REORGANIZING THE EXECUTIVE BRANCH

Since before 1940, a series of reports has urged the state to reorganize its executive branch. The purpose, in the words of the most recent study, is to "make a system of government responsive to the needs and demands of the people in the most efficient, effective manner possible."[33] Some reformers also contend that such changes will save taxpayers a great amount of money, although experience from other states refutes that claim.[34] In effect, reorganization calls for structural changes in the executive branch so as to make departments and agencies more accountable to the governor. It often entails grouping related functions under common command, limiting the number of departments, and providing the governor with sufficient staff to assist in exercising control over the state's bureaucracy. In Oklahoma such studies inevitably include a recommendation for making certain elected administrators subject to gubernatorial appointment. For example, in 1967 the Governor's Management Study Committee urged a reduction in elected officials from thirteen to four—a lieutenant governor, attorney general, secretary of state, and examiner/inspector.[35]

In 1986, partly in response to growing awareness of the need to provide for more effective coordination of the executive branch, the legislature approved a cabinet system of government for the state. The law provides for at least ten but no more than fifteen cabinet areas.[36] It also created a twenty-five-member Reorganization Council, consisting of state officials, legislators, and private citizens, to recommend the final cabinet arrangement. In its January 1, 1987, report the council proposed fifteen cabinet secretaries to the new governor, after which Republican governor Henry Bellmon announced his own cabinet structure and secretaries. Six of the newly named cabinet members were elected executives, such as the state treasurer, the auditor and inspector, and the insurance commissioner. Most of the others were heads of agencies, with two exceptions—the education secretary and the social services secretary. The law also stipulates that "each cabinet area shall consist of executive agencies, boards, commissions, or institutions with similar programmatic or administrative objectives." Presumably, then, the plethora of state boards and commissions would be subject to some perhaps very limited degree of coordination and oversight under the cabinet system thus created.

It was not until the last week of his last legislative session that Governor Bellmon obtained senate confirmation for all of his cabinet appointees.[37] So the much-heralded reform of the executive branch got off to a shaky start. Democrats, particularly in the house, quickly raised several objections to the cabinet arrangement. First, they professed to be shocked at its cost, which Speaker Jim Barker in 1987 said would exceed $640,000. The Speaker said he and other Democrats thought the system would draw from existing staff of the governor with no additional costs. Barker also objected to the arrangement that put certain appointed secretaries over elected officials such as the state superintendent of public instruction. In addition, he said that the system created chaos and jealousies among the heads of agencies. "I think it was a bad idea," said Steve Lewis (D-Shawnee), then chairman of the House Appropriations Committee. "We can't make it work," he said. "The peo-

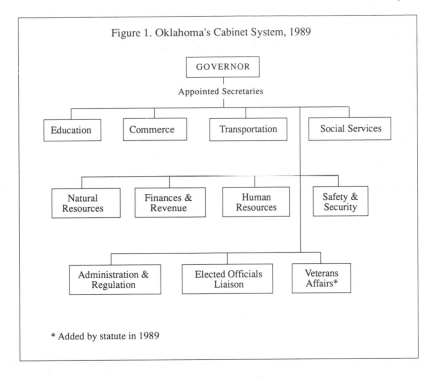

Figure 1. Oklahoma's Cabinet System, 1989

* Added by statute in 1989

ple want access . . . to us, to agencies, to the governor, not go through some secretary. . . . It's not Governor Bellmon's fault," he added. "This thing's a mess." Other Democrats objected to adding what they called another layer of bureaucracy.

Republicans, on the other hand, came to the cabinet's defense. "It's in its infancy," said Rep. Frank Davis (*R*-Guthrie). "It hasn't been given a chance. It can save millions and millions of dollars and provide more accountability." According to former house minority leader Rep. Walter Hill (*R*-Turpin), the issue is really strengthening the executive branch by giving the governor more control over the administration of state government. House Democrats were not persuaded and pushed for a vote to kill the cabinet system. It passed 63 to 33, but the measure died in the senate.

Finally, in October 1987, Governor Bellmon announced he was removing the seven elected officials—all Democrats—from his cabinet. The reason given: to "streamline" the cabinet. "We believe this new system should be more effective," the governor said, as he issued an executive order setting the number of cabinet secretaries at ten rather than the original fifteen.

Figure 1 shows the next cabinet structure after the removal of the elected officeholders. Unlike the president's cabinet, some of the secretaries do not control major operating departments (education, for example, remains under the jurisdiction of the elected superintendent of public instruction and the Board of Regents for Higher Education). If a cabinet member lacks operational responsibility for an agency, that person becomes little more than a staff adviser to the governor. Achieving a cabinet system modeled after the national cabinet would require further constitutional amendment abolishing more elected administrative officials (e.g., superintendent of public instruction) and eliminating certain constitutionally established boards (e.g., Commission for Human Services, which oversees the operation of the Department of Human Services).

Even though the cabinet system had a rocky beginning, evidence shows that the public favors executive branch reorganization. Some 58 percent of 566 respondents in a 1987 statewide survey said they favored the implementation of the "cabinet-like reorganization of the executive branch."[38] Certain elected administrative offices seem better prospects for gubernatorial appointment than others, although retaining the elected status of each has its defenders. The primary criterion for separate election might be the extent to which the function performed by the office requires true independence, as the auditor and inspector might, for example. Some argue that the attorney general also plays a vital watchdog role, although at the national level, of course, this office acts as the major legal adviser to the chief executive. In any case, the need-for-independence argument is harder to make for at least four currently elected offices—superintendent of public education, state treasurer, labor commissioner, and commissioner of insurance. Requiring the governor and lieutenant governor to run as a team would also strengthen the chief executive's control over the administration of state government. These changes would all require constitutional amendment, of course.

Why such resistance to reorganizing the executive branch, not just in Oklahoma, but in other states as well? First, government reorganization does represent a rather drastic change. Not only do such proposals create apprehension among those immediately affected (bureaucrats at all levels), but legislators may be skeptical if not hostile. They may fear that reorganization puts too much power in the hands of the chief executive, upsetting the balance between the two major branches. The various agencies, especially the semi-independent boards and commissions, enjoy their autonomy; they argue that their mission is so special that they must be permitted to operate free of direct gubernatorial influence. Clientele groups, which often develop special relationships with state offices, likewise want "their" agencies to remain somewhat removed from the governor's control. Finally, opponents can always draw on a long-standing distrust of concentrated power among the American people. After all, we like our separation of powers and checks and balances. Thus efforts to bring about extensive reorganization of the executive branch of state government will always be an uphill battle. In Oklahoma more battles by far have been lost than won. But the issue refuses to die, as shown by the 1989 recommendation of the Constitutional Reform Commission to place the cabinet system in the Oklahoma Constitution. With strong backing from Governor Bellmon, Oklahomans would have had the chance to vote on the commissions's recommendations in the 1990 elections. The state question, which was signed by enough voters to be placed on the ballot, called for the governor and lieutenant governor to run as a team, the reorganization of the executive branch into cabinet departments headed by cabinet secretaries, and greater gubernatorial control of appointments to state boards. The question was quashed in June 1990, however, by the state supreme court's finding that the constitution's one-subject rule for such measures had been violated.

CONCLUSION

More than any other single official, the governor bears responsibility for the quality and direction of state government. It is an onerous and burdensome task, one that requires political courage, exceptional management talent, strong leadership skills, the ability to work effectively as a negotiator, and an immense tolerance for frustration. The presence or absence of these personal qualities undoubtedly contributes more than anything else to gubernatorial success. Yet the lack of sufficient formal powers may seriously handicap even the most skilled leader. We need to understand the limitations of the governor's formal authority, in part because states can act to strengthen the office of the chief executive.

Oklahoma ranks somewhat below most other states on formal powers of the governor, primarily as a result of the limited administrative and reorganization powers vested in the office. Strengthening the position would require either abolishing many of the separate boards and commissions or bringing them under some form of genuine cabinet system. In addition, further reductions in the number of elected state administrators would have to occur.

Some states have done much more than others to strengthen the office of the governor. With certain exceptions, strong-governor states tend to be those with higher incomes and a better-educated populace located outside the South.[39] States with traditionalistic political cultures, on the other hand, are more likely to have weak governors.[40] As a state's population becomes more sophisticated and its people are forced to grapple with ever more complex problems (nuclear waste disposal, acid rain, and economic diversification, to name a few), the need for a stronger chief executive becomes more compelling. We might conclude that as Oklahoma continues to evolve toward a more modern, heterogeneous state, the pressure may build to furnish its chief administrator with a set of more effective tools to do the job. Yet, as the recent brouhaha over the cabinet system shows, the changes may not come easily.

impeached, convicted, and removed from the bench by the legislature in May 1965 for accepting ten thousand dollars in bribes.[4] In this instance, corruption brought institutional reform. On May 3, 1966, a constitutional amendment was adopted that created a special judicial court to facilitate removal of unfit judges. In July 1967 an amendment was approved that provided for the extensive reorganization of state courts.

THE JUDICIAL PROCESS—WHAT COURTS DO

In essence, the basic job of the courts is to resolve disputes by deciding lawsuits (cases) between the persons (parties) involved in the dispute. Most cases are tried according to highly technical rules that are all but incomprehensible to the ordinary citizen. Oklahoma does provide, however, for informal trials of civil cases in the small-claims division of the district court when the amount in controversy does not exceed twenty-five hundred dollars. Regardless of the procedural complexity of the case, the court must have legal authority—that is, jurisdiction—to decide the dispute before it can resolve the matter.

Original and Appellate Jurisdiction

In Oklahoma, as in the federal system and the other states, courts may possess original jurisdiction (the power to decide the case for the first time) or appellate jurisdiction (the power to review the decision of a lower court).

Courts of original jurisdiction are frequently referred to as *trial courts* because they are the courts where the actual case trial takes place. Any trial court has two basic functions en route to reaching a decision: (1) it must decide questions of fact, and (2) it must decide issues of law. If a jury is used in an Oklahoma trial court, it is empowered to decide only questions of fact; the judge rules on issues of law.

Once the trial court has decided a case, the losing party may seek review of the trial court's decision by an appellate court (sometimes referred to as a *court of appellate jurisdiction*). These courts normally do not become involved in disputes over the facts of the case. Instead, their attention is focused on alleged errors concerning points of law that appear in the record to the proceedings in the trial court. If the appellate court decides that the trial court's handling of the case was proper or that errors were harmless and could not have affected the outcome of the case, it affirms (upholds) the lower court's decision. If, however, the appellate court finds a significant error on a point of law by the trial judge, it may (1) reverse the decision in the

CHAPTER EIGHT

The Judicial System

James J. Lawler and Robert L. Spurrier, Jr.

Oklahoma's judicial system illustrates well the theme of transition in state politics. Despite the conservative tradition associated with Sooner politics, Oklahoma is above the national average among state courts for modernization and professionalism and incorporates many of the features of the model court system advocated by judicial reformers.[1] In a 1973 ranking of state judicial systems, for example, Oklahoma was slightly above the median on a scale measuring legal professionalism.[2] To a considerable degree, the state's judicial system also conforms to the norms advocated in the Municipal League's Model State Constitution.[3] The judicial system is relatively centralized and unified, the minor judicial positions of justice of the peace and magistrate have been eliminated, and appellate court judges are selected by means of the so-called merit system, or Missouri Plan. Yet reluctance to change in some areas has created significant problems for the Oklahoma judicial system—workload disparities, trial backlogs, and lack of funding—at the same time that the state is experiencing a substantial increase in litigation, largely resulting from the decline in the energy and agricultural sectors of the economy.

Modernization of the judicial system, however, is a relatively recent event. Changes primarily occurred in the 1960s, partly in response to one manifestation of Oklahoma's individualistic political culture: corruption. Former Oklahoma Supreme Court justice N. S. Corn, who was convicted of federal income tax evasion, confessed to have taken bribes while serving on the court. Corn's testimony implicated two former colleagues, Justices Earl Welch and Napoleon Bonaparte Johnson. Justice Welch resigned from the supreme court in the face of impeachment proceedings. Justice Johnson was case so that the loser becomes the winner or (2) send the case back for a new trial in the trial court (i.e., reverse and remand the case). Although appeals are available, in most cases the decision of the new trial court is not challenged by the loser, and the judicial process comes to an end.

Criminal and Civil Law

Criminal cases are those in which a person (the defendant) is charged with violating the law. The state statute or city ordinance (legislative law) prohibiting the conduct also provides for penalties that may be imposed by the government against the violator after guilt is proved in a court of law. Penalties may include fines, jail terms, or even death.

As in other states, most criminal cases in Oklahoma are disposed of without a trial by means of guilty pleas. From July 1, 1985, to June 30, 1986, approximately 58 percent of felony cases and 71 percent of misdemeanors were settled in this fashion.[5] Typically, guilty pleas are the result of a controversial process called plea bargaining in which the accused agrees to plead guilty or pleads guilty in return for a recommendation of leniency by the prosecutor. Despite considerable criticism of plea bargaining, the criminal justice system in Oklahoma depends heavily on the process to avoid the major costs and time demands of trials.

We should also note that the law applied in criminal cases is more highly codified than in civil cases. Unlike some states, Oklahoma does not use common law (see below) as a source of criminal law, although common law may provide a basis for interpreting legislative enactments. The state penal code, for instance, states: "No act or omission shall be deemed criminal or punishable except as prescribed or authorized by this code."[6]

Finally, another distinctive feature of criminal justice is the sentencing process. Oklahoma is one of only six states permitting jury participation in noncapital sentencing, although it is used in only about 1 percent of the cases. Defenders of jury sentencing assert that it allows for public input to the judge; critics claim that lay jurors lack the experience and expertise required for rational sentencing decisions and that the regional differences between juries can lead to a lack of uniformity in sentencing and some unusually long sentences.

Civil cases involve all cases not governed by criminal law. Examples include suits for personal injury, damage to property, divorce and child custody, breach of contract, and many others. The plaintiff in the case (the person, corporation, or government agency filing the case) is seeking legal

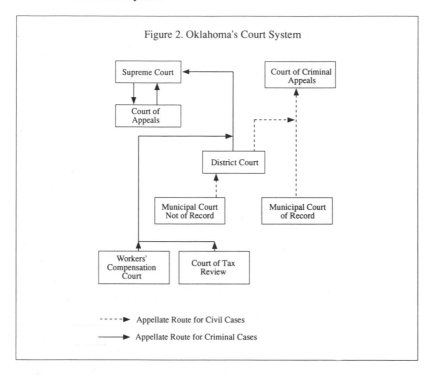

Figure 2. Oklahoma's Court System

- - - - -▶ Appellate Route for Civil Cases

————▶ Appellate Route for Criminal Cases

lief against the defendant through the judicial process. In a civil case the plaintiff usually has the burden of proof, but that burden is not as heavy as that of the prosecution in a criminal case.

A large percentage of Oklahoma civil law is uncodified and is based on common law. Common law is a traditional body of judge-made rules derived from accepted norms and legal precedents, some inherited from England before American independence. Thus, judges have greater flexibility in fashioning appropriate rules and remedies in civil law than in criminal law.

As with criminal cases, an overwhelming percentage of civil cases never go to trial. Nearly 75 percent of civil lawsuits handled by district courts between July 1, 1985, and June 30, 1986, were defaulted, withdrawn, settled, or voluntarily abandoned before trial.[7]

ORGANIZATION OF OKLAHOMA COURTS

Compared to the organization of courts in many other states, the judicial system in Oklahoma has a relatively simple structure. Figure 2 is a schematic display of the organization of Oklahoma's state courts and the routes along which cases proceed if the decision of a trial court is appealed.

Trial Courts

District Courts. In most states a variety of different specialized trial courts have jurisdiction to decide cases in limited areas. Oklahoma followed this pattern until an amendment was added to the state constitution in 1967. This amendment simplified (by consolidation) the court structure by greatly reducing the number of specialized trial courts and transferring functions to courts of general jurisdiction: the district courts.

The district court is the basic trial court in Oklahoma. It has original jurisdiction over almost all civil cases arising under state law and is the court of original jurisdiction for all cases involving charges of violation of state criminal statutes. Oklahoma has twenty-six judicial districts. All but four include more than one county. The district court system has seventy-one district judges, seventy-seven associate district judges, and sixty-two special judges. District and associate district judges have judicial authority over any case within the jurisdiction of the court; special judges have less extensive authority.

Specialized Trial Courts. Municipal courts also are trial courts in Oklahoma, but their jurisdiction is limited to criminal cases involving a violation of city ordinances. Only cities with populations exceeding two hundred thousand (Oklahoma City and Tulsa) have municipal courts of record (all other municipal courts are not courts of record). The distinction between the two types of municipal courts is significant. A decision of a municipal court of record can be appealed directly to the Oklahoma Court of Criminal Appeals on the basis of alleged errors on points of law that appear in the record. An appeal from a nonrecord municipal court takes the case to the district court for a trial *de novo*—a complete new trial on questions of fact and issues of law.

Two other specialized-jurisdiction courts serve as trial courts for claims for benefits under the state workers' compensation law and for challenges to the legality of tax levies. The workers' compensation court is a nine-judge court of record that has exclusive original jurisdiction over workers' compensation claims. The court of tax review is a court of record composed of three district judges designated by the governor. It has exclusive original jurisdiction over tax levy disputes.

Finally, the court on the judiciary (not shown in Fig. 2) is a specialized judicial tribunal established to deal with allegations of misconduct or disability of judges. It is not a court in the normal sense of the term and is best viewed as a mechanism for removing judges.

Appeal Courts

Unlike district courts, which have general jurisdiction over a wide range of civil and criminal cases, the appellate courts in Oklahoma are specialized and consist of two tiers: (1) the intermediate court of appeals and (2) the two courts of last resort—the state supreme court and the court of criminal appeals.

Intermediate Court of Appeals. Oklahoma, Idaho, and Iowa are the only states in which the state supreme court determines which civil cases will be heard by an intermediate court of appeals. In Oklahoma the intermediate court of appeals is divided into four permanent, three-judge panels, or divisions. Two of the divisions sit in Oklahoma City and two in Tulsa. Some particularly important cases are decided by all twelve court of appeals judges sitting *en banc* (i.e., as a single panel). This court, which considers only civil cases assigned to it by the Oklahoma Supreme Court, was created by the legislature in 1970 for the purpose of reducing the workload of the supreme court. The presence of an intermediate appellate court is an important factor in increasing the effectiveness of courts of last resort.[8]

When an appeal in a civil case is referred to the court of appeals by the supreme court, a three-judge division considers the issues of law raised in the appeal and decides the case by majority vote. If no further judicial action is forthcoming, the decision of the court of appeals is final. Court of appeals decisions, however, do not establish precedents that are binding on other state courts unless they are approved and given precedential authority by a majority vote of the supreme court.

The losing party in the court of appeals may petition the Oklahoma Supreme Court to review the decision. In order for this review to occur, a majority of the justices must vote to issue a *writ of certiorari,* a discretionary court order that directs the lower court to send the records of a case up for further review. If the writ is granted, the supreme court considers the case in much the same way as if the case never had been referred to the court of appeals. If the supreme court denies the petition, the case comes to an end, unless, of course, a question of federal law is involved and the case is selected for review by the United States Supreme Court.

Courts of Last Resort. Oklahoma is one of only two states (the other is Texas) that has two courts of last resort: the supreme court and the court of criminal appeals. The Oklahoma Supreme Court is the highest state court for civil cases, and the Oklahoma Court of Criminal Appeals is the highest state court for criminal cases.

The supreme court has appellate jurisdiction over decisions of the district court in civil cases, the workers' compensation court, the court of tax review, and certain judicial decisions of administrative departments and agencies of state government (the Corporation Commission, the Insurance Department, the Tax Commission, and the Banking Board or Banking Commissioner). In addition, the supreme court has original jurisdiction over challenges to the sufficiency of initiative and referendum petitions that seek to place issues on a statewide ballot for determination by a vote of the people. The supreme court also adjudicates court cases involving the executive and legislative branches of state government.

Since 1917 the supreme court has consisted of nine justices and is supported by staff lawyers and other administrative personnel. The supreme court serves as the court of last resort for civil cases in Oklahoma as long as the case involves only issues of state law. If federal law is a concern, it is possible to petition the United States Supreme Court to review the decision of the Oklahoma Supreme Court. In practice, such requests are seldom granted by the U.S. Court.

In addition to deciding cases, the Oklahoma Supreme Court performs some other functions important to the operation of the judicial system. The court serves as the management agency for state courts (considering budgetary matters and the like), the agency for licensing and disciplining lawyers, the supervising agency for the Oklahoma Bar Association, and the authoritative source of information in response to questions concerning the meaning of Oklahoma law when such questions are certified to it by federal court.

Although all appeals in civil cases are taken directly from the district court to the supreme court, not all appeals are decided by the court. As noted above, the supreme court may refer a case to the intermediate court of appeals. In practice, justices of the court allow this decision to be made by the chief justice. If the supreme court keeps a case for decision, the justices decide the case by majority vote. In most cases a ruling of the court is explained in a written "opinion" that provides the reasoning for the decision. A decision of the supreme court is binding on all other courts in cases of similar circumstances; in effect, it sets a precedent for the judicial system. Although other state courts in Oklahoma are obligated to follow supreme court precedents, the court has the authority to overrule one of its own precedents in a later case.

Appellate jurisdiction over criminal cases is possessed by the Oklahoma Court of Criminal Appeals, a five-judge (as of January 1989) court located in Oklahoma City. Unlike the Oklahoma Supreme Court, the court of criminal appeals cannot refer cases to any other court, but it, too, bases its decision on issues of law that were developed in the trial court. Except in the most unusual circumstances, the court of criminal appeals will not reconsider decisions of questions of fact that were made by the original jurisdiction court. If a question of federal law is raised in an appeal, further action is possible if the U.S. Supreme Court decides to review a decision of the Oklahoma Court of Criminal Appeals.

SELECTION AND REMOVAL OF JUDGES

Selection

Oklahoma does not use a single method for selecting judges. Instead, different approaches are used depending on the court in question. Before court reforms in 1969, state judges were elected on partisan ballots. Since then, partisan ballots have been eliminated as a means of judicial selection. Table 4 summarizes the numbers of courts and judges, terms of office, and selection/retention methods for major state courts.

Appeal Courts. Judicial reforms of the late 1960s mandated that supreme court justices and judges of the court of criminal appeals be selected by a "merit system" based on the so-called Missouri Plan, originally adopted by Missouri in its 1945 state constitution. Merit selection was extended to judges of the court of appeals through statutory changes in 1987. Judicial selection/retention criteria under this plan include a judicial nominating commission, appointment by the governor, and review by voters after a judge has been in office for at least a year.

The Judicial Nominating Commission is a thirteen-member body composed of six lawyers selected by members of the Oklahoma Bar Association (one member from each of the six congressional districts), six nonlawyers appointed by the governor (one member from each congressional district), and a thirteenth member (a nonlawyer) selected by a vote of at least eight of the other members. If eight votes cannot be obtained to select this last person, the governor makes the appointment. Members of the Judicial Nomi-

Table 4. Characteristics of Major Courts in Oklahoma, Fiscal Year 1991

Court	Number of Courts	Number of Judges	Term of Office (years)	Method of Selection and Retention in Office
Supreme Court	1	9	6	Governor appoints from list of three names from Judicial Nominating Commission; nonpartisan retention ballot after one year of service
Court of criminal appeals	1	5[a]	6	
Court of appeals	1[b]	12[c]	6	
District courts	26			
District judges		71	4	Nonpartisan, competitive election
Associate district judges		77	4	Nonpartisan competitive election
Special judges		62	No set term	Selected by district judges[d]
Workers' compensation court		9	6	Governor appoints from list of three names from Judicial Nominating Commission; no retention ballot, but may be reappointed
Court of tax review	1	3	No set term	Governor appoints three district judges

a. Three judges until January 1989.
b. Four divisions, two in Oklahoma City and two in Tulsa.
c. Three judges in each division.
d. District judges in judicial administrative district.

nating Commission serve six-year terms, and the expiration dates are staggered so that wholesale change in membership is unlikely.

When a judicial vacancy occurs, or is certain to occur because a judge has failed to file for reelection, the commission prepares a list of three lawyers who are qualified for the position and who have agreed to serve if appointed. The three names are submitted to the governor, who selects one of the three for appointment to the vacant position. If the governor fails to make an appointment within sixty days, the choice is made by the chief justice of the Oklahoma Supreme Court, although this procedure has never been carried out.

The newly appointed judge takes office and serves for at least one year. At the next statewide general election following completion of one full year in judicial office, the judge's name is placed before the voters on a nonpartisan, noncompetitive ballot (sometimes called a *retention ballot*) to serve the remainder of the six-year term. Voters are asked whether the judge should be retained in office and mark either "yes" or "no" on the ballot. If "no" votes are in the majority, the position becomes vacant and the Judicial Nominating Commission begins the process again. As of 1989, no justice or judge in Oklahoma has been defeated in a retention election. Some district attorneys did mount, however, a strong campaign in 1986 to unseat a court of criminal appeals judge. If justices or judges wish to serve another six-year term, they file for reelection and again face the voters on a retention ballot. There is no limit on the number of terms that judges may serve in Oklahoma.

Studies of the Missouri Plan in other states indicate that the selection/retention procedure does not necessarily result in true merit selection, nor has it eliminated politics from the judicial selection process. Rather, political action has shifted from the electoral arena to gubernatorial and bar association politics.[9] Nevertheless, the Missouri Plan has resulted in considerable emphasis on professional credentials in selecting judges to appeals courts.

Trial Courts. Although Oklahoma now has a single selection method for appellate court judges, that is not the case for trial court judges. Even within the district court there are two different selection methods. District judges and associate district judges continue to be elected through a system that permits opponents on the ballot, although such competition is nonpartisan in nature. These judges serve four-year terms and are almost always reelected if they seek another term. Because party labels do not appear on the ballot, the voters must rely almost entirely on name recognition to make their choice, and incumbent judges usually are better known than their opponents. Also, as judges, they occupy a position of respect in the community, which enhances their chances for victory.

Special judges of the district court are appointed rather than elected. They are selected by the district judges from the state judicial administrative district and serve at the pleasure of those district judges. Hence, they do not have a set term of office. In practice, district judges in the judicial administrative district defer to the choices of the district judges in the judicial district in which the special judges serve.

In specialized-jurisdiction trial courts in Oklahoma a variation of the selection method is found. The Judicial Nominating Commission provides three names from which the governor selects a person to fill a vacancy on the workers' compensation court. Nine judges serve on the court for six-year terms, but they do not go before the voters on a retention ballot. Instead, at the end of a six-year term the Judicial Nominating Commission prepares a new list of three names for consideration by the governor; state law permits reappointment of the judge whose term has just expired. The court of tax review does not have separate judges per se. The governor designates three district judges, and they serve indefinite terms. Finally, municipal judges are selected according to the terms of the city charter for each particular city, and most are appointed by action of the city council or city commission.

Removal

There are several methods by which judges in Oklahoma may be removed from office against their will, although by far the most common way for judges to leave the bench is by voluntary retirement or resignation. Special judges of the district court may be removed at any time by action of the district judges in that judicial administrative district because they serve at the pleasure of district judges. The voters may remove district judges and associate district judges by voting them out of office, although once again this is unusual. Voters also can remove judges from the supreme court, the court of criminal appeals, and the court of appeals by a majority of "no" votes on the retention ballot, but that never has happened. In practice, then, other strategies are more likely to be needed if judges are to be removed from office when circumstances warrant.

In the bribery scandal of the 1960s involving certain members of the Oklahoma Supreme Court, the method used to bring about removal from office was the political process of impeachment by the Oklahoma House of Representatives and trial in the Oklahoma Senate. This process resulted in the removal of Justice Johnson in 1965. Following that experience, the Oklahoma Constitution was amended to provide for a special judicial tribunal— the court on the judiciary—to deal with cases of alleged misconduct or disability of judges. The trial division of the court on the judiciary is composed of nine members, eight of whom are district judges selected according to a seniority system. The ninth member is a lawyer chosen by the Oklahoma Bar Association. The trial division hears cases against judges for misconduct or disability when charges are filed by the Oklahoma Supreme Court, the chief justice of the supreme court, the attorney general, the Oklahoma House of Representatives, or the executive secretary of the Oklahoma Bar Association. Complaints from citizens are directed to a three-person council on judicial complaints established by the legislature in 1974. If the council finds substance to a complaint, it may refer the matter to the chief justice with the recommendation to take the matter to the court on the judiciary. When a charge is filed against a judge, the trial division selects a prosecutor from a list of names submitted by the Oklahoma Bar Association.

The losing party in a case before the trial division of the court on the judiciary may appeal a decision to the appellate division of the court on the judiciary. Unlike most appeals in the Oklahoma court system, this is an "equity appeal" in which the appellate division may hear new witnesses and take additional evidence as it considers matters of fact and law on appeal.

The appellate division of the court on the judiciary is composed of two justices of the supreme court selected by that court, one judge of the court of criminal appeals selected by it, and six district judges (again selected according to a seniority system). The appellate division may affirm, reverse, or modify a decision of the trial division, or it may enter a new decision in the case. The decision of the appellate division is final.

Since its creation in 1969 the court on the judiciary has removed only four judges from office and compelled another to retire.[10] Still, that represents more judicial discipline activity than Oklahomans have witnessed since statehood through the mechanism of impeachment and trial. In 1988, to illustrate how the court on the judiciary operates, supreme court Justice Hargrave filed a petition with the court on the judiciary calling either for removal of District Judge Joe Cannon for gross partiality and oppression in office or for his retirement because of physical disability. Judge Cannon accepted medical retirement in an agreement that included dismissal of the other charges. The court on the judiciary thus represents a potentially potent force to remedy incompetence, corruption, or abuse in the judicial branch.

CENTRALIZED, PROFESSIONAL JUDICIAL ADMINISTRATION

The Oklahoma Constitution (Article VII) establishes a centralized court system, with power vested in the supreme court. Oklahoma's judicial system is more centralized than those in more than two-thirds of the other states.[11] In addition to centralizing the court system and giving the supreme court broad powers over judicial administration, Oklahoma has provided a professional court administrator's office to assist the supreme court in management of the state court system. The Administrative Office of Courts was established in 1967 "to assist the Chief Justice in his administrative duties and to aid the Court on the Judiciary."[12] The director of the office is appointed by the supreme court and serves at its pleasure.

With a staff of twenty-seven in 1988 and a budget of more than $5 million, the office is relatively small in comparison to other offices in more populous states. Yet it remains "the key to efficient justice in Oklahoma . . . because of the increasing dependence of judges on the managerial and statistical skills that the office provides."[13]

DECISION MAKING AT THE TOP

Oklahoma Supreme Court justices and judges of the court of criminal appeals resemble their counterparts in other states in that the overwhelming majority spent their childhood in the state in which they hold judicial office. Eight of the nine supreme court justices and all three (in 1988) of the judges of the court of criminal appeals were born in Oklahoma or neighboring states.[14] All hold law degrees from Oklahoma law schools, although one also holds an LL.M. from New York University. Graduates of the University of Oklahoma Law School provide a majority on both courts. All but one of the supreme court justices and all of the court of criminal appeals judges are Democrats. Although two members of the supreme court are women, all members of the court of criminal appeals are men. In most respects the Oklahoma courts of last resort are considerably more homogeneous than the U.S. Supreme Court.

Despite this homogeneity, it is surprising that the Oklahoma Supreme Court has one of the highest dissent rates in the nation. In 1966 and 1972 the supreme court ranked seventh in number of dissenting opinions among the highest courts of the fifty states, with rates of 26.5 in both years.[15] The dissent rate in 1966 was more than twice the average for all states. During 1987 dissents were reported in a majority of the cases for which full written opinions were provided. Justices Rudolph Hargrave, Ralph Hodges, and Robert Simms, often voting together, led in the number of dissents with more than nine each in 1987. Each of the nine justices dissented at least once. Few of the dissenting votes were accompanied by written opinions, so the reasons for disagreements are difficult to ascertain. Still, the patterns of alignment seem relatively fluid, with most of the justices sharing a moderate, basically "centrist" legal orientation. The dissents seem to reflect a tradition of individualism among the justices, relating more to differences on procedural matters than to differences in social or economic values.

Disagreements among judges at times have been particularly significant on the court of criminal appeals. The court changed from a rather liberal body in the 1950s to a conservative one in the 1960s with the election of Judge Hez Bussey. In the mid-1980s some judges and lawyers called for enlargement of the court because of consistent differences between Judge Bussey and Judge Tom Brett, with Judge Ed Parks holding the swing vote. Such abrupt changes in the direction of the court resulting from a single change in court membership threaten stability and predictability in criminal law. The political response to this problem was enactment of legislation (effective in January 1989) to increase the size of the court of criminal appeals to five judges.

Elsewhere in the country, state courts have increasingly interpreted state constitutions to extend protection of individual rights beyond the requirements of the United States Constitution.[16] Although the Oklahoma Supreme Court is not in the vanguard of this "new judicial federalism," the court has used Article 2, Section 7, of the Oklahoma Constitution to extend procedural due process in personnel actions beyond the federal requirements of due process.[17] Despite the traditionalism of the state and the largely "home grown" character of the judges, the Oklahoma Supreme Court has occasionally made controversial decisions on public policy—for example, in developing a defense of "economic duress" in contracts,[18] in abandoning the common law doctrine of sovereign immunity[19] (immunity was partly restored by the legislature), and in extending protection for riparian water rights.[20]

The reforms of the 1960s have helped to control the more blatant manifestations of politics in the judiciary. Nonetheless, the judicial process inevitably involves choices by human decision makers, and interpersonal relations can influence the outcomes. Increases in litigation and limited financial support present formidable challenges to these "only human" judges as they attempt to perform their duties responsibly and effectively.

THE COURT CRISIS

System overload, rather than corruption, is the major challenge facing the Oklahoma court system today. On a per capita basis Oklahoma was the ninth most litigious state in the nation in 1984, with approximately 6.6 lawsuits filed per one hundred Oklahomans.[21] The number of cases filed in Oklahoma courts has been growing at an annual rate of approximately 5 percent. The high level of litigation partly reflects the decline in Oklahoma's oil industry, leading to increasing litigation concerning foreclosures and debt enforcement. The litigation also reflects a national trend: lawsuits in federal courts across the nation have nearly tripled since 1970.

Compounding the caseload crisis in the trial courts is the unequal distribution of cases among districts. In 1984 the average caseload for a district judge per year was 2,500. In some districts judges handled as many as 8,066 cases per year, while in others judges had as few as 536 cases per year.[22] Unequal workloads led to a recommendation by a fifteen-member special commission in 1986 that the legislature redraw judicial district boundaries. This recommendation turned out to be politically controversial, particularly since it would affect the workloads of rural judges. The legislature took no action on the recommendation. According to Chief Justice Doolin of the Oklahoma Supreme Court, lack of funding for additional personnel to handle increased loads has seriously strained the resources of many districts. Some trial judges must type their own judgments and orders, while others must "delay trials because they don't have a court reporter."[23]

During the last half-decade Oklahoma has shifted from a pattern of 70 percent state legislative funding of the courts from general revenues to one of 78.5 percent of judicial funding from fines, fees, and forfeitures. This attempt to put the courts on a "pay as you go" basis has its critics and defenders; without doubt, however, legislative funding is still critical to the judiciary.

A heavier appellate caseload has imposed extraordinary strains on the supreme court—more than doubling the number of cases in the last ten years (for fiscal year 1989 the number of cases filed had reached 186 per month) and increasing the court's backlog of cases almost threefold (from 800–900 in 1973 to 2,942 at the end of fiscal year 1989). In an effort to reduce the backlog, the supreme court has made extensive use of a "fast track" system (referred to as *accelerated docketing*) for relatively routine or single-issue cases that are reviewed by two five-justice panels (with the chief justice sitting on both panels). Instead of involving detailed written opinions, decisions are announced in short memoranda. In addition, more cases are being referred to the four divisions of the court of appeals to allow the supreme court to concentrate on cases of greater public importance.

Legislative efforts to assist the courts with the litigation crisis have been forthcoming, at least to a limited extent, in the form of tort reform (limiting awards of punitive damages and permitting the courts to require a plaintiff in a lawsuit deemed frivolous to pay the legal expenses of the successful defendant) and provision for alternative dispute resolution. The Oklahoma Dispute Resolution Act is designed to encourage arbitration and mediation as alternatives to the courtroom. A two-dollar surcharge on civil case filing fees provides funds for the alternative dispute-resolution program in the state.[24] Although such laws show some responsiveness to the problems the courts are facing, they do not match the magnitude of the crisis.

The financial conservatism of the state coupled with the resistance to basic changes, such as much-needed court redistricting, reduce options open to judicial officials seeking a solution to the caseload crisis. A paradox of the judicial system in Oklahoma is that it is able to function as effectively as it does with heavy demands for justice and limited resources. Reform efforts of the 1960s modernized the court system in Oklahoma, reduced the role of partisan politics in judicial affairs, and enhanced judicial professionalism. Now it seems that Oklahomans must demand that the next step be taken: adequate funding for the judicial system must be forthcoming. Reforms are not self-executing; fair and speedy justice as well as professionalism are not without associated costs.

CHAPTER NINE

Political Participation, Parties, and Interest Groups

America has long prided itself on being a government by, for, and of the people. The people cannot govern themselves directly, however, in modern, complex societies. Today's democracies require mechanisms for translating the interests, preferences, and needs of the citizenry into public policy. So our system provides for certain basic representative institutions— primarily legislative bodies and elected chief executives. But more is required. Fair and frequent elections are essential to ensure that all groups have a reasonable chance to be heard in the electoral arena. Elections engender campaigns, and campaigns mean organization, money, media, and modern marketing techniques. Historically, political parties have been the principal device linking the people to the government, mainly through campaigns and elections. Indeed, until about the middle of this century, American parties played the dominant role in the most basic electoral functions of representative democracy: recruiting and nominating candidates for office, structuring political debate, raising money, organizing and mobilizing the electorate, and informing the people about issues and candidates.[1] The political party system in the U.S. has undergone enormous change in recent years, with the advent of television, the growth of interest groups, and the increase in the use of direct primaries for candidate selection. To understand popular political behavior in any state, we must examine not only political parties, but interest groups and other means by which people influence their government.

POLITICAL PARTICIPATION AND DIRECT DEMOCRACY

People participate in the political process primarily by voting. Yet Americans vote at much lower rates than in most European democracies. For example, only 50.1 percent of the voting-age population in this country cast ballots in the 1988 presidential election, the lowest turnout rate since 1924. Historically, voter turnout in Oklahoma hovers around the U.S. average. In 1988, voting-age Oklahomans cast their ballots at a 48.7 percent rate. For the eight presidential elections beginning in 1960, Oklahoma's age-eligible turnout rate of 56.6 percent compares favorably to the national mean of 56.3 percent. So Oklahomans seem to respond to the various forces that affect electoral participation in much the same way as the nation as a whole.

Voting turnout in the Sooner State varies by region. As discussed in earlier chapters, the southern part of Oklahoma, especially the southeastern section of Little Dixie, was the most heavily affected by migration from southern states. Politically, that means two things—less voter participation and more support for Democrats. Traditionalistic states, with their emphasis on paternalism and elite domination, generally have lower turnout rates than other states. Those living in the southeastern quadrant of Oklahoma would thus be expected to vote less frequently than people living in other parts of the state. Another factor should contribute to lower rates of voting in Little Dixie: the area generally is the poorest and least well educated in the state. Voting studies always show significant links between political participation and certain socioeconomic characteristics. In every country the better educated and wealthier groups tend to vote more regularly than do others.[2]

Recent elections in Oklahoma reflect this regional pattern—the highest rate of voter turnout occurs for those counties in the northwestern part of the state. If we examine the average vote for governor in 1982 and 1986, for example, nine of the thirteen counties with the highest average turnout (one standard deviation from the mean) are located in the northwestern quadrant of the state (north of Interstate Highway 40 and west of Interstate 35). Eleven of the thirteen high-voting counties are in the northern half of the state.

This regional variation in voter turnout tends to mirror a similar pattern of party voting. The southeastern quadrant of the state is the most heavily Democratic, the northwestern area the most staunchly Republican. Before continuing with this discussion, though, we need to consider another form of voting behavior, in which people cast ballots not for candidates or parties but directly for or against substantive issues.

Despite low levels of voter turnout across the country, some futurists see the U.S. moving inexorably toward a more participatory democracy. John Naisbitt argues in *Megatrends* that we have already "pulled the essence of political power out of the hands of our elected representatives and reinvested it into two main areas: (1) the direct ballot vote of initiatives and referenda, and (2) grassroots political activity."[3] Naisbitt may overstate the case. Yet direct voting on questions of public policy has increased substantially in a great number of states, including Oklahoma.

The initiative brings an issue to a public vote through a petition process. Initiative petition circulators in Oklahoma have ninety days to gather enough signatures to put a measure on a statewide ballot. The referendum works in two ways: the legislature may place a proposition on the ballot, or some dissatisfied group can gather enough signatures on a petition to force a public vote on some legislative act. A referendum on an act of the legislature rarely happens. A large percentage of legislation carries the emergency clause (requiring two-thirds approval of both houses) that makes the law effective on signature of the governor. If no emergency clause is attached, however, the law does not go into effect until ninety days after the legislature adjourns. During that ninety-day period the referendum petition process can take place. With enough signatures, the people can vote on that issue.

The way this process works is illustrated by an organized effort to overturn the education reform and tax increase bill passed by the legislature during the 1989–90 special session. For months, supporters of the bill sought enough votes in the senate for the emergency clause to eliminate the opportunity for a referendum vote sought by a group calling itself STOP New Taxes. In the end, senate leaders persuaded enough senate Democrats to vote for the emergency, thereby forcing STOP to concentrate its efforts on the more arduous and lengthy initiative process to repeal the new law. Given the likelihood of appeal in the Oklahoma Supreme Court from the proeducation forces and Governor Bellmon's opposition to the petition, a vote on the STOP measure could be delayed until November 1992, nearly two and one-half years after the reforms took effect.

Oklahoma's constitution, for all practical purposes, can be amended only by a vote of the people, either (1) through the initiative process (requiring signatures of 15 percent of the total votes cast in the last general election for the state office receiving the highest number of votes; a change in law requires signatures of only 8 percent); or (2) by legislative referral. Between 1970 and 1988, Oklahoma voters cast ballots on 102 state questions (initiative or referendum propositions). Some of them were technical and noncontroversial, necessary to update or expunge certain wording in the constitution. Others were among the most contentious political issues confronting state voters. As mentioned in chapter 1, such hot items as pari-mutuel betting and liquor-by-the-drink have appeared on Oklahoma ballots in recent years, primarily through the initiative process. Additionally, in the mid-1970s the voters shortened the statewide ballot by abolishing the position of commissioner of charities and corrections and making the previously elected offices of commissioner of labor, chief mine inspector, and secretary of state subject to gubernatorial appointment (in 1988 the people reversed themselves and voted to make the labor commissioner an elective office again). During the same period the terms of county officials were lengthened from two to four years. Some citizens view these devices of direct democracy as a "tremendous safeguard" enabling groups to bypass the established representative system and appeal directly to the citizens.[4] Others see these provisions as a tool of special interests which use them as a veto mechanism to protect the status quo.[5] Either way, the initiative and referendum will likely grow in importance. Undoubtedly, Oklahomans will continue to face an average of eight or ten of these measures every election year.

The financing of these questions became an issue in the 1990 legislature. The Oklahoma Constitution prohibits corporate contributions to elections, and state statutes limit the amount of individual contributions to a single campaign. The U.S. Supreme Court, however, has ruled that corporations have a First Amendment right to contribute to initiative and referendum campaigns without any limits. In Oklahoma, groups campaigning on state questions must report contributions in excess of two hundred dollars annually. These reports have revealed recent corporate contributions in excess of twenty thousand dollars to state question campaigns. Oklahoma Common Cause and the Oklahoma League of Women Voters supported legislation that passed the 1990 legislature to require more stringent reporting of such campaigns to bring to light the source of support for or opposition to state questions. The bill, however, was vetoed by the governor because he felt it would inhibit the ability of the people to use the initiative and referendum. It is almost certain that future legislatures will work further on this matter if corporations and wealthy individuals continue to finance heavily state question campaigns.

POLITICAL PARTIES AND PARTISANSHIP IN OKLAHOMA

Is the "party over," as political columnist David Broder once asked?[6] The answer depends in part on what one means by *political party*. Throughout the 1960s and 1970s the willingness of the American voter to claim identification with one of the two major parties waned considerably. Now, however, some observers see a resurgence of the two parties. This renewal comes not so much because identification with the parties has increased (it

Table 5: Party Registration in Oklahoma, 1969–88

	Democrat, (%)	Republican, (%)	Independent, (%)	Total Registration
1969	76.8	22.2	1.0	1,210,992
1979	75.1	23.1	1.8	1,361,194
1988	66.9	30.4	2.7	2,026,625

Source: Oklahoma State Election Board, *Oklahoma Elections: Statehood to Present,* vol. 1 (Oklahoma City, July 1988), C2–C3.

has not), but because of stepped-up party activity and stronger organization in the national arena, especially among Republicans.

With the rise in independent voting and ticket splitting, some observers argue that parties have become only hollow shells. They say that parties have no real power or importance and that elections are now dominated by candidate organizations that emphasize personality, media, and high-priced consultants. According to a recent *New Republic* article, for example, "our system of national politics has become candidate-, rather than party-, centered. It is a competition among individuals, and organizations that represent nothing but those individuals."[7] As we spell out in more detail below, this picture of the parties as bygone relics may be exaggerated. First, though, let us explore a bit more the question of party adherence and identification.

Partisanship and Party Identification

In Oklahoma prospective voters must register with the county election board as a Democrat, Republican, or independent. Even though a recent change in state law authorizes the two parties to allow independents to vote in primary elections, neither party has done so. Hence, most people register with one of the parties. Historically, as a border state, Oklahoma has been dominated politically, at least at the state level, by the Democratic party. This dominance is still reflected in the voter registration totals, although the Republicans have made recent gains.

The figures in Table 5 show the changes in party registration over about the past two decades. These numbers reveal a gradual slippage in Democratic strength, with the largest drop, not surprisingly, occurring in the 1980s.

Registration, of course, does not tell the whole story; people often vote

Table 6: Party Identification in Oklahoma and the Nation (in Percent)

	Oklahoma (October 1986)	U.S. (April 1987)
Democrat	41	39
Republican	30	31
Independent	29	30
	100	100

Source: For Oklahoma, telephone interview with Kenneth D. Bailey, *Bailey Oklahoma Poll,* Tulsa, January 20, 1987. For the U.S., *Daily Oklahoman,* May 24, 1987.

contrary to the way they are registered, especially in Oklahoma, where the Republicans do not always field a full slate of candidates in some heavily Democratic counties. Thus some Republican sympathizers may register as Democrats so they can vote in primary elections for legislative and county elections. The other commonly used measure of partisanship is party identification. How do Oklahomans compare with others across the country in their identification with the two major parties? The Gallup Poll regularly asks a random sample of the American public the following question: "In politics, as of today, do you consider yourself a Republican, a Democrat, or an independent?" A similar question was put to a random sample of 664 Oklahoma residents in an October 1986 telephone survey. The figures in table 6 compare party identification in Oklahoma with the U.S. Perhaps surprisingly, despite the state's Democratic heritage, Oklahomans now identify with the major parties in about the same proportion as do other voters around the country.

Party Competition

Since most authorities view parties as an indispensable link in the process by which a free people chooses political leaders, healthy competition among the major parties is considered quite desirable. Without competitive parties, voters have no real electoral choice, and the party in office will not have an out party to serve as a watchdog. However, party competition varies considerably from state to state. We once spoke of the "solid South," for example, to indicate the traditional Democratic dominance in that region as an outgrowth of the Civil War. The South is certainly not solid anymore, particularly in national elections. In fact, along with whites under age thirty and

Table 7: Vote for President in Oklahoma, 1960–88

Election	Voted Republican (%)
1960	59.0
1964	44.3
1968	47.7[a]
1972	73.7
1976	50.0[a]
1980	60.5
1984	68.6
1988	58.4
Average	57.8

Source: U.S. Bureau of the Census, *Statistical Abstract 1989,* p. 242, and ibid., *1978,* pp. 505–6.

a. Candidates with most votes.

Hispanics, white southerners have shown the largest recent swing toward the GOP. Cavanaugh and Sundquist offer this observation: "That the Republican party should be rising spectacularly in the South should not surprise anyone. The wonder is that its ascent has been delayed so long. Ever since the Democratic party committed itself in the 1930s to an activist, interventionist economic and social policy, conservatives have not had a congenial home in it. But changing party loyalties is like changing churches; people do not do so easily."[8]

As we noted in the first chapter, Oklahoma has strong southern ties. So we might expect to find a significant growth in Republican strength in the state over the past few decades. Can we now say, for example, that Oklahoma is a genuine two-party state?

As with many issues involving politics, there is no easy answer to the question of party competitiveness in Oklahoma; it depends considerably on how we measure party competition. Since 1960 Oklahoma has appeared in the GOP column in presidential elections almost exclusively. The percentage vote shown in table 7 for president in Oklahoma shows that, counting 1960, the state voted Republican in seven of the last eight elections (in 1964 Oklahoma went for Lyndon Johnson). The average of these eight elections, 57.8 percent, is considerably above the U.S. average Republican vote for president during the same period—50.4 percent. Clearly, then, Oklahomans prefer the GOP when balloting for the nation's highest office.

In state elections, however, another picture appears. Aside from Republican Henry Bellmon's election as governor in 1986, the Republicans have captured only four other statewide offices since 1974; Republican Tom Daxon was elected auditor and inspector in 1978, Robert Anthony (1988) and J. C. Watts (1990) captured seats on the Corporation Commission, and Claudette Henry beat the incumbent state treasurer in 1990. Most research analyzing two-party competition among the states considers only state offices. Probably the best-known measure of party competitiveness for the states was first developed by political scientist Austin Ranney in the mid-1960s. His index includes the average percentage Democratic for four components: (1) vote for governor, (2) seats in the state senate, (3) seats in the state house, and (4) all terms in which the Democrats controlled the governorship, senate, and house.[9] This index of party competition has been calculated for four different time periods between 1946 and 1980.[10] Each time Oklahoma appears in the "modified one-party Democratic" category. Although Republicans have increased their proportion of registered voters, however, and the state has voted Republican in most presidential elections since 1945, has two GOP congressmen and one GOP U.S. senator, elected a Republican governor in 1986, gained a few more legislative seats, and even elected four Republicans during the 1980s to secondary state offices, Oklahoma still does not have a true two-party system as customarily defined by political scientists.

Party Differences

With individual commitment to party now so tenuous, one might wonder if the differences between the two major parties may also have lessened. This conjecture assumes, obviously, that meaningful differences between Democrats and Republicans existed at one time. Despite occasional references to "Tweedle Dum" and "Tweedle Dee," or former Alabama governor George Wallace's 1960s statement that there wasn't "a dime's worth of difference" between the two parties, historically and currently a cleavage is discernible.

Since 1940 the two parties have generally drawn their core support from a divergent social, economic, and ethnic base. From the days of the New Deal until the mid-1970s, at least, Democrats were more likely to be "blue-collar workers, those with lower educational levels, those with lower income, ethnic groups of more recent immigration, racial minorities, and Catholics," whereas Republicans were more apt to be "higher status people—middle class individuals, those with high incomes, whites, Protestants and those of northern European stock."[11] A survey of Oklahoma voters during the 1970s confirms this general tendency: "Democrats draw their support disproportionately from less educated and lower income segments of society and from blacks, whereas the college educated and higher income individuals are disproportionately Republican."[12]

The parties divide on political ideology as well, although these differences may be faint indeed among average voters. Still, in James Reichley's words, "in general, at the state and local levels outside the South and at the national level, the Republicans have been the more conservative party and the Democrats the more liberal."[13] The aforementioned 1970s survey of Oklahoma voters also asked about ideological self-perceptions. Among those identifying as Democrats, 29 percent said they were either very conservative or slightly conservative. Among Republicans the figure was 50 percent.[14] But the real ideological split appears among party activists. For example, among Oklahoma delegates to the two national party conventions in 1984, only 7 percent of the Democratic delegates considered themselves conservative or extremely conservative. A resounding 84 percent of the Republican delegates said they were in one of the two conservative categories; 23 percent said they were "extreme conservatives."[15]

Despite some of these stark philosophical differences among the party's leadership, the official Democratic party in Oklahoma is not very concerned with issues, much less ideology. Some would argue that, in fact, the party stands for very little, primarily because it tries to encompass such an assortment of views and groups from across the state. This historical appeal to diverse interests coupled with the hard-line conservatism of the state's Republican party contributes to the success of Oklahoma Democrats. *Oklahoma Observer* editor Frosty Troy offers these thoughts about the state's dominant party:

> Oklahoma's Democratic Party reminds you of some simple-minded Goliath—aged, obese, and disoriented.
>
> But in this metaphor, no matter how still the behemoth stands, little David, in the person of the Republican Party, can't topple it. In preparing for a firing squad, Oklahoma Republicans form a circle. . . .
>
> Because the Oklahoma Republican Party favors the repeal of everything back to and including the 19th century, the Democratic colossus prospers far beyond its own contributions to the commonweal.
>
> With all its flaws, the Oklahoma Democratic Party remains home for most

Oklahomans because it is a large comfortable place accommodating all sorts
of viewpoints—from intellectuals to eccentrics, from rednecks to leftists,
from mossback conservatives to wild-eyed liberals.[16]

As we said earlier, partisanship in the state reflects regional variations. If
we again examine the average vote for governor by county for the 1982 and
1986 elections, we can get a feel for some of these regional differences. The
average Democratic percentage among all counties for the two elections was
59.9 percent (Democrat George Nigh won reelection to the office of governor in 1982 with a decisive 62.3 percent of the two-party vote; Republican
governor Henry Bellmon, on the other hand, received only 51.6 percent of
that vote in 1986). Of the seventeen counties with the highest Democratic
vote (one standard deviation above the mean), all but one (Sequoyah) are located in the southern half of the state. Moreover, ten of them were in the
southeastern quadrant of Oklahoma, the true Little Dixie area. The north-
east-southwest urban corridor, which includes Oklahoma City and Tulsa,
tends to be somewhat in the middle in its partisan voting habits, although the
two largest cities now vote pretty solidly Republican. When the 1982 and
1986 elections are combined, we find that these two big urban counties—
Oklahoma County and Tulsa County—voted 45.4 percent and 41.9 percent
Democratic, respectively. Tulsa's combined Democratic vote was the lowest
of any of the seventy-seven counties. These same two gubernatorial elections exhibit the relationship discussed earlier regarding voter turnout and
partisan voting. The correlation is rather striking; the higher the voter turnout, the more likely the county voted Republican ($R = .53$).

Some variation in partisan preference is also apparent for certain identi-
fiable groups. Studies of minority and ethnic voting in Oklahoma are rare,
however. Research done in the 1970s does show, as expected, that black
Oklahomans strongly prefer the Democrats.[17] Unfortunately, almost nothing
is known about Oklahoma Indian voting behavior. As an economically depressed group, a majority of Indians would likely be in the Democratic column. Yet the 1988 election found Native American leadership split, with
some tribal leaders favoring Dukakis and some favoring Bush.[18] One thing
does seem obvious, however. As a group, American Indians in Oklahoma
are largely without political power. They are not as geographically concentrated as blacks, and indeed, many still live scattered throughout small towns
and the rural countryside. No one ever speaks of the Indian vote. In fact, it is
not clear just how much political self-consciousness Indians have as a group.
The impression is that Native American voting participation and other forms

of customary political activity may be quite low. This unusually low level of involvement in the politics of the dominant culture may be the result of several factors.

Historically, of course, Native Americans have had extensive interaction with the federal Bureau of Indian Affairs (BIA). This relationship has been a troubled one, with the BIA normally acting quite paternalistically toward its charges. Paternalism certainly does not breed feelings of political power. Second, like blacks, Indians have experienced discrimination, making it more difficult for them to succeed politically without considerable effort. Finally, many Native Americans seem to remain uninvolved largely by choice; they appear to be more concerned than most other groups with family and tribal affairs. Yet evidence suggests that Oklahoma Indians are not totally apathetic politically. On the contrary, newspaper stories of intratribal disputes appear regularly, along with frequent accounts of conflict between Native American tribes and various government agencies over jurisdictional and sovereignty issues. Indeed, Indian political activism has been quite visible in recent years; it is just not played out in the mainstream political arena. Quite rationally, Indian groups have invested their primary political energies in those matters of greatest direct concern to them—in battles over tribal leadership and in actions against the federal, state, or local governments when issues of Indian sovereignty are at stake.

Party Organization

Political parties in Oklahoma, as elsewhere, are formally organized under their own rules in a hierarchical fashion. At the bottom of the pyramid stand the precinct committees, some 2,350 in Oklahoma. The next level is the county committee. Both parties also have congressional district committees along with, of course, the state committee at the top of the party structure. Composition of the state committee varies by party. The Republican state committee, for example, encompasses a large number of members, including two elected members (one of each sex) from each county, (plus the county chair and vice-chair), the state chairperson (and vice-chair), several auxiliary chairpersons (e.g., Teen-Age Republicans, Federation of Republican Women), all Republican statewide elected officials and members of the Oklahoma legislature, Republican members of Congress, and several immediate past chairpersons. GOP party rules also provide for a regular biennial state convention in odd-numbered years. The state convention elects the state chair and vice-chair for two-year terms. Oklahoma Democrats generally have a similar organizational configuration, although the party's state committee is even larger than the GOP's committee.

Despite their hierarchical appearance, state party organizations in Oklahoma, as elsewhere, do not really control the county and precinct organizations. American parties are notoriously decentralized. The pyramidal organizational structure—from the precinct level to the national party committees—is deceptive. As the late V. O. Key, Jr., once put it, each successive layer of party organization has an independent concern about elections in its geographical area; "collaboration comes about through a sense of common cause rather than exercise of command."[19]

INTEREST GROUPS

Interest groups have been a prominent part of the American political scene from the early days of the republic. In recent years, with the decline of parties, interest groups (sometimes called pressure groups or lobbies) have become an even more important institution for articulating a diverse public's needs and preferences to those in positions of official power. A recent poll shows that almost half the U.S. population (45%) believes that organized interest groups best represent their political interests, compared with only 34 percent who thought that either of the major political parties does so.[20]

Organized interests and lobbyists have long been active in Oklahoma politics. In 1947 American journalist John Gunther identified five major groups that he claimed "all . . . [had] something to do with running Oklahoma": the Baptist church, oil interests, the aged, the education lobby, and the county rings.[21] Similarly, writing about Oklahoma politics in the 1960s, Enid lawyer and political activist Stephen Jones found these five groups still dominant but added two powerful interests: labor unions and newspapers.[22] Yet ascertaining the amount of influence, or even the current level of activity, of various groups proves illusive. Previous assessments have placed Oklahoma among the strong interest-group states largely owing to the power of a few economic interests (chiefly oil) and the lack of a strong two-party system.[23] Most authorities think interest-group strength increases in the presence of weak parties. In any event, to gauge the current level of interest-group activity in Oklahoma, we gathered information on the activities and perceived strengths of various groups by contacting directly all registered lobbyists in the state along with all members of the Oklahoma legislature.

Lobbyists and Group Strength

Under state statutes, any person (1) who spends in excess of $250 in a calendar quarter for lobbying activities, (2) who receives compensation in excess of $250 in a calendar quarter for lobbying services rendered, or (3) whose employment duties in whole or part require lobbying (regardless of whether the individual is compensated for the service above normal salary) must register each year with the Council on Campaign Compliance and Ethical Standards.[24] In April 1986, 343 lobbyists were registered, representing more than three hundred different organizations. The total number of registered lobbyists for 1986 is up 313 percent from 1976, when only 83 were registered.

According to the 1986 registration list, the largest number of lobbyists ($N= 74$) work for various business organizations (excluding petroleum). The next largest group ($N= 46$) represent realty and insurance companies, while the banking and financial community employs about 40 lobbyists. Petroleum and mining interests rank fourth with 25 lobbyists. If one considers all of these as part of business more generally defined, obviously and quite unsurprisingly business groups dominate the lobbying scene. Notice also that several of the strong pressure groups identified in earlier research do not appear among the groups employing the largest number of lobbyists. And the top three categories—general business, realty/insurance, and banking/finance—were not mentioned previously as powerful interests. Whether this more recent list reflects a true shift in power relationships over time is difficult to say.

Actually, few authorities agree on just how the influence of an organized interest should be measured. Most studies rely on a reputational approach, often using legislators as respondents to a questionnaire. So we should not overemphasize the number of lobbyists working for various interests in the state. Numbers of organizations or lobbyists do not always translate into true strength. As Sarah Morehouse reminds us, such characteristics as size of membership, money, organizational cohesiveness, and the status of a group probably contribute to lobbying success more than anything else.[25]

Just how do legislators in Oklahoma perceive group strength? A 1986 survey asked legislators to list and rank the most influential or successful interest groups in Oklahoma during recent legislative sessions (table 8). Sixty-four specific groups (e.g., AFL-CIO, Oklahoma Education Association, Trial Lawyers Association) or general lobbies (e.g., senior citizens, news media, farmers) were identified.

Four lobbies are viewed as especially powerful: (1) education, (2) labor,

Table 8: Influential Lobbies in Oklahoma: State Legislators' Perceptions

Lobby	No. of 1st Rank Mentions	No. of 2nd Rank Mentions	No. of 3rd Rank Mentions	No. of 4th Rank Mentions	Weighted Influence Score[a]
Education	54	10	12	8	278
Labor	7	16	14	10	114
Professional groups	4	16	12	15	103
Banking/Finance	7	13	5	5	82
Public employees	2	6	5	2	38
Oil	2	2	7	8	36
Business	3	4	2	6	34
Agriculture	2	1	6	6	29
Realtors/Insurance	3	1	3	3	24
Human Services	0	3	3	4	19

Note: Figures are based on a mail survey conducted by two of the authors, summer 1986. Of 149 senate and house members, 87 responded.

a. Weighted aggregate influence score was derived by multiplying number of 1st rank mentions times 4, 2nd rank mentions by 3, 3rd rank mentions by 2, and 4th rank mentions by 1 and summing the products.

(3) professional groups, and (4) banking/finance. Only two of these four groups appear on earlier lists of significant lobbies in Oklahoma—education and labor. The other six categories fall considerably below the top four in the eyes of most legislators.

Here we might ask what happened to certain obviously important groups in the state—oil and agriculture, for example. No doubt, these two interests remain important in the state's overall political system. Yet recently, their political efforts have concentrated on the nation's capital more than the Oklahoma legislature. This situation prevails perhaps most obviously with agriculture; farmers are vitally concerned with federal price supports and marketing controls. Even in the 1960s, historian Stephen Jones observed the same tendency for Oklahoma oil interests; their influence was more evident on the national than the state scene.[26] This situation continues today. For example, when Ronald Reagan ran for president in 1980, oil interests contributed substantial sums to the Republican party. Nearly 25 percent of the money donated to the national GOP came from Texas and Oklahoma.[27] During the 1990 elections the Phillips and Kerr-McGee oil companies targeted Muskogee Democratic congressman Mike Synar for defeat because of his strong environmental record. Oil still wields considerable influence in Oklahoma City (ranked sixth by legislators), but the real political muscle is applied in Washington.

Asking legislators which interest groups are the most powerful is only one way of gauging group strength. Outside the narrow compass of legislative politics, other political interests may be pivotal in affecting public affairs, as, for example, in mobilizing support for or against a constitutional amendment. On moral issues, for example, the Baptist church was once the guardian force in the state. Some special interests may even be perceived as so powerful in their area of concern that no sane politician would dare cross them. Certain so-called "single-interest" groups might fit this category. In a populist frontier state like Oklahoma, no elected official should underestimate the strength of the gun lobby, for example. A legislator told one of the authors that she had never received such intense pressure from a group as when she announced her support of stronger antismoking laws. The tobacco lobby, even with its narrow focus, can be extremely powerful (if not always successful) when its interests are threatened. But single-interest groups are not likely to show up on legislative lists of influential state interests. Their scope is too narrow and their legislative activity too intermittent.

Lobbying Techniques

Interest-group representatives employ a variety of strategies and techniques in the furtherance of their causes. Such activities might be grouped into three basic categories: legislator-assisting, influence-seeking, and organizational-directed.[28] In 1986, Oklahoma lobbyists were asked to identify which, if any, of twelve specific techniques they used to advance their legislative goals. They were also queried as to effectiveness or importance of each technique in achieving goals.

Most of the twelve techniques are widely applied (table 9). In fact, with the single exception of using the press, more than two-thirds of the group representatives employ each of the lobbying strategies. Personal contact with legislators proves to be the most popular activity, undertaken by about 98 percent of all respondents. This technique was also considered the most

Table 9: Lobbying Techniques Used by Oklahoma Lobbyists

Activity and Technique	Lobbyists	
	Use Technique (%)	Mean Effectiveness[a]
Legislator-assisting		
Helping draft legislation	85.1	4.0
Appearing before committees	86.9	3.5
Presenting research results	81.6	3.5
Mean scores for 3 techniques[b]	84.5	3.6
Influence-seeking		
Personal contacts with legislators	97.7	4.2
Personal contacts with elected/ politically appointed executive personnel	85.1	3.7
Supporting a legislator at election time	82.0	3.7
Using the press	62.5	3.1
Mean scores for 4 techniques[b]	81.8	3.7
Organizational-directed		
Mobilizing public opinion behind a bill	69.7	3.7
Letter-writing campaigns	80.3	3.6
Joint lobbying by several organizations	84.6	4.0
Using clients to lobby legislators	82.8	3.9
Mounting grassroots lobbying efforts	74.5	4.0
Mean scores for 5 techniques[b]	78.4	3.8

Note: Figures are based on a mail survey conducted by two of the authors, summer 1986; $N =$ 168.

a. Range is from 1 (ineffective) to 5 (very effective).

b. Mean scores are for each lobbying activity area. Scores are calculated by summing percentage usage and effectiveness and dividing by the number of techniques in the activity area.

effective. A considerable correspondence appears between the frequency of use of each activity and its score on the effectiveness scale, with the possible exception of the item "mounting grassroots lobbying efforts," which was employed by only three-quarters of the groups but was tied for second place in effectiveness (with "helping draft legislation" and "joint lobbying by several organizations"). Little variation in usage occurs among the three basic categories of activity. As a group, lobbyists tend to favor slightly "legislator-assisting" tactics (84.5% average score). Less popular are those actions designed to mobilize and direct organizational efforts, although even here the average usage is 78.4 percent.

Lobbyists clearly rely on many different devices to get the attention of legislators. What they want most for their time, money, and effort is access. Few interest groups expect campaign contributions, for example, to guarantee a legislator's vote. As Tony Borthick, executive director of the Oklahoma Trial Lawyers Association, put it: "The thing you're looking for is just access, being able to talk with them."[29] Gaining access can take interesting forms. Consider the example of Charlie Morgan, the unsuccessful Democratic nominee for state corporation commissioner in 1988. Part of his recent court testimony provides an unusual perspective on the legislator-lobbyist relationship, as the following case illustrates.[30]

Morgan, a small oil operator who served in the legislature from 1973 until 1988, appeared in court in 1987 testifying he was broke. His legislative pay had been garnisheed to satisfy a court judgment against him for breach of contract. Here is what Morgan had to say about how lobbyists helped him during his legislative days:

QUESTION: How much does it cost you to live a month?

ANSWER: Not very much, not while the legislature is in session, that is what the lobbyists do up there, feed me pretty good. I haven't had any new clothes, not in a good while. That is legal, too, the lobbyist deal is. As long as they register and don't spend more than $35 a day on me.

QUESTION: How often are they able to do that for you?

ANSWER: Well, I don't eat $35 a day's worth, but I eat with one of them every night, just about. If you would like to see my calendar it is up there. But, we all do.

QUESTION: What about lunch time?

ANSWER: You bet, I grab one of them for lunch, too. . . . They are just wanting my time, and that is the only time I have for them is about lunch time and dinner time, the rest of the time I am in committee meetings.

Perhaps Morgan exaggerates a bit; surely not all legislators dine with lobbyists constantly. But this exchange does reveal one of the common ways lobbyists make personal contact with legislators.

Interest Group Influence in the Legislative Process

Although lobbyists have some effective techniques at their disposal, real success depends on a receptive audience. Legislators were asked the following question: "Overall, how would you rate the influence of interest groups on the legislative process in Oklahoma?" Ten percent ranked the influence of special interests as "crucial," 44 percent as "very important," and 43 percent as "important."

In another series of questions we asked legislators to evaluate the influence of lobbyists on the political system. Their answers reveal an ambiguity about the role of lobbyists in the legislative process. Perhaps surprisingly, 62 percent of the lawmakers felt that lobbyists have a "very" (12.6%) to a "somewhat" (49.4%) overall positive influence on Oklahoma politics. Yet legislators were leery of the amount of influence exerted by interest groups. They also expressed concern over the degree to which group representatives' actions promote the public interest. About 47 percent rated interest groups as "somewhat" to "very" overly influential. Similarly, a majority of the legislators (52.9%) said that lobbyists are "somewhat" or "very likely" *not* to act in the public interest. Finally, in general, members of the legislature assigned high marks to the honesty and integrity of lobbyists; about 80 percent believe that lobbyists are honest and provide accurate information.

Lobbyists, Political Action Committees, and Campaign Expenditures

Oklahoma law regulates lobbying by relying almost exclusively on two requirements—registration and disclosure of expenditures. All registered lobbyists must file expenditure reports with the Oklahoma Council on Campaign Compliance and Ethical Standards any time an expenditure on any one member of the legislative, executive, or judicial branch exceeds $37.50 a day or $300 is spent on any one official in a twelve-month period.[31] In addition to expenditures made by lobbyists, every candidate for state office and every political party and organization that receives annual campaign contributions exceeding $200 must file a report with the council. Thus the expen-

diture records of lobbyists and the amounts spent by political action committees (PACS) to influence election outcomes can be examined as an additional
means of assessing the potential influence of certain groups.

A word about PACS here. Political action committees in Oklahoma are
groups other than party or candidate committees that collect and spend
money to influence the outcome of elections. PACS proliferated wildly in the
1980s, having been created by every conceivable group across the political
spectrum from the National Abortion Rights League to the largest of all, the
National Conservative Political Action Committee (NCPAC). Although PACS
are most visible in national elections, they operate in every state as well,
generally behind the scenes with virtually no state regulation other than the
laws governing campaign finance and lobbying in general.

The Council on Campaign Compliance and its predecessors in Oklahoma
provide no published records of PAC or lobbyist contributions. All completed
expenditure forms are placed in file cabinets or large cardboard boxes. Thus,
determining how much various groups spend to influence public policy is
not easy. In the fall of 1986, however, the *Daily Oklahoman* gathered information on the amount of PAC money spent by groups favoring and opposing
tort reform, one of the hottest political issues of the late 1980s. The following
example shows how PACS mobilize when an issue arises of intense concern to
them.[32]

The battle over tort reform has erupted around the nation as the result of
the rising cost and decreasing availability of liability insurance. Proponents
of tort reform blame high jury awards in personal injury lawsuits and want to
limit the amount of money defendants can be awarded. Those who oppose
tort reform (primarily trial lawyers) blame bad investment practices by insurance companies for recent losses. They claim that the tort reform movement
seeks to deprive citizens of their access to the courthouse. According to the
Daily Oklahoman, the PAC of the Oklahoma Trial Lawyers Association,
which opposed significant change in the existing law, contributed $187,200
to political candidates in the 1986 election. Nineteen PACS that lined up favoring the tort reform issue donated some $316,538 to political candidates in
Oklahoma for that same year. According to the *Daily Oklahoman,* PACS or
groups supporting tort reform and their total contributions to Oklahoma candidates in 1986 were United Community Bankers PAC, $46,537; Oklahoma
Medical Association PAC, $38,000; Oklahoma Realtors PAC, $34,500; Oklahoma Independent Petroleum Association PAC, $36,050; and Certified Pub-
lic Accountants PAC, $28,652.

Generally, PACS prefer contributing to the campaigns of incumbents and especially to those of legislative leaders. Labor union PACs donate almost exclusively to Democrats; other groups are more likely to divide their money between candidates of both parties. Some candidates, especially powerful incumbents, receive money from PACs with competing interests. For example, in 1988 Democratic house Speaker Jim Barker accepted money from labor, which is opposed to a so-called right-to-work law, and from business groups, which generally support right-to-work laws. Basically, of course, PACs help candidates they think will help them.

CONCLUSION

Ferment and change, above all, seem to characterize the party system today, at least in national politics. It is much harder to determine the degree to which new and exciting developments are happening within the Oklahoma party system. The state Democratic party continues to function largely as it has for decades. It remains an umbrella group, home to an enormously divergent set of interests. Largely devoid of ideology, accommodationist in outlook, plagued by personalistic primary contests, the Democratic party in Oklahoma finds it hard to develop strong voter allegiance. Perhaps as the state GOP grows stronger, Sooner Democrats will be forced to reconsider what kind of party they want. Oklahoma Republicans, on the other hand, continue to build their party. Beneficiaries of a generally conservative outlook among the state's electorate and buoyed by Ronald Reagan's widespread appeal and to some extent George Bush's initial popularity, the state GOP has high hopes for the future. Yet the Republican party still includes a sizable ultra-right contingent that remains hostile to moderate political leaders, including GOP governor Henry Bellmon. This group could inhibit the party's search for new and enlightened young talent. To capitalize on the state's movement away from its traditionalistic heritage, the state GOP may need to broaden its political outlook to encompass more than the narrow right-wing political philosophy embraced by much of its leadership in the past.

Despite growing Republican strength, most authorities still consider Oklahoma a modified one-party state primarily because of Democratic dominance in state and local elections. But how long will that situation last? The GOP continues to rack up impressive victories in the state's two largest metropolitan areas. As the Oklahoma City and Tulsa areas continue to lead the state in growth and modernization, the GOP seems poised to benefit politically. Little Dixie will surely persist in its Democratic ways, although Republican inroads are apparent here, too. But as that area's population continues to dwindle, its influence wanes even in the Democratic party. Yet Republican gains will come slowly; old voting habits for local and state offices die hard.

As Oklahoma moves gradually away from its traditionalistic past, the strength and influence of certain interest groups also change. In recent years such issues as branch banking and tort reform have forced financial and professional interests to engage in legislative lobbying as never before. Although these particular issues may recede, interest groups organized around the service, financial, and information sectors of the state's economy will become even more prominent in the future. Indeed, as the state becomes less dependent on oil and agriculture, special interest influence should also become more diversified and pluralistic.

CHAPTER TEN

Financing Government in Oklahoma

Each year the state of Oklahoma spends more money than ever before. Where does it come from? Taxes, of course, one might reply. True, but in fact, more than 40 percent of the money Oklahoma collects comes from sources other than state taxes. Just how much has state revenue gone up since 1978—50 percent? 100 percent? or 150 percent? It may surprise you to know that Oklahoma's state revenue increased by about 111 percent between 1978 and 1988.[1] How does this figure compare with other states? Is Oklahoma a spendthrift, comparatively speaking, or does it lag behind other states in raising revenue? Because revenue increases in Oklahoma in the mid-1980s slowed to a virtual halt, since 1978 Oklahoma state revenue has increased at a somewhat slower pace than the U.S. average of 147 percent.

Besides considering how much it costs to operate state government in Oklahoma, we take a look at where the money goes. In addition, the process of allocating these funds—the budgetary process—is considered. Periodically, we make comparisons with other states or to the U.S. as a whole. Some of these comparisons include finances of the state government alone, and others include both state and local finances. The combined revenue and expenditure comparisons are necessary on occasion because considerable variation exists among the various states in what is called *functional assignment*. This term refers to whether the state or one of its subdivisions has legal responsibility for performing a particular government function. Many public programs, such as road building or education, are financed and provided by both the state and its local subdivisions. In some instances, however, one arena of government rather than the other handles certain activities. To elaborate a bit more, in 1988 the state government in Oklahoma spent 50.5 per-

Table 10: Major State Government Tax Sources in Oklahoma,
Fiscal Years 1978 and 1989

	1978	1989
	(%)	(%)
Income	28.6	32.9
Sales	19.2	22.6
Gross production (including oil and gas extraction)	18.5	11.1

Source: Oklahoma State Expenditures in Brief (Oklahoma City: Kerr Foundation), 1978 and 1989.

Note: Percentage calculations are based solely on state taxes, which exclude federal receipts and fees, tuition, and other charges collected by the state.

cent of combined state and local expenditures (after intergovernmental transfers).[2] In Texas, on the other hand, state government spent only 37.7 percent of the combined amount expended by state and local governments. In effect, some states are much more fiscally centralized than others. The best comparisons among states, then, really should include combined state and local revenues and expenditures.

REVENUE SOURCES

We begin by considering where the money comes from to run state government. Taxes constitute just over half of state revenue in Oklahoma (57.7%). This category has been increasing as a proportion of the total every year for the past decade; in 1978, for example, taxes were only 46 percent of the total. Changes have occured in federal aid as well. In 1988 this source represented 24 percent of all state funds; in 1978 federal assistance was 27 percent of the total. The remaining state funds come from a variety of sources such as fees, licenses, and permits.

Since taxes are so important, let us take a closer look at their composition. The figures in table 10 show the proportion of tax revenue produced by the three dominant tax sources for 1978 and 1989. This eleven-year comparison conceals some rather large changes in state finance that took place in the early 1980s as a result of the oil boom. At its peak, in 1982, taxes on oil and al gas production reached almost 30 percent of total tax receipts.

Table 11: State and Local Revenue Sources in Oklahoma and
the Nation, 1988 (in Percent)

	U.S. (Average)		Oklahoma
Taxes	59.9		56.2
Sales	21.5	24.4	
Property	18.2	10.6	
Income	15.4	11.3	
Other	4.8	9.9	
Federal aid	16.2		16.3
Charges and miscellaneous	23.9		27.5
	100.0		100.0

Source: U.S. Bureau of the Census, *Government Finances in 1987–88* (Washington, D.C.: Government Printing Office, 1990).

How does Oklahoma compare with other states? Here we include state and local governments for reasons stated above. The latest information for this purpose is for 1988 and comes from the U.S. Bureau of the Census.[3] The figures in table 11 contrast general revenue sources for all states and local governments in the U.S. with the same sources for Oklahoma. Oklahoma does not differ greatly from national averages on the basic sources of state and local revenue; the state receives about the same in federal assistance but derives relatively more from charges, fees, and miscellaneous revenue than do other states. Perhaps of greater interest are the subcategories under taxes. Oklahoma's local governments, including schools, rely much less heavily on the property tax than do other states, for reasons elaborated in chapter 12. Income taxes, including personal and corporate, are less significant among Oklahoma tax sources as well. The largest deviation from national figures is for the "other" tax category, primarily because of the still prominent place of oil and gas taxes in Oklahoma's revenue scheme.

Examining the basic sources of revenue does not provide any information on the level of taxation in a given state, so additional comparisons of relative tax burden (or effort) among the states are often made. Probably the most common is revenue per capita. If we look at only the revenue that state and local governments collect on their own (omitting federal aid), Oklahoma's per capita revenue for 1988 is $2,091. For the nation as a whole, the figure is $2,480, again for state and local own-source revenue. Thus Oklahoma falls about 16 percent below the U.S. average on this measure and ranks thirty-eighth in the nation.

A better way for calculating the relative revenue effort of a state, the Representative Tax System (RTS) was devised by the U.S. Advisory Commission on Intergovernmental Relations (ACIR). This measurement is applied to both state and local governments, but only taxes are considered. The RTS is the preferred comparative measure because it is more inclusive: it does not rely on revenue per person or on revenue based on merely the per capita income of a state's residents. It includes virtually all of the taxable resources available to a state and its localities. The calculations themselves are a bit involved, but the basic idea is simple. The ACIR develops a measure of a state's tax capacity; it then compares the actual amount of taxes collected with that capacity and derives a ratio. Tax capacity is the amount of money a state would raise if it taxed its resources (income, property, sales, and so on) at the same rate as the average state. A tax effort index is then derived by dividing the state and local taxes actually collected by the state's tax capacity and standardizing to 100. For example, a tax effort index of 115 indicates that a state is 15 percent above the national average.

The latest figures (1986) show Oklahoma to have a tax capacity of 98, 2 percent below the national average. The state's tax effort, however, is only 85, 15 percent lower than the average state,[4] and forty third in the nation. This figure may go up when tax effort is next calculated, because Oklahoma lawmakers raised taxes in 1987 after an increase just two years before. It is worth noting, however, that Oklahoma's tax effort exceeded the 80 percent mark for the first time only in 1985. We should also add that Oklahoma's tax capacity has been declining since the mid-1980s (primarily because of deflated petroleum and agricultural commodity prices), while its tax effort has gradually risen.

For which taxes is Oklahoma out of line with other states? Table 12 gives the tax effort figure for eight basic state and local taxes. Oklahoma now levies at an above-average rate for only two major taxes—licenses, including motor vehicle license tags, at 138 percent, and severance (oil, gas, and minerals) at a tax effort of 108. The state falls way below average on two—corporate income, which Oklahoma taxes at only 52 percent of the average

Table 12: Oklahoma's Tax Effort Index for Major State and Local Taxes, 1986

Tax	Oklahoma Index[a]	National Rank
General sales	94.5	26
Selective sales	95.9	27
License	137.6	7
Personal income	96.3	29
Corporate income	52.2	42
Total property	54.6	46
Estate and gift	88.5	26
Severance	108.4	11
	84.7	43

Source: Advisory Commission on Intergovernmental Relations, *1986 State Fiscal Capacity and Tax Effort* (Washington, D.C., 1989).

a. 100 is the U.S. average.

state, and property tax, with a tax effort of 55 percent. The state's effort in taxing corporations, however, will likely move higher as a result of the legislature's actions in 1990. To help pay part of the costs of a comprehensive education reform package, including sizable increases in teacher salaries, lawmakers raised corporate taxes about 10 percent.

Where does the tax burden fall in Oklahoma? Do some income groups pay proportionately more than others? Economists have long recognized that the principal sources of state and local revenue—sales and excise taxes particularly—are regressive in their impact. That is, they fall most heavily on those with the least ability to pay. Such taxes hit the poor the hardest because low-income families tend to spend a greater percentage of their earnings on consumer goods such as groceries. A recent study by Citizens for Tax Justice (CTJ) gives a good picture of how the tax burden looks in Oklahoma. As a share of income, Oklahoma sales and excise taxes (e.g., on gasoline, tobacco, and alcoholic beverages) take six times as much from poor families as from rich (for 1987).[5] The lowest-income families spend 7.6 percent of their meager income for those taxes, the sixth highest rate in the nation. Taxes on food purchases, for example, take about twenty times as big a percentage from the poor as from the rich in Oklahoma, according to the study. Oklahoma is one of sixteen states that do not exempt groceries from the sales tax. The CTJ recommends that the legislature eliminate the sales tax on food and perhaps consider retrieving that lost revenue by taxing services used primarily by the well-off, such as jewelry repair and lawn care, and by bringing state income taxes more in line with the ability to pay. Indeed, many Oklahoma lawmakers are sensitive to the regressive nature of the sales tax. Again, to fund part of the 1990 educational reforms, the legislature increased the state sales tax by one-half cent. Democratic senators, however, negotiated an annual sales tax refund of twenty dollars per person (increasing to forty dollars after the first year) for all families earning less than twelve thousand dollars a year. To some degree, this move will help lessen the impact of the sales tax increase on the poor.

Income taxes are the least regressive major tax, but sales taxes, partly because they seem fair (everyone pays the same rate) and are relatively painless, are more popular with the public. No doubt, most state and local governments will continue to rely on both, but the income tax is clearly preferable where tax equity is an issue. In addition to increasing sales and corporate income taxes, the 1990 legislature boosted the individual income tax by progressively raising the rates in all but the lowest income brackets.

People always complain of high taxes, and Oklahomans are no exception. Yet for decades Oklahoma has been a low-tax state. Perhaps the willingness of state officials to raise taxes four times since the mid-1980s (1984, 1985, 1987, and 1990) reflects more than an immediate concern for dealing with revenue shortfalls induced by the state's stagnant economy. Governor Bellmon's 1989 call for a special session to raise taxes to improve common education, although criticized strongly for its specific tax increases, drew significant public support for its intent. In contrast to the three tax increases in the 1980s, which were in response to deep revenue shortfalls, the one in 1990 was intended to stimulate the state's economy by improving the quality of Oklahoma's troubled public school system. Could it be that state leaders are now beginning to recognize that some states with a very strong economic base also have relatively high taxes (e.g., California, Massachusetts, and New York)? States seeking economic development have become more and more aware that good public services, education especially, can be important inducements to high-quality industry.

We might also note here that a second transition in Oklahoma's revenue sources is occurring—the movement away from a heavy reliance on oil and gas taxes. Such sources of revenue fueled the boom times for state government in the early 1980s, but when oil prices tumbled, so did state revenue. Political leaders now seem to recognize that such a tax roller coaster is not a good way to run state government. The following discussion illustrates some of these recent changes.[6]

At the height of the oil boom, Oklahoma state coffers overflowed with oil and gas taxes. In the words of Associated Press writer Bill Johnson, "At the time when the 'oilies' were drinking champagne from their cowboy hats and treating Rolex watches like something made by Timex, the gross production tax on oil and natural gas accounted for 21.5 percent of the state's general fund revenue." But when the boom collapsed, the state was forced to make enormous adjustments and make them quickly. For fiscal year 1988, with "drilling rigs rusting in outdoor lots and capped wells overgrown with weeds," taxes on oil and gas represented only 7.6 percent of state revenue.

According to Harry Culver, public information officer for the Office of State Finance, "In FY-83, the oil and gas industry was like a ruling dinosaur, albeit a welcome one, whose health spelled life or death for the state's economy." Today, the dinosaur hasn't vanished, "but his reign was weakened as other economic elements migrated into his former territory."

In some ways the state government has adjusted more rapidly to the oil boom and bust than the overall economy of the state. "We are not very diversified economically, but we have a very diversified tax base," is the way Alexander Holmes, director of state finance, puts it. "We still need to get out there and get more industry." In fact, Holmes's claim of a very diversified tax base may be overstated. A recent study of state-local tax systems ranks Oklahoma thirty-first in diversity. Oil and gas remain important, of course. In fact, despite the recent slump in prices, most observers assume that the petroleum industry will be a vital part of the Oklahoma economy for a long time. The natural gas industry especially has a bright future over the long run. Yet most people would agree with the statement by a *Norman Transcript* editorial writer: "Petroleum can never again be the tail that wags the dog." Another slightly different but certainly more colorful way of saying it can still be seen on an occasional bumper sticker: "Lord, please send another oil boom. I promise not to blow this one."

Table 13: State Government Spending in Oklahoma, Fiscal Years 1978 and 1989
(in Percent)

Function		1978		1989
Education		44.7		42.1
Elementary and secondary schools	46.6		48.9	
Higher education	42.5		41.2	
Health services		16.5		18.6
Transportation		12.3		11.4
Social services		12.7		12.5
Other		13.8		15.4
		100.0		100.0

Source: Oklahoma State Expenditures in Brief (Oklahoma City: Kerr Foundation),
1978 and 1989.

EXPENDITURES

Less than half of all state money in Oklahoma is appropriated annually by the
legislature.[7] The rest is legally dedicated or "earmarked"; it must be spent
(without further legislative authorization) for predetermined purposes. For
example, county governments receive some earmarked gasoline tax revenues for road maintenance and construction. The largest amount of earmarked money goes to state highways from what are called road-user taxes
(on gasoline and oil). For years, two cents of the state sales tax in Oklahoma
was pledged for human services (e.g., welfare). The earmarking of the sales
tax was undone by the legislature in 1987. The state's Department of Human
Services now depends on general fund appropriations for its share of state
funds.

The big four, or really the big one and the three dwarfs, is one way of
looking at state spending. Education dominates state spending; only three
other functions make up at least 10 percent. Table 13 offers a comparison of
state government spending for 1978 and 1988.

The state of Oklahoma spent a bit less proportionately on education in

Table 14: State and Local Government General Expenditures in Oklahoma and the Nation, 1988 (in Percent)

Function	U.S.		Oklahoma	Per Capita Rank[a]
Education		34.4	37.7	
Elementary and secondary	24.1		25.4	43
Higher	8.9		11.2	26
Welfare		12.6	12.6	25
Health and hospitals		8.8	10.1	
Highways		7.9	9.5	32
Public safety[b]		8.1	6.9	
Other		28.2	23.2	
		100.0	100.0	

Source: U.S. Bureau of the Census, *Government Finances in 1987–88* (Washington, D.C.: Government Printing Office, 1990), pp. 26–29, 107–8. General expenditures omit utility, liquor-store, and insurance-trust spending.

a. Includes Washington, D.C.

b. Includes only police, fire, and corrections.

1988 than it did in 1978, with elementary and secondary schools still the principal beneficiaries. Otherwise, health spending crept up a bit, transportation (highways, mostly) remained steady, and social services declined slightly.

A brief check against national averages is useful at this point. Here again we include local governments to provide a more accurate basis for comparing Oklahoma with other states. When compared to the nation, Oklahoma spends a slightly larger proportion of its state and local funds on education— 37.7 percent compared to 34.4 percent (table 14). Accordingly, both public schools and higher education reflect higher than average percentages. The only other area in which Oklahoma departs much from U.S. figures is for public safety, where the state falls below average—6.9 percent compared to 8.1 percent for all states. We can also note where Oklahoma ranks on some of these measures when we consider spending per person. The state is close to the middle on welfare and higher education and below average for per capita public school and highway spending (table 14).

Education expenditures, however, customarily are calculated for each student rather than per capita. Oklahoma does not do so well on that basis. For 1988 the U.S. average expenditure per pupil for elementary and secondary schools was $4,209; Oklahoma spent only $3,051, for a rank of forty-fourth.[8] In higher education Oklahoma does even worse. According to a national report, Oklahoma ranked last in the nation in 1984 for the amount spent for each student in the state's various institutions of higher education.[9] The reason: Oklahoma was low on legislative appropriations per student and low on tuition. Some states are high on one and low on the other, but not usually low on both. Being near the bottom on the two measures puts the Sooner State in last place.

The Budget

Some authorities view public budgeting from two seemingly contradictory perspectives. On the one hand, many political scientists, such as Aaron Wildavsky, argue that the allocation of money constitutes the ultimate political act. Describing the federal budgetary process, Wildavsky has written, "If politics is regarded in part as conflict over whose preferences shall prevail in the determination of national policy, then the budget records the outcomes of this struggle . . . [thus] the budget lies at the heart of the political process."[10] On the other hand, those with a management orientation emphasize the rationality of the budgeting process, at least in ideal form. The budget becomes an essential management tool.[11] Perhaps the budget is both—a preeminent expression of policy and an indispensable management instrument. In any event, no one doubts the critical nature of the budgetary process for all governments. Frequently, for example, the Oklahoma legislature has difficulty adjourning on time because of the protracted battles over who gets what from the state treasury.

The Budgeting Process

Oklahoma operates under an executive budget system that requires the governor to prepare and submit a budget to the legislature. The state continues to use the line-item budget. Such a format essentially shows proposed expenditures by department and agency for various categories: salaries, materials, equipment, travel, and so on. The governor's budget also displays the amount actually spent for each of these categories for the preceding two years, the amount requested by the agency for the coming year, and the governor's recommended amount. For the past several years, gubernatorial budgets have also provided workload data and expenditures by activity. For example, under the Department of Health, seven programs are listed, including local health services (e.g., county health services supported by the state), environmental health services (air quality, food protection, waste management services), and personal health services (immunizations, maternal and child health programs, central lab services). Expenditure totals (past and proposed) are then shown for each of these subcategories of activity.

Departments are required to submit their estimates for financial needs by September 1 for the next fiscal year's (July 1–June 30) budget. These estimates go to the director of state finance, who is appointed by and may be removed freely by the governor. The finance office and its budget analysts scrutinize these agency requests along with cabinet secretaries normally for the purpose of recommending reductions to the governor. As discussed below, the constitution requires the governor to submit a balanced budget.

In all, the process of preparing the budget is highly incremental, ordinarily reflecting only small changes from year to year. Agencies, building on what they received in previous years, almost always ask for more; budget officers invariably reduce these requests; and the governor makes the final decisions on what eventually goes to the legislature. This process is an annual affair, although in recent years proposals have been advanced to shift to a biennial budget process. According to Governor Henry Bellmon, a biennial system of budgeting would permit shorter legislative sessions and more efficient expenditure of tax money. The legislature would devote its time to budget bills in even-numbered years, leaving odd years open to nonappropriations issues. A newly elected governor would also benefit from a biennial budget, according to Bellmon. Under the current arrangement, a governor is elected in November and must have a budget formulated and ready for presentation when the legislature convenes in February. "It makes for an extremely hectic process," said Alexander Holmes, director of state finance. He added that a new chief executive still could initiate programs in the nonbudget legislative session.[12]

A 1989 constitutional amendment may help alleviate the budgetary problems facing a newly elected governor. The voters approved a proposition to shorten the legislative session which also sets the first day of the session on the first Monday in February (the final legislative day is the last Friday in May). So a new governor has several more weeks than before to modify his predecessor's budget for the fiscal year beginning on July 1.

The legislative group with the most power to affect the budget is the General Conference Committee on Appropriations (GCCA). It consists of members appointed by the presiding officers from the house and senate, primarily from the appropriations committees from the two houses. The GCCA works closely with the leaders of both houses and the governor to hammer out the details for agency budgets and to balance the state budget, which are then sent back to both houses and the governor for final passage. The governor, of course, can exercise regular veto powers over budget bills he or she does not like or even resort to the line-item veto if the bulk of the measure is acceptable.

Balancing the Budget

All states except Vermont require a balanced budget. Oklahoma enacted its first constitutional amendment mandating a balanced budget in 1941. Since 1941 this provision has been amended several times, primarily to modify the formula by which the state's revenue is to be estimated. Until recently, the State Board of Equalization[13] had to rely on a complicated formula designed to yield conservative estimates of state revenue. That provision was changed by constitutional amendment in 1985. Now the equalization board, in December must certify the amount of money the state may budget for the coming fiscal year based on 95 percent of an "itemized estimate" made by the board, except for appropriated federal funds that can be certified for their full amount. This estimate is to consider any increase or decline in revenues that "would result from predictable changes in the economy." Any revenues received beyond 100 percent of the certified amount are deposited to a "rainy day fund," the Constitutional Reserve Fund, which can be used for emergency purposes as determined by the governor and legislature. The certification process applies only to anticipated revenue; the legislature may appropriate any cash on hand. In no case, however, can the total amount exceed the previous year's appropriations by more than 12 percent, adjusted for inflation. The Board of Equalization also meets after the monthly apportionment of funds in February, at which time it may adjust the original certified estimate to allow for changes in economic conditions and later in response to legislation affecting revenues.

In practice, the current arrangement for ensuring a balanced budget involves precise estimates of revenue furnished to the board by the Office of State Finance. This office compiles revenue estimates from several sources, mostly from the Oklahoma Tax Commission, which is also the state's tax-collecting agency. For example, according to finance director Alexander Holmes, the Oklahoma Tax Commission operates one of the five most sophisticated income-tax estimating models in the country. The commission also employs various computer models to estimate revenue from oil and gas production. Other sources of revenue include the state treasurer, for interest earnings, and the state insurance commissioner, for insurance premium fees. In all, Holmes maintains, the revenue-estimation process in the past few years has been "awfully close, especially given the massive shocks the system has taken" as a result of the state's economic turmoil.[14]

CONCLUSION

Historically, the state of Oklahoma and its local governments have taxed and spent less than the average state, when the state's capacity to fund public services is taken into account. Recent figures show the Sooner State with a rank of forty-third in the nation on tax effort, although that position is likely to rise when the next tax effort calculations are done, because of recent tax hikes by state government. In general, when Oklahoma is compared to other states on revenue sources, we find a lower reliance on property taxes and income taxes and, not surprisingly, a much higher dependence on oil and gas taxes. The lion's share of state government spending goes for education, both public schools and higher education—about 45 percent in recent years. However, when per pupil spending is considered, the situation changes: according to the most current data (1984), Oklahoma ranks forty-sixth on this measure for elementary and secondary schools and last in the country in spending per student in higher education.

The budgetary process in Oklahoma involves both the governor, who is not only responsible for submitting the budget but must ensure that it is balanced, and the legislature, especially the General Conference Committee on Appropriations. The fights can be long and even bitter at times over the fundamental question of the level of taxation and also, of course, over which government programs will get more than others. Partly because the budget battles consume so much legislative time and energy, some reformers contend that a biennial budget would permit better planning and allow the legislature to make more effective use of its time without being distracted constantly with questions of money.

Budgeting and financial affairs are complicated and perhaps boring to many citizens. Nonetheless, nothing a state government does is more critical than deciding who will pay and who will benefit from government spending. The process of making these fiscal decisions represents the ultimate political value judgment. At times it can bring forth the wrath of newspaper editorial writers and induce consternation among a variety of special interests. But as Harry Truman once said, "if you can't stand the heat, stay out of the kitchen." Political controversy may ensue, but perhaps more than in any other area statesmanship by state and local elected officials is essential when tough taxing and spending decisions must be made.

CHAPTER ELEVEN

Contemporary Policy Concerns

UNDERSTANDING PUBLIC POLICY

What is public policy? Why is the policy process important? Before examining contemporary issues on Oklahoma's policy agenda, let us address these basic questions.

One expert defines public policy as "whatever governments decide to do or not to do."[1] This definition captures the essence of what Peter Bachrach and Morton S. Baratz call the "two faces of power."[2] The first face of political power is action; government officials can pursue a purposive course of action to deal with a problem or matter of public concern.[3] The second face of political power is deliberate inaction. Because political leaders control the public policy agenda, they may confine the "scope of decision making to relatively 'safe' issues."[4] Most of us are quite aware of the first face of power. We may experience firsthand the results of state action to address various policy concerns. Oklahomans must now buckle up when they drive, most restaurants must provide nonsmoking sections, and residents can now bet on horse races. All of these changes are the result of relatively recent state legislation. The second form of power is more subtle and often overlooked. Nevertheless, it helps explain why some issues are acted on and others are not, or why some groups are included in the policy process and others are excluded. Bachrach and Baratz argue that unless organized interests mobilize and push a particular issue, the matter may never reach the policy agenda.[5] We might add that this is particularly true in Oklahoma, where the status quo is resistant to change because of the state's traditionalistic political culture and a frontier individualism that runs counter to collective action.

As pointed out earlier, the political system in Oklahoma largely ignores the interests of American Indians. How might such excluded groups push their political preferences? In March 1988 Governor Henry Bellmon, in an "apparently unprecedented action,"[6] sent personal letters to the leaders of thirty-six Oklahoma Indian tribes inviting them to suggest Indians for appointment to state boards and commissions. According to Bellmon aide Allen Wright, a descendant of the Choctaw Indian Allan Wright, who coined the name *Oklahoma* to mean "Land of the Red People," the invitation was the result of lobbying by Bobby Bighorse, a retired roofer and member of the Cheyenne-Arapaho tribe. Bighorse asserted that "no administration from the first governor to the present governor has ever actively sought Indians to set on their boards and commissions." In the past state officials have only asked Indians "to come dance for us." They never said "come and help us. We know that Indians are just as smart as anybody else, have just as good an education as anybody else." Bighorse claims that the invitation "is a very historical thing. . . . This shows that the State of Oklahoma and the current administration are looking at Indians as other than being dancers, drunks, and stuff like that."

Policy making thus brings various interested parties into the governmental arena, where they compete for scarce resources. Because government resources are limited, different individuals or groups win, lose, or draw in the policy process. For example, when the legislature appropriates $1 million for a new student loan program, those same funds cannot go to build bridges or extend welfare benefits to the poor. Given limited resources, quite naturally the highway lobby would rather see the money spent on the construction of new bridges, the welfare lobby on aid to the poor, and the school lobby on education.

Another example further illustrates the notion of winners and losers in the policy process. Paying taxes is not an activity most Oklahomans enjoy. Some individuals, groups, and transactions, however, are exempt from taxation. Harry Culver, an official in the Office of State Finance, reports that "Oklahoma grants tax preferences of nearly $800 million a year."[7] In total, 132 tax exemptions have been identified. Some of the more costly include exemption of (1) medical services and advertising from sales taxes, (2) homesteads from ad valorem taxes, and (3) diesel fuel for nonhighway use from motor fuel taxes. Those who are the beneficiaries of exemptions are tax policy winners; those who are not are tax policy losers. If all tax exemptions were nullified, the state would have about an additional $800 million to spend, or tax rates on other items could be lowered, of course. With a base established for understanding the essential meaning and nature of public policy, we now turn to a discussion of contemporary policy concerns in Oklahoma.

OKLAHOMA'S PUBLIC POLICY AGENDA

In recent years a multitude of concerns has made it to the state policy agenda. Even though many of the issues are not new, they often required the support of prominent groups to force policy makers to address perceived problems. Several of these contemporary policy matters have been highlighted in previous chapters. In chapter 1, for example, we noted that currently much is being made about Oklahoma's "image problem." The assumption, right or wrong, is that the state's image needs to be refurbished to lure more people and industry to Oklahoma. Several studies have been conducted recently that have made recommendations on how the state could improve its image. The state is funding foreign trade offices in Tokyo, London, Singapore, and Beijing, for example, to overcome the lack of knowledge about Oklahoma, to recruit foreign capital, and to sell state products. Domestically, state government has united with the state tourist industry to mount campaigns to attract out-of-state visitors by advertising the virtues of the Sooner State.

Two other major policy concerns were identified in chapter 2—school desegregation and the current dispute over Indian sovereignty. Unfortunately, space does not allow for a detailed discussion of these or the many other controversial issues confronting Oklahomans, such as right-to-work, tort reform, workers' compensation, ethics in government, responses by state leaders to fiscal stress, and prison overcrowding. Rather, in this chapter we focus on the issue that has once again captured the lion's share of attention in both the public and private sectors: economic development.

As explained in chapter 4, the pragmatic, transition politics pursued by state leaders since the end of World War II in many respects were abandoned during the 1970s. Economic diversification took a back seat to the oil boom. State coffers were awash with tax money from oil and natural gas production, and economists predicted the state would benefit greatly from an even higher escalation of energy prices. With the collapse of the petroleum industry in 1982 (coupled with a depressed agricultural sector), the prosperity of the 1970s slipped away and attention returned to broadening the tax base and diversifying the state's economy. The 1980s were marked by the return to the pragmatic politics of the days before the oil boom.

ECONOMIC DEVELOPMENT

The Inspiration for Economic Development Programs

Currently across America, economic development is viewed as one of the major issues, if not "the" issue, facing state and local governments. Almost every day the media report on some new economic development initiative passed by a state legislature or pursued by city officials. Economic development (or economic diversification, economic renewal, economic expansion, etc.) is important for several reasons. First, such programs have a wide political appeal. The bottom line, so to speak, of such policies is to create new jobs and increase economic activity and opportunities.[8] The careers of political officials may be tied to their success in promoting policies that enhance economic opportunities for their constituents. Second, the creation of new jobs and potential increases in population can have positive consequences for local economies. Retail sales, land values, building construction, newspaper circulations, and service-oriented businesses are likely to experience increases as local economies expand. At the same time, state and local governments benefit from economic growth through the collection of more taxes. Finally, creating jobs helps combat social problems, such as unemployment, poverty, and crime. Given these potential benefits, no wonder economic development appears so appealing.

The Difference between Economic Growth and Economic Development

What exactly constitutes economic development is not really clear. Sociologist Craig St. John, for example, suggests that a distinction must be made between economic growth and economic development. He argues that during the 1970s and early 1980s Oklahoma experienced economic growth as a result of soaring prices for petroleum and good prices for farm commodities. The economy expanded and the number of dollars in circulation increased, but the economic base of the state did not change fundamentally; economic growth occurred largely without development. In contrast, "true" economic development requires making fundamental changes in a state's economic base: "Growth comes with development but development means much more than just increasing the circulation of money through the economy."[9] Economic development, suggests St. John, actually means economic diversification and long-range policy planning. The economic growth Oklahoma experienced during the 1970s was tenuous because it depended so heavily on world petroleum and agricultural commodity markets. Once these markets collapsed, so did the state's economy. Clearly, Oklahomans cannot control international markets. But state business interests can pursue economic development strategies that permit downturns in a particular sector to be absorbed within a diversified economy.

Despite the warnings of St. John and numerous other scholars,[10] all too often short-term, unplanned economic growth has been confused with genuine economic development—long-term, planned initiatives to produce a stable, diversified economy. Cities, for example, have engaged in "smokestack chasing" or "industrial prospecting" without first evaluating the adequacy of local infrastructures and labor skills. State and local governments often become contestants in an almost unbridled governmental version of "Let's Make a Deal" to see who can offer firms the best tax incentive and/or industrial park development package regardless of any potential cost to taxpayers. In short, as Enid F. Beaumont and Harold A. Hovey note: "State and local economic development strategies typically evolve incrementally, without an underlying economic theory except that more jobs are good and less jobs are bad."[11]

Economic Development Initiatives in Oklahoma

Without doubt, Oklahoma is in dire need of economic development programs, as a few statistics will show. In a ranking of percentage changes from 1985 to 1986, Oklahoma placed thirty-eighth nationally in new business incorporations and forty-eighth in job growth.[12] According to *Inc.* magazine's annual ranking of states' abilities to stimulate entrepreneurial activity, Oklahoma held the forty-third spot in 1986 and slipped to forty-seventh place in 1987.[13] Compared to other states, in 1986 Oklahoma did fare better on Grant Thornton's (a Chicago-based accounting and management consulting firm) index of manufacturing climate—twenty-fifth rank among the states.[14] In addition to these more traditional "business climate" measures, the Corporation for Enterprise Development (CFED), a Washington, D.C., economic development research group, analyzes seventy-eight factors deemed to be

Table 15: The 1990 Development Report Card

	Economic Performance Index	Business Vitality Index	Development Capacity Index	State Policy Index
Alabama	D	B	D	C
Alaska	C	C	B	C
Arizona	C	C	C	F
Arkansas	D	C	F	C
California	B	B	B	B
Colorado	D	B	A	F
Connecticut	A	B	A	B
Delaware	A	C	A	C
Florida	B	B	D	C
Georgia	C	A	D	C
Hawaii	A	D	B	C
Idaho	C	D	C	C
Illinois	D	C	B	B
Indiana	B	B	C	A
Iowa	C	D	D	A
Kansas	C	D	D	B
Kentucky	F	B	F	C
Louisiana	F	F	F	D
Maine	B	A	D	C
Maryland	A	A	A	A
Massachusetts	A	B	A	B
Michigan	C	C	C	A
Minnesota	B	C	A	A
Mississippi	D	C	F	C
Missouri	C	C	C	B
Montana	D	D	C	D
Nebraska	C	D	C	F
Nevada	A	C	C	F
New Hampshire	A	A	C	F
New Jersey	A	A	A	B
New Mexico	F	C	C	C
New York	C	A	B	A
North Carolina	C	A	C	D
North Dakota	D	F	D	D

Table 15 (*continued*)

	Economic Performance Index	Business Vitality Index	Development Capacity Index	State Policy Index
Ohio	B	D	C	A
Oklahoma	D	F	D	A
Oregon	C	B	A	B
Pennsylvania	B	B	A	A
Rhode Island	A	C	B	B
South Carolina	C	D	D	D
South Dakota	D	C	C	D
Tennessee	D	A	D	D
Texas	D	C	B	D
Utah	B	C	A	C
Vermont	A	A	B	D
Virginia	B	A	B	B
Washington	C	C	A	C
West Virginia	F	D	F	C
Wisconsin	B	D	C	A
Wyoming	C	F	C	D

Source: Corporation for Enterprise Development, *The 1990 Development Report Card for the States* (Washington, D.C., 1990), p. 1.

determinants of current and future state economic growth. Each state is graded along four dimensions:

1. Economic performance—employment growth, income per capita, equity, job quality, and quality of life;

2. Business vitality—competitiveness of existing businesses and ability to spawn new ones;
3. Development capacity—human and capital resources, infrastructure capacity, amenities to attract and retain talent; and

4. State policy strength—effectiveness of governance and regulation, tax policy, commitment to enabling capital mobilization, improved education and research, and help for distressed communities.[15]

Table 15 displays the development report card for each state for 1990. Rather than ranking states numerically as in other indices, the CfED simply assigns a letter grade for each development category. Given the state's current economic woes and low job growth, not surprisingly Oklahoma was graded a "D" for economic performance. The state fared worse for business vitality—a grade of "F." This grade basically means that existing firms in the state are competitive but have room for substantial improvement. The grade of "D" for development capacity seems on target; as we document shortly, the state badly needs to undertake improvements in human capital and infrastructure. Finally, the grade of "A" for economic development policy reflects the changes in development-related policies made by state policy makers in the late 1980s.

A host of economic development studies have been either commissioned by state leaders or undertaken by public and private sector groups. For example, in 1986 a group of professors from the University of Oklahoma, Oklahoma State University, and Rose State College submitted to Oklahoma 2000, Inc., an organization affiliated with the Oklahoma State Chamber of Commerce, a report entitled, *State Policy and Economic Development in Oklahoma: 1986*. In February 1987 the Oklahoma Academy for State Goals released its final report and recommendations in *Strategy for Economic Expansion in Oklahoma*. On January 7, 1987, the Cambridge, Massachusetts, consulting firm of Counsel for Community Development, Inc., submitted to the Joint Fiscal Operations Committee of the legislature a study called *Oklahoma: Tools for a Global Competitor*. In 1988 the Hudson Institute, an Indianapolis think tank, released its report on ways to improve Oklahoma's future, which includes recommendations on economic development policies and institutions. Finally, Oklahoma Futures, a group of public and private sector leaders, issued its first five-year economic development plan for the state.[16] Collectively, these reports contain literally hundreds of pages of facts, figures, analyses, and recommendations. The sheer number of reports demonstrates the commitment of public and private interests to economic development. But as the adage goes, actions speak louder than words.

The state legislature has been very active in the state's economic development efforts.[17] In 1986, for example, the Department of Commerce (DOC) was created, combining the state's two major economic development agencies. The DOC's primary mission is to provide support to Oklahoma firms and local communities in their efforts to diversify, expand, and increase competitiveness. Incorporating many of the recommendations suggested in the Counsel for Community Development's report, sweeping economic development initiatives were passed in the Oklahoma Economic Development Act of 1987. This bill created Oklahoma Futures as a policy development board to advise the Department of Commerce. The board includes leaders from private industry, labor, agriculture, and the public sector. The 1987 act also established the Oklahoma Center for the Advancement of Science and Technology (OCAST) to develop and enlarge the state's research programs; the Oklahoma Capital Investment Board to oversee a pool of money to be loaned to Oklahoma businesses; the Executive Bond Oversight Commission and the Legislative Bond Oversight Commission to review state bond issues; and the Oklahoma Development Finance Authority (ODFA) to replace the Oklahoma Development Authority. The new authority assumes the duties of the one it replaced but has greater bonding capacity. Funding for these programs has increased sharply despite a stagnant state budget. Between fiscal years 1987 and 1988, state funding for the research and development programs operated by the DOC grew from $3 million to $11 million. In September 1988 the voters overwhelmingly passed two state propositions on economic development. One allows the ODFA to issue $100 million in bonds to underwrite economic expansion; the other permits OCAST to receive up to 1 percent of the annual legislative appropriation for economic development loans and grants to persons and companies. The 1989 legislature gave OCAST almost $16 million in state funds.

The mainstays of Oklahoma's economy were not forgotten either. In 1988 the petroleum industry was given a break. Any incremental production that is the result of an enhanced recovery project is exempted from the gross production tax for three years, or until the cost of the project is recovered. The Oklahoma agricultural linked deposit program created an innovative financing plan to aid the distressed agricultural sector. This legislation authorizes the state treasurer to invest up to $25 million annually at below market value with state banks. The banks must agree to make loans to agricultural businesses that propose to produce, process, or market alternative products or to distressed farms and ranches that develop an approved management plan. Another 1988 piece of legislation, similar in operation to the agriculture linked deposit program, authorizes the state treasurer to create a small business linked deposit program that could provide more than $125 million in new loans for small businesses.

Finally, economist Larkin Warner argues that Indian tribal governments possess "special advantages in state economic development."[18] Enterprises located on Indian lands, for example, may enjoy the benefits of paying no local property taxes, state taxes, or payroll tax for unemployment insurance. Additionally, a business can be shielded from lawsuits under the sovereign immunity of the tribal government, can have independent access to federal designation as a foreign trade zone, and can benefit from low-interest financing through tribal issue of tax-exempt bonds. Despite these and other advantages, Warner asserts that economic development on Indian lands is retarded because of poor relations between the state of Oklahoma and Indian tribes over the issue of tribal sovereignty and occasionally because of unstable and fractious tribal politics. Nevertheless, progress is being made. In 1987, for instance, an Indian economic development specialist was added to the staff of the Oklahoma Department of Commerce. Since then, the attorney general has cleared the way for tribal governments to secure economic development loans from the state backed by bonds created by the legislature in 1987. And in 1988 the legislature passed Senate Bill 210, which allows the state to enter into cooperative agreements with Indian tribes. Warner warns that if the special economic development advantages tribal governments possess are to be fully realized, "proactive intergovernmental relations" between the state and Indian tribes will be required.

In sum, 1987 and 1988, in particular, were pivotal years in Oklahoma's effort to place in operation policies and institutions that will facilitate planned, long-range economic development. Associated with the drive for economic development have been two other concerns: (1) improving the state's human capital by emphasizing the crucial role of education in economic development and (2) studying and addressing the state's infrastructure needs.

IMPROVING HUMAN CAPITAL THROUGH EDUCATION

One of the high-priority recommendations offered by the Counsel for Community Development in its 1987 report to the legislature was: "invest in Oklahoma's most important asset—its people—through the highest quality common education, higher education, and continuing education."[19] In fact, the development of human capital through education is inextricably linked to economic development. The logic is straightforward: a principal factor affecting location decisions of firms is the cost and quality of labor. An educated labor pool from which to draw is a prime asset to business. A strong vocational education system facilitates training and retraining needs of the work force. Finally, "states with robust economies have world-class research universities located within their boundaries. Often, high tech companies are attracted to communities with outstanding universities or are founded due to the spin-off from research carried out at these institutions."[20] One needs only to look at Boston, Austin, and North Carolina's Research Triangle for examples of this last point.

Unfortunately, Oklahoma's educational system needs considerable attention. According to statistics released by U.S. Secretary of Education William J. Bennett in February 1988, among the twenty-eight states that use the
American College Test (ACT) as the dominant college entrance exam, Oklahoma ranked twenty-fifth.[21] Scores on the ACT range from 1 to 36, with a
1987 national average of 18.7. Oklahoma's average was 17.7; only West Virginia, Louisiana, and Mississippi had lower averages. Bennett's report card
to the states also revealed that Oklahoma in 1987 ranked thirty-first in high-
school graduation rates (71.6%), thirty-ninth in expenditure per pupil for
public school students ($3,146), and forty-first in average teacher's pay
($22,060).[22] Of all these measures, test scores, of course, most nearly ap-
proximate achievement. On that basis the system of public education in
Oklahoma does not have much to be proud of, with the notable exception of
Oklahoma's vocational-education schools, which are regarded as some of
the nation's finest.

To deal with one of the major funding problems of common education,
lawmakers have recently tackled the difficult issue of property tax reform.
The process of property tax assessment in Oklahoma is quite complex and
political. For years each of the state's seventy-seven counties was allowed to
set tax ratios between 9 and 15 percent. Despite successful reform efforts
aimed at narrowing the tax ratio spread, significant disparities in tax assessment remain among counties. The linkage between property taxes and education funding is discussed at some length in the next chapter; for now let us
note that in 1987 about 63 cents of every common school dollar came from
state government—tenth rank nationally. In contrast, local support for
schools amounted to only 17.5 cents, forty-sixth rank nationally. According
to former house Speaker Jim Barker, "The disparity between strong state
support and . . . [the state's] low per pupil spending can largely be traced to
comparatively low property tax contributions to public education."[23]
Current legislative strategies to reform the property tax system basically involve
equalizing assessment practices across counties, tightening controls over
county assessors in evaluating property, and making it easier for local governments to support local programs. Because tax reform often spells tax increases
to many, such proposals have been unusually controversial. Legislators tread
lightly, for example, when the discussion turns to property tax increases. This
caution was evident after a blue-ribbon panel recommended to the 1989–90 special session of the legislature that a portion of the costs for education reform
could come from the property tax. That proposal was quickly discarded for fear
of repercussions from property owners, particularly farmers.

Property tax reform may not be the only answer to school funding problems. Fundamental changes in the state's property tax system may be slow in coming. In the meantime, other proposals have been advanced to provide additional funds for local schools. State leaders have become more concerned than ever that the state's economic growth may be hampered by an underfunded educational system. As noted above, in July 1989 Governor Bellmon called a special session of the legislature to consider major modifications in the state's tax system to raise more money for education. Although his plan was rejected decisively, other leaders agreed on the need for significant new revenues for common schools.

The actions of the legislature and other major public opinion shapers during the special session are illustrative of the struggle to propel the state forward. Soon after the special session met in August, legislators determined that the governor's plan was deficient because it failed to include education reforms and its tax proposals were unacceptable. It proposed to reduce the state's tax base by doing away with the property tax, historically the principal local funding source for schools and county government, and to expand the sales tax to include most services. The legislature called on a blue-ribbon panel, Task Force 2000, chaired by Tulsa oil man George Singer, to develop a package of school reforms and tax recommendations for the legislature when it reconvened the special session in November 1989. The Task Force report recommended sweeping education reforms in the areas of school consolidation, school accountability, curriculum and testing, accreditation standards, increases in minimum salaries for teachers, class-size reductions, longer school years, the equalization of school funding, performance review of teachers and administrators, and removal of those deemed incompetent. The Task Force also made controversial recommendations for the state to mandate preschool and full-day kindergarten programs, programs for the parents of three-year-olds, and registration of children educated in home schools. To fund the reforms, the Task Force offered several alternative tax increase proposals that amounted to more than $300 million annually.

The proposals were incorporated into a house bill authored by house Speaker Steve Lewis and senate president pro tempore Bob Cullison. Before the bill was signed into law in April 1990, it elicited some of the most dramatic moments in recent legislative history. Early in the process, conservatives successfully killed provisions to force any state regulation of home schoolers, and friends of the tourism industry deleted a provision to lengthen the school year by ten days even though Oklahoma's school year is one of the shortest. The bill, however, continued to move through the legislature. As it did so, a joint conference committee inserted a compromise on preschool and mandatory kindergarten programs, programs that the house had earlier removed. The same committee failed to reach agreement on controversial provisions regarding parental choice of schools and mandatory school consolidation which senate Republicans demanded in return for their votes for the bill.

Democratic leaders were able to secure a majority of votes in both houses to pass the bill. Much more difficult, however, was the two-thirds majority for the emergency clause, which Governor Bellmon and the legislative Democratic leadership agreed would be essential to thwart a planned effort against the bill by a citizens' group seeking to put the measure to a popular vote. In the house the final vote on the emergency clause had to wait about a week after the vote on the bill itself as legislators mourned the tragic death of Representative Bill Brewster's two children in a plane crash. Final action in the senate took months and came only after negotiations nearly collapsed several times. In the end, it took a week of school closings, during which educators marched at the capitol in support of the reforms, and a marathon meeting of the senate Democratic caucus before the emergency clause passed. The final vote was heavily partisan, with only one Republican senator breaking ranks to vote with the Democrats for the emergency clause.

What about higher education? In 1987 J. R. Morris, Regents' Professor at the University of Oklahoma, declared that Oklahoma was "America's most poorly funded higher education system." In fiscal year 1984 "no state in the United States . . . provided fewer dollars per student from state appropriations and tuition and fees [than Oklahoma]." If state appropriations and tuition and fees are considered separately, in 1984 Oklahoma ranked thirty-eighth in state appropriations per student and fifty-first (including the District of Columbia) in tuition and fees. Morris surmises:

> The sad reality is that all of the comparative gains of the late 70s and early 80s have been lost. As recently as the period from 1980 to 1984, Oklahoma ranked 7th in the nation in increased revenues to higher education. . . . By 1983, probably for the first time in the state's history, Oklahoma had achieved nationally competitive faculty salaries, leading the nation in percentage salary increases for that five-year period. Beginning early in 1983 and continuing today, budget reductions and lack of salary increases have essentially returned Oklahoma's over-all funding level to the pre-boom period.[24]

To address the need for higher education funding, the Regents for Higher Education approved substantial tuition hikes throughout much of the 1980s. Nevertheless, in 1988 Oklahoma still ranked fortieth out of the fifty states in tuition per student, thirty-eighth in state-appropriated funds per student, and forty-first in average salary of professors at the state's two flagship universities.[25] Yet college students complain about tuition hikes, and substantial tax increases in the near future seem unlikely. So the state is in a bind. The existing tax structure will generate only modest new revenue over the next few years, and every state agency will compete for its share of the small increase. How much can higher education really claim? And if state leaders give the colleges and universities a large boost in funding, how will that money be used?

Oklahoma's system of higher education has been criticized for years for emphasizing quantity over quality. The state supports twenty-six public institutions of higher learning: two major comprehensive universities, ten regional and senior universities (including six former teacher colleges), and fourteen two-year institutions. For a state of just over three million people, some citizens have long contended that Oklahoma has too many colleges and universities. The State Regents for Higher Education disagree, and in any event closing any of the institutions would be difficult. Still, some evidence supports the view that Oklahoma higher education stresses access above all. For example, the state ranks ninth in the country in the number of full-time college students per high-school graduates in the state.[26] Perhaps even more telling is the way funds are allocated within the state's system of higher education. The constitution directs that the legislature must make one lump-sum appropriation to the state's higher regents. That group then has the responsibility of dividing the funds among all the competing institutions. Until 1987 the process employed by the regents was based heavily on enrollment. Some recognition was given to the much higher costs of graduate education and research, but the University of Oklahoma (OU) and Oklahoma State University (OSU) remained under constant pressure to keep enrollments up to avoid reductions in state funding.

An effort is underway to begin decoupling enrollment from higher education funding, although it will be a slow and difficult task. At least one peculiarity arises from the state's historic enrollment-driven system. More than anything else, the reputation of a university is intimately tied to the quality of its faculty, especially the faculty that teaches graduate courses and conducts scholarly research. Probably the best way of attracting and retaining a superior faculty is to pay it well and provide it ample support for research. Faculty salaries at OU and OSU consistently lag far behind national averages and are regularly near the bottom among the universities of the Big Eight. On the other hand, faculty salaries at the so-called regional universities, especially Central State University (CSU), the largest of the group, often considerably surpass regional averages. In fact, over the past decade or so average faculty salaries at CSU have generally exceeded those at the two flagship universities (when fringe benefits are included, OU and OSU salaries are higher). If higher education is to be a cornerstone in the quest for high-quality economic development, the long-standing arrangement for funding institutions of higher education must be modified. More money alone is not enough; the allocation of those funds is also critical. Yet any significant changes that would benefit the two major universities at the expense of others would be quite controversial and difficult to achieve.

Before leaving the discussion of education, we need to touch briefly on Oklahoma's superb system of vocational-technical education. More than two hundred thousand Oklahomans enroll each year in some phase of vo-tech education, in programs operated through the twenty-four area vo-tech districts, the public high schools, or the skills centers and inmate training centers. Local taxes are the prime source of vo-tech funds, but state and federal support is provided as well. The *Oklahoma Observer*'s Frosty Troy, a big booster of the state's vo-tech system, claims that it ranks among the very top in the nation. In his words, "Vo-tech today is the difference between success and failure in the state's drive for economic development. Not everybody needs a doctorate. Somebody has to nurse the sick, man the technician slots, program and service computers, and otherwise deal with the routine of today's technologies."[27]

Finally, we do not wish to sound overly pessimistic regarding education in Oklahoma, although the shortcomings of the common schools and the system of higher education are very real. Still, things have improved, and evidence shows that the people of the state do support educational progress. A recent statewide poll conducted for the Oklahoma Education Association by Kielhorn and Associates is revealing.[28] Some 73 percent of the respondents think more money is needed to improve public schools; 45 percent want improved colleges and universities. Perhaps most encouraging of all the poll results is the willingness of 51 percent who say they would vote for higher taxes if the money went to improve public schools.

The business community is increasingly committing itself to education, as noted by Frosty Troy: "After years of doing everything to get out of the oil recession except the right thing, it looks like Oklahoma's political and business leaders are finally on the right track. . . . For years a lot of people in Oklahoma's business community were willing to do anything but raise the revenue for the excellence they sought in education. Now they realize that states such as Massachusetts, Wisconsin, Minnesota and others saw education as an investment, not an expense. They're booming.''[29]

INFRASTRUCTURE NEEDS

Another critical ingredient in economic development is the quality of a state's infrastructure. Providing basic services such as roads and highways, waste collection and disposal, and clean drinking water are the responsibilities of state and local governments. The condition of local infrastructures can seriously impinge on business decisions to relocate or expand.

In order to determine the status of Oklahoma's infrastructure in 1985, the Department of Economic and Community Affairs (now the Department of Commerce) initiated a major study. An infrastructure database was created using government documents and assessments from federal, state, and local agencies and survey information collected from local governments. Some of the principal findings of the study were:

1. More than 26 percent of municipal water systems and 50 percent of sanitary systems in Oklahoma will probably have to increase capacity to accommodate any new industrial demands.

2. Oklahoma ranks second in the nation in the number of structurally deficient bridges. The cost of replacing inadequate bridges on state highways, county roads, and city streets exceeds $1.3 billion.

3. Among water systems, difficulties with distribution systems appear to be the most widespread problem. Only half the cities, towns, and rural water districts in Oklahoma report adequate distribution systems.

4. For more than 30 percent of rural and municipal water systems, water supplies are vulnerable to potential contamination from agricultural and petroleum activities.

5. By 1991, 42 percent of municipally operated solid-waste facilities will exhaust disposal capacity.

6. Siting of new refuse disposal facilities is one of the most difficult problems facing cities and towns in Oklahoma.[30]

The report also offered some stark bottom-line estimates of infrastructure needs and funding requirements. Between 1985 and the year 2000, infrastructure *needs* (i.e., operations, maintenance, construction, interest, and repairs) will require $24 billion in 1985 dollars, or $1.52 billion per year. Assuming spending at current levels, continuation of federal and state programs, and oil prices at 1985 levels, infrastructure *spending* will total $17 billion ($1.08 billion per year) by the year 2000. Thus, in 1985 dollars, unless user fees are increased or alternative sources of revenues are made available, infrastructure spending will fall short of infrastructure needs by $7 billion.[31]

The legislature has begun to respond to the demand for more public works spending. During the 1987 session the gasoline tax was increased and millions of new dollars were directed to state and county road programs. At the same time, the governor and lawmakers authorized feasibility studies designed to expand the state's toll-road programs. The Oklahoma Turnpike Authority subsequently issued bonds for new turnpikes in the Oklahoma City and Tulsa metropolitan areas and for a two-lane turnpike from Ada to Davis. The 1988 legislature established a revolving loan program of about $2 million to assist communities in constructing wastewater treatment facilities and placed a question on the ballot lowering the requirement for passing local bond issues for streets and bridges from 60 percent of the voters to a simple majority (it subsequently passed).

CONCLUSION

The call for true economic development in Oklahoma does not require justification; the need is real and immediate. Overdependence on hydrocarbon and agricultural industries places the state at a disadvantage in a volatile world market. Oklahoma can no longer afford to confuse short-term economic growth with the real purpose of economic development—long-term, planned economic diversification. Oklahoma leaders have recognized that the state had to improve on its traditional economic development strategies of "smokestack chasing" and dogmatic attachment to a low tax base. The legislature, in cooperation with other public and private interests, has begun to set in place those structures and institutions that eventually can make Oklahoma more competitive in today's global economy. How can state leaders build on what they have started and demonstrate a key characteristic associated with maturity—patience? Results will not be immediate and will be hard to measure. As one expert notes, "it is too early, if indeed it will ever be possible, to measure precisely just what any program or agency did for the economic development of its state."[32]

The Oklahoma Economic Development Act and other related legislation made a start, a good start in fact. But as St. John notes, economic develop-

ment is "the achievement of a matrix of . . . activities that by their own pro-
ductivity create new opportunities for development."[33] Creation of departments and commissions that provide venture capital and facilitate issuance
of bonds is not enough. The same can be said of legislation that provides tax
incentives for this or that business or enterprise. All too often economic development has been viewed simply as a process of the government's lower-
ing business costs.[34] Incentives may be necessary in the competition for
firms, but they alone are not sufficient. Included in the matrix of activities to
foster long-term growth should be an educated populace and local living environments that promote quality of life and entrepreneurial innovations. In
years to come historians and political analysts may label the mid-1980s as the
period of economic development maturity. If the economic development
seeds planted are to come to fruition, however, policy makers must address
human capital and infrastructure needs.

CHAPTER TWELVE

Local Government in Oklahoma

Many of us seem to prefer government at the local level—the grassroots—to other, "higher" arenas. Although much of the attraction to a grassroots political ideology has a distinct nostalgic quality, perhaps even a longing for a time that never really existed, scholars and ordinary citizens alike seem to agree that the local community is indeed the cradle of democracy. According to political scientist Richard Dagger, the city is readily accessible to its residents, closely tied to their interests, and likely to promote the sense of community usually associated with citizenship.[1] A picture of government in Oklahoma thus would not be complete without considering those units that govern its cities, counties, and local schools.

MUNICIPAL GOVERNMENT

Before examining specific features of Oklahoma municipal government, we first take a brief look at where people live in the state. Most Oklahomans live in cities, which the Census Bureau considers any urban place of twenty-five hundred or more population. According to that standard, exactly two-thirds of Oklahoma's 1980 population was urban. These approximately two million people represent an increase of almost 16 percent over the city population of 1970. But this growth in urban dwellers was outpaced by the increase in rural areas (table 16). Reversing a long-term downward trend, the number of Oklahomans residing in rural areas actually went up by more than 23 percent between 1970 and 1980. The land still has an attraction for many people.

Even though rural areas in Oklahoma have shown a healthy population gain in recent years, the two largest metropolitan areas represent an increasingly dominant part of the state. The Oklahoma City and Tulsa Metropolitan

Table 16: Urban/Rural Population Changes in Oklahoma, 1960–80

	1960 Population	Change 1950–60 (%)	1970 Population	Change 1960–70 (%)	1980 Population	Change 1970–80 (%)
Urban	1,464,789	+28.5	1,740,161	+18.8	2,014,617	+15.8
Rural	863,498	–21.1	819,692	–5.1	1,010,649	+23.3
Total state	2,328,284	+4.3	2,559,253	+9.9	3,025,266	+18.2

Source: U. S. Bureau of the Census, *Statistical Abstract, 1973* (Washington, D. C.: Government Printing Office, 1973), p. 19; *Statistical Abstract, 1964*, p. 16; and *Statistical Abstract, 1981*, p. 12.

Statistical Areas (MSAS)[2] represented some 50.4 percent of the total state population for 1980. Officially, Oklahoma now contains four MSAS with part of a fifth represented by several eastern Oklahoma counties that are associated with Fort Smith, Arkansas, but the two largest metropolitan areas completely overshadow the others. Overall, about 59 percent of Oklahomans live in metropolitan areas. We should note also that since 1980, Oklahoma's population growth has slowed considerably. According to the Census Bureau, between 1980 and 1988 the total increase was only 8 percent (to about 3.26 million).

Urbanization and Political Consequences

Does this bimodal population distribution between the two dominant metropolitan areas and the rest of the state have any political consequences? First, as chapter 9 showed, the trend toward more Republican voting in Oklahoma has been accentuated by the electoral behavior of the state's two largest areas. Tulsa County has traditionally been a Republican stronghold, but until the 1980s Oklahoma County was more of a swing county. Through the late 1960s, the Oklahoma County vote for president, for example, was rather evenly divided between candidates of the two parties. But of more significance is the contrasting voting patterns between the two metropolitan areas and the outlying parts of the state.

As we noted before, the southeastern part of the state, Little Dixie, is the most Democratic of any geographic area. The northwestern area, on the other hand, consistently votes Republican. As a result, the nonmetropolitan vote in Oklahoma tends to lean Democratic in most elections, at least for nonpresidential contests. The biggest rural-urban voting split for a major of-

Table 17: Oklahoma Gubernatorial Elections, 1970–86:
Oklahoma and Tulsa Counties versus Balance of State

Election	State % Republican	Oklahoma & Tulsa Counties % Republican	Balance of State % Republican	Urban Counties, Balance of State % Difference
1970	48.1	57.9	43.3	14.6
1974	36.1	45.5	31.4	14.1
1978	47.2	53.9	43.9	10.0
1982	37.6	47.5	32.6	14.9
1986	47.5	54.5	44.0	10.5
Mean	43.3	51.9	39.0	12.8

Source: Oklahoma State Election Board, *Election Results and Statistics* (Oklahoma City: State Election Board, 1970, 1974, 1978, 1982, 1986).

fice occurs in gubernatorial elections, for reasons not altogether clear. The smallest division appears for presidential elections. These findings suggest that when the contest involves strictly state issues or personalities, the outlying areas tend to adhere to their historic Democratic party allegiance. Table 17 shows the rural-urban difference in recent votes for governor. Democrats controlled the chief executive's office from 1970 until 1986, yet in three of the five elections the two large counties went Republican. The two deviant elections were 1974, when current senator David Boren ran quite well all across the state, and 1982, when incumbent governor George Nigh carried every county in the state in his reelection bid. Still, the average difference in Republican vote between the two largest counties and the remainder of the state was 12.8 percent for all five elections, not a small difference.

Why are the two large counties more likely to vote Republican than other places in the state? No definitive answer can be provided, but several possible explanations come to mind.[3] First, many large cities around the country tend to vote Democratic because such places are the natural home of the traditional Democratic constituency—organized labor, minority groups, Roman Catholics, and the poor. This situation is more likely to prevail for large, old, central cities in the Northeast and Midwest than elsewhere. Newer urban areas such as those found in the South, Southwest, and West are not as likely to contain large proportions of the traditional Democratic voting block (the exception is the growing Hispanic vote in the Southwest and West). Many of these newer cities have within their legal boundaries large concentrations of white, middle-class Protestants. In older metropolitan areas such groups are more likely to be found in the suburbs. Oklahoma City especially fits this pattern. Moreover, such cities depend less on a manufacturing base, which ordinarily means fewer labor unions, less political power for such groups, and consequently fewer Democratic voters. Again, this is the case for Oklahoma City. In fact, capital city politics are noticeably influenced by the chamber of commerce and a staunchly conservative daily press. Likewise, in Tulsa a strongly Republican press, coupled with the presence of powerful oil interests, contributes to a heavily pro-Republican political milieu. Compared to many old, northern cities, the two largest cities in Oklahoma also contain relatively small black populations.

Becoming a City

In Oklahoma it is easy to become a city; no minimum population is required for legal incorporation. In early July 1987, for example, it was announced that a new municipality was to be created, called "Fireworks City," with a population of two: a husband and wife who own a fireworks business. The legislature, of course, has something to say about what cities are and what they can do. First, the law states that any incorporated place of one thousand or more people is legally a "city." Unless further action is taken locally, it is organized under one of the statutory forms of city government. If the community contains fewer than a thousand people (except by population loss), it is officially a "town." The legislatively prescribed form of government for towns is a three-member board of aldermen. If the community's population is over two thousand, it can become a home-rule city. Among other things, this status permits the city to adopt its own charter and to choose its own form of government.[4]

City-State Relations

In general, courts have taken a strict view of the subordinate legal status of city governments. The best-known statement of the relationship between the state and its municipalities is known as Dillon's Rule, after Judge John Dillon, who first articulated it in 1868 when he was chief justice of the Iowa Supreme Court. Basically, the rule declares that cities possess only three kinds of governmental power. First, they can exercise those powers that are expressly granted by the state; second, those that are necessarily implied from the expressed powers; and third, those that are vital for carrying out local governmental responsibilities. As expected, the application of these broad principles may lead to conflict and litigation. So despite home rule, states continue to keep close rein on their municipalities. If an act of city government, even in a home rule city, lies within a field that has been dealt with by state law, courts may invalidate the municipal action.[5] States have retained particularly close control over municipal finance. Cities must seek statutory approval for any new taxes. The Oklahoma legislature, for example, did not grant cities the right to levy a municipal sales tax until 1965. Such a tax, of course, must be approved by local voters. Although cities can levy an income tax (none do), they are not allowed to impose a "commuter" or earnings tax—a levy on persons working but not living in the city.

Conflict between state and municipal law can erupt over almost any issue. Disputes often entail attempts by cities to enact regulations in an area covered by state law. Consider liquor laws. Most states provide rather detailed statutory regulations concerning the conditions under which alcoholic beverages may be sold, including limits on hours or even days of operation. Sunday sales might be restricted, for instance. As the following example shows, cities on occasion may seek to impose more stringent requirements, but the courts usually do not permit them; the sale of liquor is an area of public concern preempted by the more inclusive powers of the state.[6]

Soon after the voters of the state approved liquor-by-the-drink (in September 1984), the city council of Oklahoma City passed a local ordinance requiring small neighborhood restaurants serving beer and wine to close at midnight. State law, however, allows all establishments serving liquor to remain open from 10 A.M. to 2 A.M. Dick Stubbs, owner of Applewoods and Muffins restaurants, objected to the city's actions. He said the city was trying to override state laws. An assistant city attorney, James Hamill, seemed to agree and so advised the city council. "The state has said they've got exclusive jurisdiction over the hours of operation," Hamill said. But council members wanted neighborhood restaurants to close at midnight or earlier. Such a change would presumably cut down on noise and boisterous behavior complaints from nearby residents.

State law clearly permits a city through its zoning laws the right to say where a liquor establishment can be located. The city may also specify items such as required parking and lighting. Hours of operation apparently are another matter. Restaurant owner Stubbs remarked, "If the city does enact this, I am sure it is going to be challenged in court."

As it turned out, no suit has been filed challenging the city's action. In fact, Hamill said that he thought the ordinance was working well. Larger restaurants located in traditional commercial zones were not affected by this change in hours. And neighborhood restaurants now seem to find it unprofitable to stay open past midnight.

States do more, of course, than restrict certain municipal practices; they also provide considerable financial support. Across the country, city governments of twenty-five thousand or more population receive about 20 percent of their general revenue from state governments. This figure is substantially more than that obtained through federal grants (around 8 percent). Yet the amount of state financial aid for cities varies enormously from state to state. Schools and welfare receive the most aid by far. In many states, such as Oklahoma, these areas are not responsibilities of city government. Consequently, Sooner State cities receive only about 3 percent of general revenue from state government. On the other hand, almost 12 percent of city revenues in Oklahoma comes from federal aid.[7]

Forms of City Government

Under Oklahoma law, cities can choose from three different forms of government. Home-rule cities may also select one of these three forms. But when the charter is prepared and adopted, home-rule cities may modify some of the specific structural features to suit local preferences. The statutory forms are (1) aldermanic, (2) council-manager, and (3) strong mayor-council.[8]

Aldermanic government, sometimes called the weak-mayor form, requires the people to elect not only a mayor and council but also a city clerk, treasurer, street commissioner, and marshal. Members of the council are elected by ward, or geographic district, for four-year terms. The mayor, also elected for four years, is the chief executive at least in name. The mayor's appointive and removal powers are limited, however, and he or she is not authorized to prepare the municipal budget. These restrictions, along with the presence of other popularly elected administrative officials, seriously reduce the mayor's formal authority, thus the name *weak-mayor form*. Few cities of any size in Oklahoma retain this essentially outdated form of government.

State law also permits a city to adopt a strong-mayor form of government. As the name implies, the popularly elected mayor has much more power than under the aldermanic arrangement. The mayor appoints and removes all department heads without council concurrence. No other administrative officials are elected by the people. The mayor also prepares the municipal budget, subject to council approval. The city council members must reside in the wards they represent, but they are elected to four-year terms by all voters in

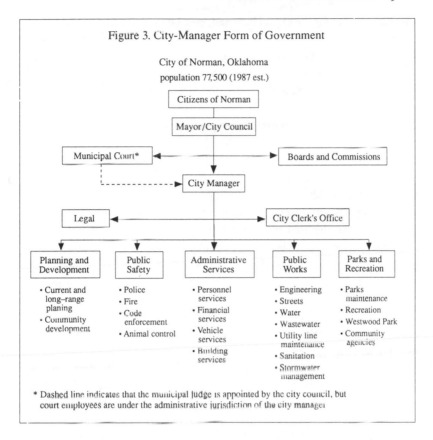

Figure 3. City-Manager Form of Government

City of Norman, Oklahoma
population 77,500 (1987 est.)

Citizens of Norman

Mayor/City Council

Municipal Court*   Boards and Commissions

City Manager

Legal   City Clerk's Office

Planning and Development	Public Safety	Administrative Services	Public Works	Parks and Recreation
• Current and long–range planing • Community development	• Police • Fire • Code enforcement • Animal control	• Personnel services • Financial services • Vehicle services • Building services	• Engineering • Streets • Water • Wastewater • Utility line maintenance • Sanitation • Stormwater management	• Parks maintenance • Recreation • Westwood Park • Community agencies

* Dashed line indicates that the municipal judge is appointed by the city council, but court employees are under the administrative jurisdiction of the city manager

the city. Most authorities consider the strong-mayor form especially suitable for large heterogeneous communities. In such cities the mayor may be required to exercise considerable political leadership. Only a few cities in Oklahoma employ this form, including Claremore, Idabel, and Warr Acres.

As the third option, state law permits council-manager government. This form calls for the election of a small city council, with primary responsibility for setting municipal policy. That group then hires a full-time administrator to carry out the day-to-day functions of city government. Council-manager cities all have mayors who carry out essentially ceremonial duties. Under the statutory plan, council members must be residents of the wards they represent but are elected at large. The city council appoints the city manager, who may be removed at any time by a majority vote of the council. The manager appoints and removes all department heads except the city treasurer and prepares the annual budget for council consideration. Figure 3 shows the council-manager plan for the city of Norman. Even though Norman operates as a home-rule city with its own charter, the arrangement here is quite similar to that required under the statutory form.

Reformers love council-manager governments. The city council bears final responsibility for the overall direction of city government. But the manager presumably brings professional expertise not only to administrative matters but to the policy recommendations furnished to the council. Because of its similarity to the corporate model, with its board of directors and chief executive officer, city-manager government appears quite businesslike. This arrangement appeals especially to medium-sized, homogeneous, white-collar communities. Although the nation's biggest cities do not use it much, most communities of over twenty-five thousand population around the country operate with the council-manager form. In Oklahoma more than two-thirds of the state's 129 cities of over twenty-five hundred population use the manager plan; nationally, the figure is about 36 percent.[9] Among state cities of ten thousand and over, only Altus, Claremore, Miami, and Tulsa have nonmanager governments.

Council-manager government has proven popular in the Sooner State for several reasons. First, the home-rule provision of the state's constitution makes changing the form of government relatively painless. Such an arrangement fits neatly with the populist view of making government more responsive to the people. So when Oklahomans become dissatisfied with municipal affairs, they can do more than throw the rascals out; they can vote out the entire form of government. Over the years, a large number of even quite small communities have done just that. On what grounds? An early analysis of city-manager government in Oklahoma reveals that in every city studied, a principal reason for the change was the feeling that the older forms of government did not provide satisfactory administrative leadership and close daily supervision of municipal affairs.[10] In addition, many city governments in the 1920s and 1930s were considered to be inefficient, wasteful, and extravagant. For example, a 1927 newspaper editorial in the *Bartlesville Morning Examiner* named two reasons for the switch to the manager plan in that city: "Taxes are too high [and] too much money is being wasted and too little results are being obtained." In many such cases the charge was brought against the "system" rather than individual officeholders. Local chambers of commerce often spearheaded such changes, a further indication of the importance of economy and efficiency arguments. In sum, changing the form of municipal government was not overly difficult, and in a relatively poor state, saving money and instituting businesslike government held special appeal.

Some observers criticize council-manager government because it does not provide for strong policy leadership. Originators of the plan thought that such leadership would be exercised by the council with perhaps the mayor as first among equals. In practice, councils and even mayors often cannot or do not provide that leadership. So the city manager must fill the void. This situation creates controversy. Occasionally, managers even find themselves accused of being dictators. Just how far should they go in providing policy guidance to the city council? No easy answers here. Recent research in Oklahoma reveals that about 42 percent of a sample of managers say they play an active role in policy leadership.[11]

Regardless of their form, most city governments constantly worry about money—where it is coming from and what to spend it on. The next section provides a brief overview of municipal revenue and expenditure practices in Oklahoma.

Municipal Finance

Historically, cities in Oklahoma have been underfunded compared to urban places elsewhere. A peculiarity in the state constitution prohibits municipalities from directly levying a property tax for current operations (property taxes, however, may be used to retire city debt). Today most cities rely heavily on the municipal sales tax. Virtually every city of any size in the state has voted at least a one-cent sales tax, more than two thirds have two or more cents, and a majority of cities are now at the three-cent level.[12]

Cities in Oklahoma obtain about 15 percent of their general revenue from intergovernmental sources (almost 80% from the national government).[13] Taxes provide the bulk of the remaining funds—about 47 percent (mostly the sales tax); charges and fees for services bring in 26 percent. These amounts diverge considerably from national norms, primarily because of the differences in the use of property taxes. For all U.S. cities, intergovernmental sources provide a full 35 percent of general revenue (only 35% of these external funds emanate from the federal government). Taxes make up 41 percent of the national total; 53 percent of this figure comes from property taxes. Charges and fees contribute about 14 percent of municipal revenue for all U.S. cities. As noted, a distinctive feature of the municipal revenue system in Oklahoma is that cities do not have access to the property tax for current operations.

Where does the money go? Perhaps unexpectedly, hospitals top the list at 14.5 percent of general expenditures. A large number of cities in the state have no municipal hospital; those that do find it an expensive activity indeed. Consider Norman's municipal hospital. Even though the Norman Regional Hospital (its official name) has a separate board and a separate budget, the Census Bureau lists its cost as part of the city's overall expenditures. The census figures for Norman show that the hospital consumes more than 43 percent of the city's spending. Consequently, the very large municipal hospital spending by such places as Norman and Midwest City causes that category to rise to the top among all cities in the state. The next highest areas of spending among cities in Oklahoma include police (12.5%), streets and highways (11.1%), fire (8.9%), and parks and recreation (6.3%).[14]

COUNTY GOVERNMENT

Legally, counties are administrative subdivisions established for the convenience of the state. Half the states (including Oklahoma) provide no home rule, so counties must abide strictly by state law. Although many states have modernized or reorganized their county governments, counties in Oklahoma still operate under a political system designed for a bygone era. This anachronistic arrangement contributed to an unprecedented scandal in the 1970s and 1980s involving kickbacks, mail fraud, and tax evasion. At the end of a five-year federal investigation in 1984, more than two hundred former and incumbent county commissioners and materials suppliers had been sentenced to jail. Only seventeen of the state's seventy-seven counties escaped unscathed. But the rest of that story comes later. First, we need to cover a few basic facts about county government.

Oklahoma counties are organized under a plural executive form imported from England about three hundred fifty years ago. County voters elect nine administrative officials. Three county commissioners, chosen by district, collectively provide what overall administration exists for the county. Counties also elect a county clerk, treasurer, assessor, sheriff, court clerk, and in most counties a superintendent of schools (eliminated by the legislature in 1990). The elected district attorney replaced the old county attorney in 1967. In addition, several boards and commissions—the board of health, excise board, welfare board—further fragment and complicate county government.

County Government Organization

Partly because most counties across the nation continue to operate under some version of the plural commissioner system, "county government organization is undoubtedly the most criticized feature of county government."[15] Critics contend that the plural executive arrangement (1) makes it difficult for voters to hold any one person or office responsible for the administrative efficiency of county government, (2) provides no means of coordination or control over the direction of county government, and (3) contributes to voter confusion and apathy because of the difficulty in comprehending how county government works or who is ultimately responsible for what the county does. So some states now permit counties to adopt more modern forms of government.

Two basic alternatives to the traditional commissioner form can be found in certain other states—the appointed administrator and the elected executive. The administrator form for counties parallels council-manager government for cities. A county administrator, with considerable authority for operating the day-to-day affairs of county government, is appointed by a county council composed of perhaps five or seven members elected either from districts or from throughout the county. The elected executive, on the other hand, looks much like the strong-mayor form of city government. The elected executive serves as the top administrator, while the board of commissioners enacts county ordinances (if a home-rule county), confirms department head appointments made by the executive, levies taxes, and adopts the budget. Three southern states—Arkansas, Kentucky, and Tennessee—now require their counties to use the elected executive form of government.[16]

Rural areas often resist efforts to permit optional forms of county government. They apparently fear that it might become the first step toward county consolidation, in which the seventy-seven counties of the state might be reduced to only twenty or thirty. Occasionally, such proposals appear in the metropolitan press, sending shock waves through rural Oklahoma. As we point out later, school consolidation has been legislatively imposed in the past on many small rural communities. Many small-town residents can be expected to oppose any similar loss of their county government resulting from a forced merger with some neighboring county. Their anxiety about the possibility that county government might become less immediately accessible to local folks stems largely from the counties' vital role in supporting the farm-to-market road system throughout the state. As the following discussion shows, building and maintaining roads represents the major activity of county government in Oklahoma.

County Finance

In Oklahoma, revenue to support county government accrues principally from three sources: intergovernmental aid, the local property tax, and charges or fees for services. According to the most recent census data, al-

most 40 percent of county general revenue in Oklahoma comes from intergovernmental sources. About 85 percent of that total was provided by
state government.[17] Property taxes provide around 30 percent of the counties' general revenue, and charges for services produce about 20 percent.
The remainder derives from a variety of miscellaneous revenue and other
taxes.

Counties in Oklahoma spend more for roads, highways, and bridges than
anything else—32 percent.[18] Nothing else comes close. Hospitals appear
next at 17 percent. Public safety ranks third with only 5 percent, mostly for
county sheriffs' departments.

The Scandal and Its Aftermath

No one knows how many years the illegal practices among county officials
had gone on before they were unearthed officially. Rumors and sporadic investigations of graft and kickbacks in county government in Oklahoma had
cropped up repeatedly over decades. Nonetheless, no person or agency was
either willing or able to pursue the problem assiduously enough to uncover
the long-term, pervasive nature of these practices. Space permits only an
overview of this sordid tale, called by some the most widespread example of
political corruption in U.S. history.

The probe of wrongdoing by county commissioners and suppliers sur-
faced officially in the spring of 1981, when federal district attorney William
Price announced indictments against ten commissioners.[19] The investigation
can be traced to efforts by Charles Muse, of the state auditor and inspector's
office, who uncovered alleged wrongdoing in Stephens County in 1978.
When no indictments were returned by a local grand jury, Muse turned to the
Federal Bureau of Investigation and the U.S. attorney's office. The subsequent federal investigation turned up essentially three forms of illegal behavior:

1. A standard 10 percent kickback from suppliers to commissioners on untold
thousands of county purchases of culvert pipe, bridge timbers, grader
blades, and other supplies and materials;

2. Flat-fee kickbacks to commissioners on lease-purchase agreements for
heavy road-building and maintenance equipment; and

3. So-called blue-sky deals or 50–50 splits with suppliers for nonexistent,
undelivered supplies and materials.

U.S. Attorney Price decided that the key to ferreting out these corrupt practices was in persuading a certain Dorothy Griffin, who operated a phony invoice mill, to cooperate with his investigation. Through a complicated procedure, this woman for years had been writing bogus invoices for transactions all over the state. One version of the scheme worked like this. Certain materials would be delivered to the county. Commissioners would ask another employee to sign the delivery invoice for the goods received; afterward nonexistent material would be tacked on the already-signed invoice. The county, of course, would write a check for the whole amount. At times, totally nonexistent purchases ("blue-sky" deals) were invoiced as well.

Griffin came under suspicion initially by the Internal Revenue Service for failure to pay taxes on unreported income. When confronted with certain evidence, she caved in and confessed all to the IRS and the FBI. Most crucially, she agreed to cooperate with Price's continuing investigation. In short, they equipped her with a hidden microphone and directed her to tape some illegal transactions involving both suppliers and commissioners. Later, another guilty supplier agreed to help. Also wired, he recorded incriminating evidence on current and past county commissioners on the pretext of warning them about Griffin.

After all the evidence was gathered, more than thirty federal agents descended on commissioners and suppliers. "Once we hit them, they began to tumble like dominoes," one agent said, "as officials and suppliers admitted their guilt and started naming names of others involved."[20] By 1984, more than 200 people had been convicted, most sent to the federal reformatory at El Reno. Of the 165 convicted commissioners, 110 were in office when indicted. Sentences averaged one to two years for those who cooperated through plea bargaining; those who went to trial received seven to twenty years. No one knows, of course, how much this monumental scandal cost the taxpayers. Equipment prices dropped by as much as 42 percent following the scandal, and U.S. Attorney Price estimated that the investigation and convictions ultimately saved some $200 million annually in equipment and material costs.

How could such widespread corruption stretching over years, if not decades, have happened? There is no simple answer, of course. One of the main reasons, according to Frank S. Meyers's comprehensive analysis, was the enormous autonomy given the commissioners. These officials, other legal responsibilities notwithstanding, are essentially road and bridge builders, each operating independently within their geographic districts. "Each commissioner operated his own 'barn'; he hired and fired his own road crews; he bought (or lease-purchased) the construction equipment for his district; and he maintained this fleet."[21] Moreover, the commissioners exercised virtually total control over county road funds. Other factors entered in as well, including the substantial political power wielded by the commissioners, the surprising lack of interest in county affairs by much of the local media and district attorneys (who were then financially dependent on county commissioners), and the Oklahoma attorney general's lack of authority to intervene in local investigations unless so requested. It is amazing still that these practices continued for so long. Remember, though, as we noted in the first chapter, individualistic political cultures tolerate a fair amount of corruption as part of the "business" of politics.

If ever a time was ripe for major reform in a political system, this was it in Oklahoma. Nonetheless, despite studies by a joint legislative committee and a blue-ribbon task force appointed by the governor, the changes were relatively minor, most aimed at tightening up purchasing procedures.[22] A centralized purchasing system was established; a bidding system was mandated for purchases of items over $750 and for lease-purchase agreements; the use of state contracts for many items was permitted; and a comprehensive receiving and inventory system was created. Another important change took place—state funding of district attorneys, which makes them financially independent of county commissioners. Despite these reforms, the basic system of county government, with its lack of centralized authority, remains unaltered.

As political scientist and close observer Phillip Simpson writes, "the informal feature of county government that seems to have contributed the most to the organized theft from counties was the almost total breakdown of the requirement that commissioners act as a board in administering the affairs of the entire county."[23] Nothing was done about the arrangement that created the little fiefdoms for each of the three commissioners. To eliminate unilateral decision making by the commissioners, the citizen task force had recommended that those officials be nominated from districts but elected from the county at large. Even that modest step was too much for the legislature. The conservative penchant for avoiding drastic action prevailed. True structural reforms such as county home rule never reached a vote on the floor of either house.

Despite its closeness to the people and the essential functions it performs, county government in Oklahoma remains notably obsolete. Unfortunately, most state and local leaders seem unaware that county modernization is not an idealistic dream. It stands as an accomplished fact, even for some southern states that, like Oklahoma, are often slow to respond to change. Or if political leaders do know of these developments in other places, they still avoid rocking the boat for fear of incurring the political wrath of the courthouse gangs, the bastions of Old Guard politics in the state.

A Further Comment on County Government Reform

Perhaps we should not oversell the promise of county government reform, especially in a traditionalistic/individualistic state like Oklahoma. Reforms can be expensive, they frequently have unexpected consequences, and they may not mesh well with prevailing cultural norms and political practices. Everyone wants honest government, so any steps taken to tighten up procurement and accounting practices, for example, are usually well received. Even here, though, the introduction of procedural changes may bring certain unforeseen results. At the least, they inevitably produce more paperwork and inject rigidities into the system in an attempt to reduce discretionary behavior. Even the modest reforms that followed Oklahoma's massive scandal produced complaints by some county officials. They grumbled about complex new rules, increased paperwork, and a loss of flexibility in purchasing.

Just as the reformer's favorite city-government model, the council-manager plan, works best in certain places—notably in medium-sized, middle-class, homogeneous communities—reform models of county government should find a more congenial home in certain settings. Most residents in rural counties might have little interest in county-administrator or county-executive forms of government even if they were available to them. Especially in the heavily traditionalistic southeastern region of Oklahoma, the more bureaucratic and perhaps impersonal nature of reform governments[24] may not fit the slower-paced, more placid, and provincial lifestyle of the small communities in this area. Here, long-time friendships and helping one's neighbor might be considered preferable to governmental efficiency or perhaps even traditionally defined honesty. Such an outlook could be seen among some residents of outlying counties when the commissioner scandal broke. In fact, the degree of popular support for some indicted or convicted commissioners in certain rural counties surprised and even shocked the metropolitan press. For example, following his indictment, a commissioner in Garvin County decided to seek reelection anyway. One of his supporters who helped plan a fundraiser for his defense said, "A person doesn't really need a friend until he's in trouble. He's a hometown cowboy and we just want to stand beside him."[25]

In short, "good government reforms" may not be compatible with certain political cultures. Reform institutions must fit the context. If they do not or cannot adapt to local conditions and the prevailing political culture, they may prove ineffective or even produce certain unintended results.

SCHOOL DISTRICTS

Next to national defense, social security, and Medicare this country spends more public money on education than any other function of government. Most of these funds come from state and local governments; the federal government provides only about 7 percent of the financial support for elementary and secondary education nationwide. In Oklahoma the state furnishes around 65 percent of the money for public schools, local government (school districts) supplies 30 percent, and the national government contributes slightly less than 6 percent.[26] Even though state government provides most of the funding, the local school districts control and operate local public education. Oklahoma has both independent and dependent school districts, with the principal difference being that dependent districts lack high schools.

A recent count of school districts in the state puts the figure at 635 (6th largest in the nation). Although it may sound like quite a large number, it is substantially less than the count of some years ago. In 1962 Oklahoma had 1,225 districts; in 1952 the number was an astonishing 2,100.[27] This enormous drop resulted from school consolidation, the forced merger of usually rural schools because of declines in average daily attendance. Although it was mandated by state law, many rural residents, who prize the presence of a separate school system in their community, strongly oppose school consolidation. Yet some reformers want even more mergers to help ensure Oklahoma's children access to a high-quality education. These advocates of change often point to other states with populations somewhat comparable to Oklahoma's. For example, Louisiana has only 66 school districts; Colorado, 176; and Kansas, 304; even Missouri, with a much larger population than Oklahoma, has only 545 districts.[28] The education reform legislation passed by the legislature during the 1989–90 special session will encourage considerable school consolidation. The combination of financial incentives to consolidating districts, higher academic standards, and stronger state sanctions for districts failing to meet the standards is expected to reduce the number of districts by at least 150, according to the legislation's architects.

Virtually all local school funding in Oklahoma comes from the property tax. Yet with all the problems of dependence on the property tax to support local schools, many people prefer to keep school operations and funding close to the local community. Other groups, such as the U.S. Advisory Commission on Intergovernmental Relations, take the opposite approach. In the mid-1970s the ACIR recommended that state government assume the predominant share of the costs of elementary and secondary education, thereby fostering equality of educational opportunity and releasing the property tax for other uses.[29] The commission insists that local policy control should be maintained; critics argue that local authority cannot really be preserved if the state controls the purse strings.

Almost every state has grappled with attempts to modify the way local schools are funded. With such heavy reliance on the property tax for local support, problems of financial equity plague school districts everywhere. Some districts contain enormous property wealth—perhaps large manufacturing firms, a public utility, or a regional shopping center—while others are dirt poor. Even before the U.S. Supreme Court, in a 5–4 decision in the 1970s,[30] ruled that public education was not a constitutional right and thus tossed the problem of funding equity back to the states, state and school officials were wrestling with how to overcome these "natural" variations in wealth among school districts. The range in per pupil funding is quite large. In the 1989–90 school year, the Frontier School District had $10,629 per pupil while Langston schools had only $2,342. The state average was $3,068.[31] A special report in Oklahoma highlights the problem: the wealthiest district in the state has more than 30,000 percent more in assessed value per student as the poorest district.[32] A sizable gap in valuation per pupil appears among counties as well, from a low of $6,086 for eastern Oklahoma's Sequoyah County (Sallisaw) to $56,763 for Grant County (Medford) to the north (1986–87 figures).[33] The usual response is some form of state aid, initially provided perhaps on a per pupil basis but increasingly designed to level up the poorer districts. Court challenges to these enormous disparities in school-district wealth have come to naught in Oklahoma. In 1987 the Oklahoma Supreme Court finally dismissed a four-year-old suit challenging the inequities of the state's system of public school finance.

State legislatures, of course, can address this imbalance in funding for local schools in a variety of ways. In Oklahoma recent efforts to change the state-aid formula to provide more money for needy districts have been complicated by a "hold harmless" arrangement. This provision in the law has kept certain districts (including Tulsa) experiencing sharp declines in student enrollment from losing money even though the new formula gives them less state aid. A compromise move passed during the 1987 legislature cut hold harmless by a third. This half-a-loaf will not begin to do the job, though, according to a 1986 comprehensive study undertaken by a Special Joint Committee on School Finance of the Oklahoma legislature.[34] The committee called for more school consolidation and a substantial increase in both state and local support; the price tag for an "optimum program" is a shocking $2 billion more per year. The report recommends about $504 million more from the district level and $1.6 billion in additional state aid. These figures are considerably more than the approximately $200 million per year that the 1990 education reform act will raise.

To ensure fairness among local districts and to avoid state subsidies to low-tax effort counties, the report urges that all counties assess real property at an average of 12 percent of market value. Such a figure seems absurdly low until one realizes that in 1985–86 half of all counties in Oklahoma had assessment ratios of 10.2 percent or less. If all counties levied at the recommended 12 percent rate, the joint committee report estimates, local schools could raise about $102 million in additional revenue. Such a change was not to be, however. Despite the joint committee's recommendation, no fundamental changes except to the hold harmless formula were accomplished in subsequent legislative sessions until the 1989–90 special session. The nearly 25 percent increase in state appropriations to public schools, an increase in weights for disadvantaged pupils, and the addition of isolation factors to the school aid formula by the legislature will help equalize state funding. Lawmakers, furthermore, asked voter approval to equalize a variety of now-local funds through the state aid formula, but that package of reforms was defeated by heavy opposition from central Oklahoma and some northwestern Oklahoma counties on July 16, 1990. Enormous disparities in dollars per pupil persist among districts across the state. A group of educators called the Fair School Finance Council has filed suit asking the courts to declare Oklahoma's school finance system unconstitutional for its inequities, as the courts did with the Kentucky, Montana, Texas, and New Jersey systems in 1989 and 1990.

SPECIAL DISTRICTS

One other unit of local government warrants mention: the special district. Oklahoma has 498 of these governmental bodies, most of which perform only one function, such as water supply, soil conservation, or even fire protection.[35] Other than their limited purpose, two conditions ensure the relative anonymity of special districts: most lack taxing authority, and many are located in rural areas (with the exception of housing authorities). The largest number in Oklahoma, some 224, were created to supply water to rural or fringe developments, where city water is unavailable. The users pay a monthly charge for the service, which is used by the water district to operate the system. Only two other special districts are widespread in Oklahoma—for housing and soil conservation. The 119 housing and community development districts largely represent independently constituted public housing authorities, governed by boards appointed by mayors. These authorities receive federal funds to construct public housing facilities, own and maintain these units, and administer such housing projects along with rent-subsidy programs. The 91 soil-conservation districts provide information, education, and technical services for land users primarily in rural areas on such matters as floodplain management and watershed preservation. Even though only 15 of all these districts possess taxing power, for 1982 they had revenue in excess of $567 million, primarily from charges for utilities and other services.

Although special districts are the most rapidly growing form of local government in the U.S., they are often criticized. Reformers in particular complain that, because of their relative obscurity, these entities are difficult to keep up with and therefore to hold accountable. Nonetheless, the fact that special districts continue to proliferate suggests they meet a need that other local governments are not addressing. In one sense these districts epitomize the pragmatism that characterizes local governments in this country; if existing local public agencies do not or cannot respond, then create another unit that will. There may be a price to pay, however. In rural areas, for example, water districts facilitate urban sprawl, and as noted above, most of these organizations are virtually free from genuine popular control.

CONCLUSION

Local governments may be closest to home, but that does not mean they are easy to understand; they can be quite varied and complex. Most of us are probably more familiar with city government than any of the others. Oklahoma has a surprisingly large number of municipalities governed under the council-manager plan, more for a state its size than perhaps any other in the country. In that sense Oklahoma appears progressive. It is another story when we turn to county government. The state continues to operate under the archaic county commissioner form with its multiple elected officials and lack of concentrated authority. In large part because this system allows commissioners to function almost as little kings or queens in their districts, the state suffered one of the worst political scandals in the nation's history. Even that shameful episode could not generate legislative support to permit counties to adopt more modern forms of government. When fundamental county government change was at stake, the forces of rural traditionalism stood firmly in opposition.

Fiscal conservatism also influences the level of financial support for all local governments in Oklahoma. The state has one of the lowest property tax rates in the nation, and it shows. Cities have survived by relying very heavily on the sales tax. Schools consume the lion's share of the local property tax, but because the assessment rates are so low, the state now provides almost two-thirds of the money for local public education. The existence of so many school districts adds to the overall local financial burden. But rural areas remain politically powerful, and school consolidation is bitterly resisted in most outlying areas.

In all, municipal governments in Oklahoma seem to be doing pretty well. With home rule available to all cities of more than two thousand people, the local citizenry can adopt a charter that suits its purposes. Cities also possess considerable financial independence. The sales tax requires a vote of the people, of course, but if the city can show the need and make its case to the public, a sales tax increase is easy. Local school districts are not as well off as city governments. Schools depend heavily on state aid, the formulas for which are complicated and subject to never-ending legislative infighting. Moreover, schools must secure voter approval for certain local taxes, and the assessment of property, which remains a major component of the local funding equation, remains with the elected county assessor.

PART IV

Studying Oklahoma Government and Politics

CHAPTER THIRTEEN

Continuing Traditions and Emerging Patterns

Throughout this book we have emphasized political culture as a way of understanding Oklahoma's government, history, and economy. The definition of the traditionalistic political culture developed by Daniel Elazar suggests that Oklahoma, along with Texas, Kentucky, West Virginia, and Florida, mixes this type of political culture with a strong individualistic tendency. John Kincaid recently summarized what Elazar understood by the traditionalistic political culture: it

> displays an ambivalent attitude toward the "marketplace" and an elitist, paternalistic view of the "commonwealth." It is rooted in preindustrial attitudes emphasizing an ordered hierarchy of social dominance laced with interpersonal, often familial and "old boy" social and political ties. Political power tends to be confined to small, relatively closed circles of established elites who may or may not be elected officials. As a result, widespread popular participation is not only not expected, but often discouraged through various direct and indirect devices. Like the individualistic political culture, those active in politics are expected to benefit personally from their activity though not necessarily through direct pecuniary gain.[1]

Oklahoma's traditionalistic political culture is the product of early settlement from southern migration, particularly in the state's southern and eastern portions. This political system has maintained itself with strong support from the Old Guard politicians from rural counties. In recent decades, however, the system has been challenged from several directions. Certainly, the recent migration from other areas of the country has brought an infusion of persons interested in seeing changes in Oklahoma. More important, the reexamination of traditional Oklahoma values has been spurred by the hard economic times following the end of the oil and gas boom in the early 1980s. Sooner political leaders have studied the state repeatedly and found numerous areas in need of reform. Although impressive changes have been made in economic development policies, other basic areas of the state's political system remain unchanged.

Political structure remains one of the biggest problems. The strongholds of the Old Guard remain largely intact thirty years after Governor J. Howard Edmondson's attack on the "county rings" and the malapportioned state legislature. County government is still fragmented in Oklahoma's seventy-seven counties by 231 fiercely independent county commissioners who rule over their individual "fiefdoms." Educational reform in 1990 was made more difficult by the state's comparatively large number of school districts. In state government nearly every governor since statehood has signed acts to streamline the executive branch, but it still remains "balkanized" with more than two hundred state agencies, many governed by appointed boards or commissions or statewide elected officials who share power with one of the nation's most structurally weak governors. Moreover, Governor Henry Bellmon's attempt to reorganize state government by constitutional amendment did not even make it to the ballot. The legislature refused to confirm his cabinet secretaries until the last days of his fourth legislative session, and some lawmakers would like to scrap the entire cabinet system.

Strong commitment to the common well-being, ordinarily absent from traditionalistic political cultures, is frequently lacking in Oklahoma. An unwillingness by competing groups to compromise too often blocks important changes. Factional conflict creates barriers to progress, as groups dig in their heels in opposition to change. The history of Oklahoma politics has often reflected such fundamental divisions as rural versus urban, one region of the state against all others, the public sector against the private, labor versus management, the University of Oklahoma against Oklahoma State University (unless both are united against all the other institutions of higher education), or the mental health lobby against the welfare system.

Although public and media pressure for reform has for the most part focused on the public sector, the private sector has been a major contributor to the state's problems during the 1980s. To a large extent, the strong resurgence of the petroleum industry in the 1970s and early 1980s threw Oklahoma off its course toward economic diversification and modernization. The story of the Oklahoma energy boom and bust is captured well in two readable studies, Phillip L. Zweig's *Belly Up: The Collapse of the Penn Square Bank* and Mark Singer's *Funny Money*.[2] Both books focus on the collapse of the Penn Square Bank, an Oklahoma City bank that played an extremely important role in financing the oil boom of the early 1980s. In response to the rash of bank failures following Penn Square's demise—thirty-one alone in 1987—the legislature finally changed the law to permit branch banking and to allow out-of-state banks to purchase Oklahoma banks that had gone "belly up."

The oil and gas boom in Oklahoma during the late 1970s and early 1980s was profoundly affected by Robert A. Hefner III and Oklahoma City's Penn Square National Bank.[3] More than any other individual, Hefner encouraged the development of the natural gas field in western Oklahoma. Hefner, the product of a prominent state family with deep roots in the political and economic history of Oklahoma, capitalized on his family influence and his own considerable personal skills to convince the world of the enormous potential of the Anadarko Basin. In fact, without Hefner, it is difficult to imagine that the incredible natural gas boom in western Oklahoma could have occurred. He played a key role in persuading Congress to revise natural gas pricing laws, which enabled him and others to drill for the deep gas of the Anadarko Basin.

Hefner has been described as "geologist-as-artist-as-hero" by author Mark Singer. By all accounts, the young Hefner was handsome, well-polished, and a convincing advocate for the potential of the Anadarko Basin. Despite limited financial resources of his own, Hefner's untiring efforts to sell others on the value of the basin attracted abundant capital. Moreover, he made his listeners believe that the basin's future development would make the state the energy center of the twenty-first century and that Oklahoma City would become one of the major cities of the western world.

Hefner found others to share and, more important, to invest in his dream. Penn Square National Bank, a comparatively small but ambitious bank, became the financial solution for him and many other Oklahoma "oilies." However, Penn Square's limited lending capacity made it necessary to seek other banking partners. The quest was made relatively easy because of the optimistic projections of future energy prices and because out-of-state banks were looking for a role in the southwestern energy boom as a way to increase profits. The partnership forged among Sooner "oilies," Penn Square, and its numerous correspondent banks fueled the incredible economic activity in the state oil patch. The end came quickly as energy price projections failed to become reality and bank regulators finally detected that the quality of the energy loans left Penn Square and the other banks badly exposed. On July 5,

1982, the closing of Penn Square by federal regulators signaled the end of Hefner's dreams for the state. At the time, the failure was the fourth largest in American history, but its accumulated impact was unquestionably the largest. Including upstream banks, the total unsecured loans totaled more than $1.4 billion. Moreover, the collapse of Penn Square caused the failure or near failure of numerous other banks in the region and throughout the nation, including Seattle First and Continental Illinois, which almost precipitated a near collapse of the entire U.S. banking system.

In Oklahoma, Penn Square was the first of a large number of failed banks, and the constriction of capital forced hundreds of state businesses into bankruptcy. The state's national reputation suffered as stories circulated of excessive financial mismanagement. Penn Square ended, at least temporarily, the "era of good feelings" that had dominated Oklahoma since the end of World War II.

Apparently, Hefner's vision of a powerful state built on the extraction of natural gas from thousands of feet below the surface will not be possible. Though some prefer to wait for a rebound in energy prices, most Oklahomans see the future of the state tied to economic diversification and improvements in the educational systems. Such achievements, however, are not simple or cheap, as the 1990 tax increase proved. Further improvements in common education will cost Sooners hundreds of millions of additional tax dollars. One of the most likely sources for these additional revenues is the much-maligned Oklahoma property tax system that for decades has escaped reform under the protection of Old Guard politics.

The fight over property tax reform involves some of the strongest interest groups in Oklahoma. Farm groups, for example, strongly opposed the reform measures that had been scheduled for the March 1989 ballot. And the issues at stake are vital for much-needed education improvements, as well as to provide additional revenues for local government. Prospects for property tax reform, apparently threatened when the legislature removed the measures from the special election ballot, brightened at the end of the 1989 session. Reformers won passage of a $4 million appropriation to begin computerization of the property tax system. The legislature appropriated an additional $10 million during the 1989–90 special session for implementation of the new system. When the plan is implemented, its architects believe that Oklahoma's administration of the property tax will be much improved and will meet national standards.

The property tax issue, and the problems incurred by those seeking to modernize that inefficient and frequently corrupt system, is similar to other major problems facing the Sooner State, such as county government reform and reorganization of the state's executive agencies. The failure to modernize the operations of state and local programs has hurt the state's image and ruined the careers of far too many public officials. Scandals in county government, higher education, and tag agencies have been altogether too common. To put this in numerical terms, Oklahoma's record of 246 public officials convicted by federal prosecutors from 1977 to 1987 ranks among the worst in the nation. Over the same period, Texas, with its much larger population, had only 272 convictions and New Mexico only 47.[4]

Too much emphasis can be placed on public spending. Of equal importance to the future of Oklahoma is whether the quality of life in the state improves or deteriorates. Quality of life (QOL) plays a big part both in retaining a state's population and in attracting new business and people from other states. Without improvements in Oklahoma's quality of life, the state can expect an increased "brain drain" of talented citizens to other states where greater opportunities and a better quality of life can be enjoyed. And it is those persons who value a high QOL who are most likely to be leaders and supporters of increased modernization for Oklahoma. Quality of life includes such matters as cultural and recreational opportunities, quality of education, crime rates, housing, and health care. Authoritative rankings of quality of life for states are not available, but Rand McNally's *Places Rated Almanac* is probably the source most often used for QOL comparison. Using nine variables, Rand McNally ranked 329 metropolitan areas nationwide, with Oklahoma City ranked forty-sixth and Tulsa one hundredth.[5] When the study was published in 1985, it ranked both cities very high on economics (Oklahoma City, 5th; Tulsa, 31st). It is reasonable to believe that the overall downturn in the state economy would adversely affect such a ranking. So quality of life, one could reasonably conclude, has suffered in recent years. Arguably, the QOL varies considerably from county to county, particularly between the state's poorest rural counties and the wealthier urban ones. In 1986 several of the poorest counties had annual per capita personal income levels of less than $8,000, considerably lower than the more than $14,000 in Oklahoma and Tulsa counties.[6]

We began this chapter with a discussion of the traditionalistic political culture. It is possible, although assuredly difficult, for a state or community to alter its political culture. Throughout this book, we have identified areas of Oklahoma life where change has occurred or where there are indications that change may occur. Nevertheless, the Sooner political culture of the future remains uncertain and difficult to predict. Certainly, the influence of forces beyond the control of Oklahomans will have a considerable impact. So will the decisions made by Oklahomans, according to the Hudson Institute's report to the Oklahoma Academy for State Goals.

OKLAHOMA IN THE CENTENNIAL OF ITS STATEHOOD

One of the most absorbing parts of the Hudson Institute's 1988 study on the future of Oklahoma is the chapter offering possible scenarios of the state in 2007, its centennial.[7] These scenarios, to a large extent, incorporate the report's major themes. The Hudson Institute emphasizes the state's dependence on two economic sectors: (1) oil and gas and (2) agriculture (particularly beef and wheat). According to the institute, both of these economic sectors, and thereby the state, are extremely vulnerable to developments beyond the control of Oklahoma's borders. For example, Oklahoma agriculture would be damaged severely either by conclusive medical evidence linking beef to heart disease or by the elimination of agriculture subsidies by the federal government (both of which eventualities the institute sees as very possible). Politically, the analysts stress the need for great change in state and local government institutions that, according to the institute, suffer from apathy and political fractiousness.

Accordingly, the report develops a series of future scenarios for Oklahoma based on two major variables: luck and management. Following are two of the Hudson Institute's scenarios for the Sooner State in the year 2007.

Good Luck, Bad Management

On November 16, 2007, Mary Franklin, a thirty-seven-year old Oklahoma City history teacher in a public school, finishes grading papers and looks outside as she prepares to go home. She notes that traffic is already heavy as some businesses have allowed workers to leave early in commemoration of Oklahoma's centenary. She thinks, as a history teacher, that the day should have been a holiday to celebrate.

Mary, somewhat depressed, reflects on Oklahoma's first one hundred years and particularly the last thirty. The state's economy was in pretty fair shape. Oil prices had increased steadily to the point that many failed to see the need for the kind of reforms pushed by some in the 1980s. All the talk of educational excellence had failed to bring about fundamental change. Sure, standards were raised slightly, as were budgets. But public education remained primarily a local matter. "The result was that the common schools of the state were scattered across an ever broader spectrum of quality. Some were excellent; many were mediocre; not a few were pathetic."

Reforms in other areas of Oklahoma government also fell short, frequently victims to political squabbling. The long-term state interests were lost among fights by all the many special interests. The good news in the energy and agricultural sectors permitted modest, steady growth in the state. State politicians took advantage of the situation to reduce taxes three times between 1994 and 2002. Some pessimists, however, warned that the state's economy still had problems. It remained too dependent on energy and agriculture. Other states, with stronger leadership, had developed their own special niches in the global economy. Now Oklahomans were forced to face up to the legacy of dependence on declining energy resources, and the rapid commercialization of alternative energy sources threatened the state's energy producers.

Mary Franklin concluded: "She was re-living the mid-1980s as she knew them from history textbooks. . . . Most of the problems that faced policymakers in the late 1980s were still there. They had simply been swept under the rug in the 1990s and during the first few years of the new century. Unfortunately, ignoring them hadn't made them go away; there they were, in 2007, more deeply entrenched and more threatening than ever."

Good Luck, Good Management

It is Friday, November 16, 2007, and state senator Jerry Walker joins thousands of other jubilant Sooners at the Capitol for a day-long celebration of the state's one hundred years of statehood. All the speakers testify "that history had fulfilled the dreams of all those men [and women] who helped usher Oklahoma into statehood just a century earlier." They also recount how Oklahoma had overcome the "prophecies of doomsayers" and had far exceeded the dreams of the most optimistic Oklahomans of the 1980s.

Senator Walker personifies Oklahoma's good fortunes. Born on a farm in rural Coal County, he and his brothers and sisters benefited from major improvements in Oklahoma's education systems. Unlike previous generations of Coal County children, the children of Walker's and later generations attended excellent local schools, thanks to the educational reforms passed by the state legislature in the late 1980s. The Walker children all went on to state colleges and received professional degrees. Consequently, they all found excellent jobs in their chosen fields in the Oklahoma City or Tulsa areas.

Educational reform was only one of the major changes made in the state's governmental structures over the previous quarter of a century. Others included executive branch reorganization that gave the governor real power over state agencies, promulgation of a new and improved state constitution, development of a strong public finance system that provided Oklahoma's education programs adequate revenues, and a strong Ethics Commission that made "integrity in government . . . an Oklahoma trademark." These remarkable reforms were made possible by a determined, bipartisan reform effort that started in the late 1980s, bringing the state to its "political maturity."

Good management decisions by state leaders contributed to the healthy state economy at the turn of the century. The strong commitment to higher education, particularly at the University of Oklahoma and Oklahoma State University, now regarded as among the nation's most outstanding institutions of higher education, has played a major role in the diversification of the state economy. However, fortune had also favored the Sooner economy. Slow and steady increased demand for and gradually higher prices for producers of oil and natural gas provided stability to those industries that, along with the entire Oklahoma economy, had suffered from decades of boom and bust. Like the energy sector, Oklahoma's agricultural economy also prospered. Early theories linking beef consumption to heart disease proved false. In fact, the beef industry in Oklahoma, recognized worldwide for its "Oklahoma Lean" trademark, had done remarkably well on both the domestic and international markets. Oklahoma remained a major wheat producer, despite the elimination of federal subsidies. Easier access to international markets, trade adjustment assistance, and other farm programs provided the basis for agricultural prosperity.

Indeed, Jerry Walker and his fellow Sooners believed themselves fortunate to be citizens of Oklahoma. The first century had been good; the second, they believed, would be even better.

A FINAL WORD

Pragmatic politics, the drive toward modernization, and economic development may be the key phrases associated with Oklahoma politics during the last quarter of the twentieth century. Perhaps at no other point in Oklahoma history has the nature of the challenges facing the state been so important. The rapidity of change in today's world does not accommodate prolonged debate over the measures that must be taken if Oklahoma is to compete with other states in a global economy. No doubt, the necessary changes will be costly and difficult for many, but not beyond the grasp of Oklahomans. Yet historian Danney Goble warns Sooners of the need to set aside their deep-seated tradition of negativism,[8] illustrated in recent years by rural opposition to property tax reform. One of the legacies of the frontier in Oklahoma is the fear of outside forces that might threaten the status quo and upset the established order. Overcoming the state's tradition of negative politics remains a principal barrier to progress.

Those who question the state's ability to rise to the occasion should review its history. Debo's 1949 *Oklahoma: Footloose and Fancy-Free* chronicles the industriousness of Oklahomans in meeting the challenges of the oil patch by educating a scientific and engineering community necessary to exploit the underground mineral wealth and by deciding to assume a leading role in the pioneering aviation industry. We conclude with a most appropriate sentence from Angie Debo: "Who said anything about quitting?"[9]

CHAPTER FOURTEEN

Studying Oklahoma Politics: A Guide to Resources

Studying Oklahoma government and politics can be both fun and rewarding. On the other hand, as we learned in preparing this book, it can also be frustrating, time-consuming, and just downright hard work. This chapter is intended to aid you in your pursuit of knowledge about the people, politics, and policies of Oklahoma by providing a guide to resources. The guide is not exhaustive; it is, however, reasonably comprehensive. Resources available to the serious student of Oklahoma politics are ample in terms of both quantity and quality. Here we offer a discussion of general resources, a guide to the use of state documents, and a topical bibliography. Finally, do not forget to seek out state and local officials not only for their firsthand knowledge of public affairs, but as a virtually unlimited source of official documents, reports, and data.

GENERAL RESOURCES

Libraries

The best place to begin your study of the state is at the library. The availability of journals, books, special collections, and government documents varies, of course, depending on the library you visit. Nevertheless, be it your local public library or one of the two dozen or so state-supported university libraries, you can start to develop an information base about Oklahoma.

The two comprehensive university libraries located in Norman (University of Oklahoma) and Stillwater (Oklahoma State University) offer the largest holdings. At both facilities computerized searches on topics of interest can be run (for a fee), master theses and doctoral dissertations are available (or dissertations can be purchased in photocopy or microfiche from University Microfilms in Ann Arbor, Michigan), and the interlibrary loan system allows access to journal articles and books not found in the library. Both libraries also have extensive government documents sections. At osu the government documents stacks are open; at ou the aid of a documents librarian is required. The University of Oklahoma is the site of the major law library in the state, although the University of Tulsa, Oklahoma City University, and the capitol branch of the Oklahoma Department of Libraries also have law libraries.

Newspapers

Another excellent source of information about Oklahoma politics is newspapers. Subscription or access to your local city daily and/or one of the three major dailies—*Daily Oklahoman, Tulsa Tribune,* and *Tulsa World*—provides an up-to-date record of major events and legislation. Be forewarned, however, that the major state dailies are not free of bias, especially the *Daily Oklahoman* and *Tulsa Tribune*. The *Daily Oklahoman* (and its afternoon edition, no longer published, the *Oklahoma City Times*) has been indexed, which makes newspaper research much easier. Subject files for many years of the *Daily Oklahoman* are on microfilm in the Oklahoma room of the Oklahoma Department of Libraries. The strong conservative strand in Oklahoma politics is quite evident in, and some would argue was shaped by, these two newspapers. As an antidote to this conservative bias, we recommend Frosty Troy's the *Oklahoma Observer*. The *Observer,* a journal of editorial opinion, is published twice monthly, except in July and December, and is reminiscent of the muckraking journalism at the turn of the century. The motto of the paper provides a clue to its contents: "To Comfort the Afflicted and Afflict the Comfortable." The daily Oklahoma City *Business Journal and Record* is an excellent review of matters of interest to the state's business community. In addition, black newspapers in Oklahoma City (*Ebony Tribune* and *Black Chronicle*) and Tulsa (*Oklahoma Eagle*) provide insight into minority concerns. The Oklahoma Historical Society maintains the best collection of Oklahoma newspapers on microfilm.

Journals and Magazines

Oklahoma-focused journals and magazines may aid in your search for information. Though not an exhaustive list, the following might be useful: *Oklahoma Cities & Towns, Oklahoma City University Law Review, Oklahoma*

Gazette, Oklahoma Journal of Public Health, Oklahoma Law Review, Oklahoma Legislative Reporter, Oklahoma Magazine, Oklahoma Quarterly, Oklahoma Review, Oklahoma School Board Journal, Oklahoma Today, Chronicles of Oklahoma, Historia (Oklahoma Historical Society), and *Tulsa Law Journal.*

Data Sources

Demographic, social, economic, and political data for the state and its cities can be found in a number of publications. Two primary sources are the *Book of the States* (various years) and the *Municipal Year Book* (various years). Comparative state and city information is also found in numerous U.S. Bureau of the Census documents (e.g., *Statistical Abstract of the United States* [various years], *County and City Data Book* [various years], *State and Metropolitan Data Book* [various years], *Census of Governments* [various years], *State Government Finances in [year]*, *City Government Finances in [year]*, *County Government Finances in [year]*, *Finances of Public School Systems in [year]*, *Federal Expenditures by State for Fiscal Year [various]*, *Labor-Management Relations in State and Local Governments: [year]*, etc.). Literally hundreds of data tapes are available through the U.S. Bureau of the Census (usually for a fee). Many of the statistics are published in government documents and can be found in the reference/documents sections of public and university libraries. The U.S. Department of Commerce, Bureau of the Census, publishes an annual *Census Catalog and Guide* that provides a complete list of holdings in the archive.

The Oklahoma State Data Center, Department of Commerce, 6601 Broadway Extension, Oklahoma City, OK, 73116–8214, (405)/843–9770, is the official state depository for census information and serves as a source of assistance to users of Census Bureau data. The Oklahoma Department of Libraries, as part of its function as a U.S. government documents repository, also has extensive census records. The State Data Center is a valuable source for economic data as well and has some affiliates throughout the state. The center publishes "Demographic State of the State," with very interesting information on population trends. These appear irregularly; so far, only three have been published.

Quite a few reports on Oklahoma's economic development have appeared in the past few years. Several of these were mentioned in chapter 11, for example. The most recent is Oklahoma Futures (the principal economic development policy planning board for the state of Oklahoma), *Oklahoma's Strategic Economic Development Plan: 1988–1993* (Oklahoma City: Oklahoma Department of Commerce, October 1988).

Another excellent source for state comparative data is State Policy Research, Inc., *State Policy Data Book* (years; beginning in 1987) (Alexandria, Va.: State Policy Research, Inc., 1987). We found its state ranking format quite helpful in writing this book. State Policy Research also publishes a bi-weekly *State Policy Report*.

Research Bureaus/Groups/Centers

Established in the late 1930s, the Bureau of Government Research, University of Oklahoma, has published a large number of monographs on state and local government and politics. Two regular monograph series have been established: the Legislative Research Series (currently about twelve monographs) and the Criminal Justice Policy and Administration Series (currently about fourteen monographs). In addition, the bureau has published about three dozen monographs of general interest to state and local scholars and policy makers. A publications list can be secured from Bureau of Government Research, University of Oklahoma, Norman, OK, 73019, (405) 325–6621. It is unfortunate that the University of Oklahoma has seen fit to terminate the bureau.

Created in 1983, the Policy Studies Group at Oklahoma State University publishes monographs focusing on policy issues relevant to the state. Currently, the holdings include about a dozen manuscripts. A publication list can be secured from Policy Sciences Group, 403 Life Sciences East, Oklahoma State University, Stillwater, OK, 74078, (405) 744–5173.

Several private-sector research ventures have been created to provide input to the policy-making process. The most important are the Oklahoma Academy for State Goals, which includes a statewide representation of political, private, and education leaders who meet annually and publish proceedings from that conference; and Oklahoma 2000, closely affiliated with the Oklahoma Chamber of Commerce, which publishes the annual *State Policy and Economic Development in Oklahoma*, directed to influence the legislature and governor.

The Center for Economic and Management Research at the University of Oklahoma publishes the *Statistical Abstract of Oklahoma* every even-numbered year. It is a compilation of statistics on the state and its local subdivisions, including sections on population, geography, finance, taxes, education, income, manufactures, energy, labor, and more. The Oklahoma Advisory Committee on Intergovernmental Relations has published *Selected Cultural and Economic Data of Oklahoma Counties* (Oklahoma City, 1990), which draws together demographic, economic, financial, and fiscal data for each of the state's counties.

Public Opinion Surveys

No regular surveys on Oklahoma are published at this time. From 1980 through 1987 the *Oklahoma Poll,* later the *Bailey Poll,* was issued periodically by Kenneth D. Bailey Research Associates in Tulsa. These polls were based on telephone surveys of about six hundred randomly chosen Oklahoma residents eighteen years of age or older. Many of the questions were about political candidates and issues, with occasional attention paid to economic issues as well. The poll results were available by subscription.

State Election Data

The State Election Board is the administrative agency responsible for the conduct of state elections and the coordination of balloting in the state's seventy-seven counties. It prints state ballots and has been the repository of election data since statehood. Until 1981 the Election Board published the *Directory of Oklahoma* and included historical data on statewide elections. The Election Board now publishes a biennial *Election Results and Statistics,* which provides county returns on all statewide elections (including state legislative races). It also publishes the *Roster of Oklahoma State and County Officers,* which lists all officers' political affiliations. The Election Board, until the creation of the Council on Campaign Compliance and Ethical Standards in 1986, was the repository of statewide campaign finance information. The council (now the State Ethics Commission) currently maintains that data.

For county and municipal election information, the researcher is forced to go to the election boards for the seventy-seven counties. There are four useful studies on Oklahoma elections (all published by the University of Oklahoma's Bureau of Government Research), although they are now out of date. See Oliver Benson et al., *Oklahoma Votes, 1907–1962* (1964); *Oklahoma Votes for Congress, 1907–1964* (1965); *Oklahoma Voting Patterns: Presidential, Senatorial, and Gubernatorial Elections* (1970); and *Oklahoma Voting Patterns: Congressional Elections* (1970). Finally, in 1988 the Oklahoma State Election Board released a comprehensive two-volume study of state elections entitled, *Oklahoma Elections: Statehood to Present.*

STATE GOVERNMENT DOCUMENTS

In addition to the university libraries, state government also has several important libraries for those interested in Oklahoma research. The Oklahoma

State Department of Libraries (ODL) is an important resource, particularly for state government documents. For recent state government reports, the Publications Clearinghouse, which publishes an annual subject index, should be consulted. The ODL also contains an Archives and Records Division with a collection of valuable historical materials about state government. It is limited because of poor records administration before 1969, but the contents of the archives are listed in the three-volume *Guide to Oklahoma State Archives*, published in 1980. The ODL maintains an Oklahoma room in the main building, as well as a law library and legislative reference collection at the capitol branch. The capitol branch contains important legislative materials, including clipping files.

For Oklahoma history, the Oklahoma Historical Society is an important resource. The most complete collection of state newspapers on microfilm is found in the newspaper room. The society also has a valuable library that is especially strong in genealogy; it houses Indian, territorial, and state manuscript collections; and it publishes numerous useful books on the state. The Oklahoma Historical Society's major publication is its *Chronicles of Oklahoma*, which has recently been indexed. For holdings of the society, see Kenny Franks and John Stewart, *A Guide to Research at the Oklahoma Historical Society and the Oklahoma State Archives* (Oklahoma City: Central Printing, 1975).

Oklahoma legislative records, like those of most state legislatures, are not as complete as congressional materials for research. Both houses publish *Journals* for each legislative session which contain valuable information on floor votes. Debates are not, however, included. Legislation passed each session is contained in *Oklahoma Session Laws. Oklahoma Statutes* is published every ten years, with annual supplements. A very useful source regarding legislative matters is the *Legislative Reporter,* a daily reporting of state capitol developments published by Oklahoma Business News. The capitol library has a legislative reference section that houses a useful collection of current and historical materials, including many legislative special reports.

In recent years the activities of the session have been incorporated into annual "highlight" reports published by legislative staff agencies and *Summary Digests*, describing bills passed. The house of representatives also issues a biennial publication, *Legislator's Guide to Oklahoma Taxes.* These reports can be obtained from the capitol branch of the State Department of Libraries.

In 1988 the state of Oklahoma developed a five-year plan. See Oklahoma

Futures, *Oklahoma's Strategic Economic Development Plan 1988–1993 (Oklahoma City: Department of Commerce,* 1988). Annual updates to the plan are also published by the Oklahoma Department of Commerce.

TOPICAL BIBLIOGRAPHY

Associated with the various chapters in this book are scores of citations. We do not repeat all of them here. Rather, in this section we begin with some essential general references and then provide a listing of suggested readings, some new and some found in previous chapters, by topic areas.

The Essentials

The most comprehensive guide to facts about Oklahoma government is Oklahoma Department of Libraries, *Directory of Oklahoma: 1989–1990 State Almanac* (Oklahoma City: Oklahoma Department of Libraries, 1989). This volume of some 750 pages is published biennially.

Often one can learn much about the people and politics of a state through literature. For example, John Steinbeck's *Grapes of Wrath* (New York: Viking Press, 1939) was mentioned numerous times in this volume. For a comprehensive bibliographic essay of Oklahoma-related literature, see Anne Hodges Morgan, "Oklahoma in Literature," chapter 5 in Anne Hodges Morgan and H. Wayne Morgan, eds., *Oklahoma: New Views of the Forty-Sixth State* (Norman: University of Oklahoma Press, 1982). Useful bibliographical resources to Oklahoma materials are Vicki Dale Withers, *A Checklist of Theses and Dissertations Relating to Oklahoma History, Completed at the University of Oklahoma and Oklahoma State University through 1973 (Stillwater: Oklahoma State University,* 1974); and Mary E. Morris, ed., *Bibliography of Theses on Oklahoma* (Norman: University of Oklahoma, Institute of Community Development, 1956).

History and politics are inextricably linked, or at least so it seems. Rennard Strickland provides an excellent bibliographic essay of historical accounts of Oklahoma in "Oklahoma's Story: Recording the History of the Forty-Sixth State," chapter 6 in Anne Hodges Morgan and H. Wayne Morgan, eds., *Oklahoma: New Views of the Forty-Sixth State* (Norman: University of Oklahoma Press, 1982). This essay, as well as the other essays in the volume, simply is required reading.

Perhaps the best book that places the fifty states in an comparative perspective is Virginia Gray, Herbert Jacob, and Robert Albritten, eds., *Politics in the American States: A Comparative Analysis,* 5th ed. (Glenview, Ill.: Scott, Foresman, 1990).

In order to understand the importance of the concept of political culture to the study of state politics, see Daniel J. Elazar, *American Federalism: A View from the States,* 3d ed. (New York: Harper and Row, 1984).

Two entertaining volumes on Oklahoma politics since the 1950s are Martin Hauaun, *He Buys Organs for Churches, Pianos for Bawdy Houses* (Oklahoma City: Midwest Political Publications, 1976), and *How to Win Elections without Hardly Cheating at All* (Oklahoma City: Midwest Political Publications, 1983).

Oklahoma Government: An Overview

Jack Strain, Leroy Crozier, and Carl F. Reherman, eds., *An Outline of Oklahoma Government* (Edmond: Bureau of Governmental Services, Department of Political Science, Central State University, 1989). This slim volume emphasizes the legal and structural features of Oklahoma government. It was written originally in 1955 by H. V. Thornton, at the University of Oklahoma, as a text for Boys State, and has been updated regularly.

James R. Scales and Danney Goble, *Oklahoma Politics: A History* (Norman: University of Oklahoma Press, 1982).

Stephen Jones, *Oklahoma Politics in State and Nation, Volume I: 1907–1962* (Enid, Okla.: Haymaker Press, 1974). The author is working on a second volume.

Anne Hodges Morgan and H. Wayne Morgan, eds., *Oklahoma: New Views of the Forty-Sixth State* (Norman: University of Oklahoma Press, 1982).

H. Wayne Morgan and Anne Hodges Morgan, *Oklahoma: A Bicentennial History* (New York: W. W. Norton, 1977).

Arrel M. Gibson, *Oklahoma: A History of Five Centuries* (Norman: University of Oklahoma Press, 1981).

John W. Morris et al., *Historical Atlas of Oklahoma,* 3d ed. (Norman: University of Oklahoma Press, 1986).

John Thompson, *Closing the Frontier: Radical Response in Oklahoma, 1889–1923* (Norman: University of Oklahoma Press, 1986).

Anne Hodges Morgan, *Robert S. Kerr: The Senate Years* (Norman: University of Oklahoma Press, 1977).

H. V. Thornton with Gene Aldrich, *The Government of Oklahoma* (Oklahoma City: Harlow Publishing Co., 1960).

H. V. Thornton with Corbitt Rushing and John Wood, *Problems in Okla-*

homa State Government (Norman: Bureau of Government Research, University of Oklahoma, 1957).

Last, but not least, those interested in Oklahoma history should read Angie Debo. Perhaps her two most important state histories are *And Still the Water Runs: The Betrayal of the Five Civilized Tribes* (Princeton: Princeton University Press, 1940), and *Oklahoma, Footloose and Fancy-Free* (Norman: University of Oklahoma Press, 1949).

Oklahoma in the Federal System

William J. Pammer, Jr., and David R. Morgan, *Responses of Oklahoma Urban Officials to Reductions of Federal Aid to Cities* (Norman: University of Oklahoma, Bureau of Government Research, 1982).

Anthony Brown and Mark R. Daniels, "Gunfight at the OK Statehouse: A Legislature's Duel with Federal Aid," in Carol W. Lewis and A. Grayson Walker, eds., *Casebook in Public Budgeting and Financial Management* (Englewood Cliffs, N.J.: Prentice-Hall, 1984).

Clara Luper, *Behold the Walls* (Oklahoma City: Jim Wire, 1979).

Jimmie L. Franklin, *Journey toward Hope: A History of Blacks in Oklahoma* (Norman: University of Oklahoma Press, 1982).

David R. Morgan and Robert E. England, "The Small Cities Block Grant Program: An Assessment of Programmatic Change under State Control," *Public Administration Review* 44 (November/December 1984): 477–82.

David R. Morgan and Robert E. England, "Evaluating a Community Development Block Grant Program: Elite and Program Recipient Views," in Terry Busson and Phillip Coulter, eds., *Policy Evaluation for Local Government* (New York: Greenwood Press, 1987).

The State Constitution

Thomas H. Doyle, "Single Statehood versus Double Statehood," *Chronicles of Oklahoma* 5 (1927): 18–41, 117–48, 266–86.

Danney Goble, *Progressive Oklahoma: The Making of a New Kind of State* (Norman: University of Oklahoma Press, 1980).

Albert H. Ellis, *A History of the Constitutional Convention of the State of Oklahoma* (Muskogee, Okla.: Economy Printing Co., 1923).

Proceedings of the Constitutional Convention of the Proposed State of Se-

quoyah (Muskogee, Okla.: Muskogee Printing Co., 1907).

Irvin Hurst, *The Forty Sixth State: A History of Oklahoma's Constitutional Convention and Early Statehood* (Oklahoma City: Semco Color Press, 1957).

Oklahoma Constitutional Studies of the Oklahoma Constitutional Survey and Citizen Advisory Committees, directed by H. V. Thornton for the Oklahoma State Legislative Council (Oklahoma City: 1950).

League of Women Voters of Oklahoma, *Study of the State Constitution*, parts 1 and 2 (Washington, D.C.: League of Women Voters Education Fund, 1966).

The Legislature

Samuel A. Kirkpatrick, *The Legislative Process in Oklahoma* (Norman: University of Oklahoma Press, 1978).

Donald R. Songer, James M. Underwood, Sonja G. Dillon, Patricia E. Jameson, and Darla W. Kite, "Voting Cues in Two State Legislatures: A Further Application of the Kingdon Model," *Social Science Quarterly* 66 (December 1985): 983–90.

Samuel C. Patterson, "Dimensions of Voting Behavior in a One-Party State Legislature," *Public Opinion Quarterly* 26 (Summer 1962): 185–200.

Jean G. McDonald, *Legislators and Patronage in Oklahoma* (Norman: University of Oklahoma, Bureau of Government Research, 1975).

Margaret Reid, *Legislator-Citizen Attitude Congruence in Oklahoma* (Norman: University of Oklahoma, Bureau of Government Research, 1981).

Larry Walker, *State Legislature Control of Federal Aid Funds: The Case of Oklahoma* (Norman: Bureau of Government Research, University of Oklahoma, 1978).

Emil Lee Bernick, *Legislative Decision-Making and the Politics of Tax Reform: The Oklahoma Senate* (Norman: Bureau of Government Research, University of Oklahoma, 1975).

Lelan McLemore, "The Structuring of Legislative Behavior: Norm Patterns in a State Legislature" (Ph.D. dissertation, University of Oklahoma, 1973).

Emil Lee Bernick, *Legislative Voting Patterns and Partisan Cohesion in a One-Party Dominant Legislature* (Norman: Bureau of Government Research, University of Oklahoma, 1973).

F. Ted Hebert, *Oklahoma Legislative Voting: A Roll-Call Analysis for 1970–74 (Norman: Bureau of Government Research, University of Oklahoma, 1978).*

The Governor and Bureaucracy

LeRoy H. Fischer, *Oklahoma's Governors*, 4 vols. (Oklahoma City: Oklahoma Historical Society, 1975–85). Covers the territorial governors and ends with Governor Nigh in 1979.

Keith L. Bryant, Jr., *Alfalfa Bill Murray* (Norman: University of Oklahoma Press, 1968). A good biographical study of the state's most colorful governor.

Elizabeth Gunn, *Representative Bureaucracy in Oklahoma: A Comparison of Citizens' and Administrators' Characteristics and Attitudes* (Norman: University of Oklahoma, Bureau of Government Research, 1982).

Legislative Reference Division, Oklahoma Department of Libraries, *Oklahoma: State Agencies, Boards, Commissions, County Institutions, Legislature and Officers, 1990* (West Publishing Co.). Updated annually.

Jean G. McDonald and David R. Morgan, "Oklahoma: A Historic Gubernatorial Succession," in Thad Beyle, ed., *Re-Electing the Governor: The 1982 Elections* (Lanham, Md.: University Press of America, 1986).

James C. Milligan and L. David Norris, *The Man on the Second Floor: Raymond D. Gary* (Muskogee, Okla.: Western Heritage Books for Oklahoma Heritage Association, 1988).

Oklahoma Reorganization Council, *Comprehensive Plan for Executive Branch Reorganization: State of Oklahoma* (Oklahoma City, 1987).

The Judiciary

Jimmie L. Franklin, *Born Sober: Prohibition in Oklahoma, 1907–1959 (Norman: University of Oklahoma Press, 1971).*

Dave R. McKown, *The Dean: The Life of Julien C. Monnet* (Norman: University of Oklahoma Press, 1973).

George B. Fraser, "Oklahoma's New Judicial System," *Oklahoma Law Review* 21 (November 1968): 373–410.

Keith L. Bryant, "The Juvenile Court Movement: Oklahoma as a Case Study," *Social Science Quarterly* 49 (September 1968): 368–76.

Elections, Political Parties, and Interest Groups

Samuel A. Kirkpatrick, David R. Morgan, and Thomas G. Kielhorn, *The Oklahoma Voter* (Norman: University of Oklahoma Press, 1977).

Robert E. England and David R. Morgan, "Interest Groups in Oklahoma: Lobbyists, Legislators, and Sooner Politics," in Ronald Hrebenar and Clive S. Thomas, eds., *Interest Groups in the Midwestern States* (Salt Lake City: University of Utah Press, forthcoming).

Jean G. McDonald, *State Legislative Competition in a Changing Party System: The Case of Oklahoma* (Norman: University of Oklahoma, Bureau of Government Research, 1982).

Dorothy K. Davidson and Deborah Rugs, *Election '84: The Oklahoma State Party Convention* (Norman: University of Oklahoma, Bureau of Government Research, 1985).

Robert Darcy, Margaret Brewer, and Judy Clay, "Women in the Oklahoma Political System: State Legislative Elections," *Social Science Journal* 21 (January 1984): 67–78.

Samuel C. Patterson, "The Role of the Lobbyist: The Case of Oklahoma," *Journal of Politics* 25 (February 1963): 72–92.

Kenneth J. Meier, *Predicting Oklahoma Elections: An Inexpensive and Accurate Method* (Norman: Bureau of Government Research, University of Oklahoma, 1979). Includes Oklahoma election statistics by county, 1970–78.

David R. Morgan and Kenneth J. Meier, "Politics and Morality: The Effect of Religion on Referenda Voting," *Social Science Quarterly* 61 (June): 144–48.

State Finance

State of Oklahoma, *Executive Budget,* submitted annually to the Oklahoma legislature. Contains governor's budget message and proposed budget.

Oklahoma State Expenditures in Brief (Oklahoma City: Kerr Foundation and Grayce B. Kerr Fund). Published annually.

Robert E. England, John P. Pelissero, and Ted P. Robinson, *Severance Taxes, Tax Bases, and Fiscal Stress in Oklahoma, Texas, and Louisiana* (Norman: University of Oklahoma, Bureau of Government Research, 1986).

David R. Morgan and Joan O'Brien, *Oklahoma State Finance: A Longitudinal and Comparative Overview* (Norman: University of Oklahoma, Bureau of Government Research, 1977).

David R. Morgan and Emily Peterson, *Oklahoma State Debt: A Longitudinal and Comparative Analysis* (Norman: Bureau of Government Research, University of Oklahoma, 1977).

Robert K. Carr, *State Control of Local Finance in Oklahoma* (Norman: University of Oklahoma Press, 1937).

Gerald M. Lage, Ronald Moomau, and Larkin Warner, *A Profile of Oklahoma: Economic Development 1950–1975* (Oklahoma City: Frontiers of Science Foundation, 1977).

Kent W. Olson et al., *Oklahoma State and Local Taxes: Structure, Issues, and Reforms,* report to the Kerr Foundation (Stillwater: Oklahoma State University, Office of Business and Economic Research, 1984).

Oklahoma Revenue, a monthly report on state government revenue collections, Office of State Finance.

Local Government

Michael W. Hirlinger and Robert E. England, *City Managers and the Legislative Process: The Case of Oklahoma* (Norman: University of Oklahoma, Bureau of Government Research, 1986).

Robert E. England, John P. Pelissero, and Ted P. Robinson, *Severance Taxes, Tax Bases, and Fiscal Stress in Oklahoma, Texas, and Louisiana* (Norman: University of Oklahoma, Bureau of Government Research, 1986).

David R. Morgan, Michael E. Meyer, and Robert E. England, "Alternatives to Municipal Service Delivery," *Southern Review of Public Administration* 5 (Summer 1981): 184–89.

Robbie Jamieson, *The Oklahoma County Commissioner Scandal: Reaction and Reform* (Norman: University of Oklahoma, Bureau of Government Research, 1986).

David R. Morgan and William J. Pammer, Jr., "Responding to Urban Fiscal Stress: The Case of Arkansas and Oklahoma," in Terry Clark, ed., *Research in Urban Policy,* vol. 2, part B (New York: J A I Press, 1986), pp. 75–88.

Frank S. Myers, "Political Science and Political Corruption: The Case of the County Commissioner Scandal in Oklahoma" (Ph.D. dissertation, University of Oklahoma, 1985).

Gerald A. Starr, "Organizational Functions and Conflict in a Regional Council of Governments: An Application of Parsonian Theory" (Ph.D. dissertation, University of Oklahoma, 1975).

Sheila S. Watson, "Decentralization, the C D B G Program, and Local Spending Priorities: A Study of Oklahoma's Small Communities" (Ph.D. dissertation, University of Oklahoma, 1988).

Charles B. Williams, "The Politics of Local Taxation: A Study of Community Leadership in Revenue Matters" (Ph.D. dissertation, University of Oklahoma, 1974).

Notes

FOREWORD

1 See James R. Scales and Danney Goble, *Oklahoma Politics: A History* (Norman: University of Oklahoma Press, 1982), p.349, and Goble, "Oklahoma Politics and the Sooner Electorate," in Anne Hodges Morgan and H. Wayne Morgan, eds., *Oklahoma: New Views of the Forty-Sixth State* (Norman: University of Oklahoma Press, 1982), p.174. Will Rogers, whose cowpunching "Oklahomely" wit was read daily by thirty million readers of his syndicated column, perfectly described this cynicism when he once explained that Oklahoma would never change from its abstinence from alcohol voted at statehood. "Oklahomans," he said, "will vote dry as long as they can stagger to the polls."

2 Oscar Ameringer, *If You Don't Weaken: The Autobiography of Oscar Ameringer* (Norman: University of Oklahoma Press, 1983), p.232

CHAPTER ONE

1 *Daily Oklahoman*, September 2, 1988.

2 Ibid., September 17 and 18, 1988.

3 H. Wayne Morgan and Anne Hodges Morgan, *Oklahoma: A Bicentennial History* (New York: W. W. Norton, 1977), p.xiv.

4 William Sweet, "The Plains States: World's Breadbasket," in Hoyt Gimlin, ed., *American Regionalism: Our Economic, Cultural, and Political Makeup* (Washington, D.C.: Congressional Quarterly Press, 1980), pp.155–71.

5 Kirkpatrick Sale, *Power Shift* (New York: Random House, 1975).

6 For example, see Robert F. Hill and Howard F. Stein, "Oklahoma's Image" (Paper presented at High Plains Society for Applied Anthropology, Denver, Colorado, March 28, 1987); "'Grapes of Wrath' Is Still Tainting Oklahoma's Image," *Stillwater NewsPress,* October 8, 1987; Gary Percefull, "Dressing Up State's Image Taking Time," *Tulsa World,* February 16, 1987; Jerry Fink, "Oklahoma Must Polish 2 Images to Get Business," *Tulsa World,* February 16, 1987; "Study Finds Others Think We're Boring," *Daily Oklahoman,* November 1, 1988.

7 Daniel J. Elazar, *American Federalism: A View from the States,* 3d ed. (New York: Harper and Row, 1984). See also John Kincaid, ed., *Political Culture, Public Policy and the American States* (Philadelphia: ISHI Press, 1982).

8 Walter A. Rosenbaum, *Political Culture* (New York: Praeger, 1975), p.4.

9 Elazar, *American Federalism,* p.119.

10 Ibid., pp.115–17.

11 Morgan and Morgan, *Oklahoma,* p.18.

12 Arrell Morgan Gibson, *Oklahoma: A History of Five Centuries,* 2d ed. (Norman: University of Oklahoma Press, 1985), p.4.

13 Information about Oklahoma as a transition zone draws from ibid., pp.4–8.

14 Ibid.

15 Morgan and Morgan, *Oklahoma,* p.135.

16 This percentage is for the year 1980. U.S. Bureau of the Census, *Statistical Abstract of the United States 1985* (Washington, D.C.: Government Printing Office, 1984), p.633. All state rankings reported in this chapter and remaining chapters exclude the District of Columbia.

17 Clarence H. Stone, Robert K. Whelan, and William J. Murin, *Urban Policy and Politics in a Bureaucratic Age,* 2d ed. (Englewood Cliffs, N.J.: Prentice-Hall), chap. 6.

18 Quoted in Alan Ehrenhalt, "Even among the Sooners, There Are More Important Things than Football," *Governing,* November 1988, pp.41–45.

19 Ibid., p.141.

20 State Policy Research, Inc., *State Policy Data Book 1989* (Alexandria, Va.: State Policy Research, Inc., 1989), table A-1 for total population as of July 1, 1988; table A-24 for rural population in 1980.

21 *Statistical Abstract 1985,* p.31; population percentages are for the year 1980 and include Eskimo and Aleut.

22 Douglas Johnson, Paul Picard, and Bernard Quinn, *Churches and Church Membership in the United States* (Washington, D.C.: Glenmary Research Center, 1971).

23 State Policy Research, *State Policy Data Book 1989*, table B-34 for 1987 non-agricultural labor force employed in manufacturing and table N-10 for 1982 percentage of union members.

24 Ibid., table G-28 for 1988 high-school graduation; table A-16 for 1987 percentage of persons aged sixty-five or older; and *Statistical Abstract 1985*, p.637, for 1982 value of agricultural products sold.

25 *Statistical Abstract 1989*, p.433, for per capita personal income and State Policy Research, *State Policy Data Book 1989*, table A-22, for 1985 persons living in poverty.

26 David R. Morgan, *Handbook of State Policy Indicators*, 3d ed. (Norman: University of Oklahoma, Bureau of Government Research, 1978), p.24.

27 David R. Morgan and Kenneth J. Meier, "Politics and Morality: The Effect of Religion on Referenda Voting," *Social Science Quarterly* 61 (June 1980): 144–48.

28 Stephen Jones, *Oklahoma Politics in State and Nation* (Enid, Okla.: Haymaker Press, 1974), p.181.

29 Morgan, *Handbook of State Policy Indicators*, 4th ed., p.77.

30 U.S. Bureau of the Census, *Government Finances in 1987–1988* (Washington, D.C.: Government Printing Office, 1990), table 33 for police and highway expenditures; State Policy Research, *State Policy Data Book 1989*, table G-14 for per pupil spending. These expenditure data include funds received from the federal government.

31 State Policy Research, *State Policy Data Book 1989*, table E-21 for state and local average wages; table G-17 for teacher salaries in public schools.

32 Jerome O. Steffen, "Stages of Development in Oklahoma History," in Anne Hodges Morgan and H. Wayne Morgan, eds., *Oklahoma: New Views of the Forty-Sixth State* (Norman: University of Oklahoma Press, 1982), p.29.

33 State Policy Research, *State Policy Data Book 1989*, table A-9.

34 Ibid., table B-34, for manufacturing employment in 1987, and Steffen, "Stages of Development in Oklahoma History," p.30, for 1950 manufacturing employment.

35 Douglas Hale, "The People of Oklahoma: Economics and Social Change," in Morgan and Morgan, eds., *Oklahoma: New Views*, p.77.

36 Oklahoma Department of Commerce, *Economic Report to the Governor 1987* (Oklahoma City, 1987), p.108.

37 Hale, "People of Oklahoma," pp.77–90.

38 This account is drawn from "Catoosans Defeat City Manager Plan," *Tulsa World*, September 1, 1982, and Linda Martin and Rob Kerby, "Old-Timers vs. Newcomers," *Tulsa World*, September 5, 1982.

39 Russell L. Hanson, "The Intergovernmental Setting of State Politics," in Virginia Gray, Herbert Jacob, and Kenneth N. Vines, eds., *Politics in the American States,* 4th ed. (Boston: Little, Brown, 1983), p.33.

CHAPTER TWO

1 Quoted in Marshall E. Dimock, Gladys Ogden Dimock, and Douglas M. Fox, *Public Administration,* 5th ed. (New York: Holt, Rinehart, and Winston, 1983), p.57.

2 The Advisory Commission on Intergovernmental Relations (ACIR) was created by Congress in 1959 to monitor the operation of American federalism and to recommend improvements. The ACIR is a national, permanent, bipartisan body composed of twenty-six members representing the executive and legislative branches of federal, state, and local governments and the public.

3 George J. Gordon, *Public Administration in America,* 3d ed. (New York: St. Martin's Press, 1986), p.136.

4 "Governors to Ink Bridge Pact," *Stillwater NewsPress,* June 4, 1987.

5 "Evaders of Traffic Tickets Can't Escape," *Stillwater NewsPress,* July 12, 1987.

6 "Bumpers Blocks State Funds," *Stillwater NewsPress,* October 18, 1987.

7 "Oklahoma Loses Legal Round," *Stillwater NewsPress,* January 20, 1988.

8 H. Wayne Morgan and Anne Hodges Morgan, *Oklahoma: A Bicentennial History* (New York: W. W. Norton, 1977), p.4.

9 Arrell M. Gibson, *The History of Oklahoma* (Norman: University of Oklahoma Press, 1984), p.31.

10 Ibid., p.34.

11 Ibid., pp.101–5.

12 Ibid., pp.104–6.

13 Ibid., pp.118–19.

14 Arrell Morgan Gibson, *Oklahoma: A History of Five Centuries,* 2d ed. (Norman: University of Oklahoma Press, 1981), pp.205–6.

15 This account of school desegregation efforts in Oklahoma was drawn from Gibson, *Oklahoma,* pp.237–39, 243–45; Michelle Celarier, "A Study of Public Opinion on Desegregation in Oklahoma Higher Education," *Chronicles of Oklahoma* 47 (Autumn 1969): 268–81; and George Lynn Cross, "Guess Who's Coming to School?" *Oklahoma Monthly* 2 (September 1976): 42–51.

16 This paragraph draws from Gibson, *Oklahoma,* pp.220–30.

17 Ibid., p.279.

18 Unless otherwise noted, data concerning recent federal spending in Oklahoma was taken from Oklahoma Department of Commerce in cooperation with Okla-

homa State University and the University of Oklahoma, *Economic Report to the Governor 1987* (Oklahoma City: Oklahoma Department of Commerce, 1987), pp.137–41, 188–89.

19 David R. Morgan, *Handbook of State Policy Indicators*, 4th ed. (Norman: University of Oklahoma, Bureau of Government Research, 1982), p.45, for the years 1970, 1975, and 1980; State Policy Research, Inc., *State Policy Data Book 1987* (Alexandria, Va.: State Policy Research, Inc., 1987), table F-1, for fiscal year 1984–85. The state's share of federal spending as a percentage of state and local revenue, however, improved to twenty-fifth for fiscal year 1986–87. See *State Policy Data Book 1989*, table F-1.

20 Ed Kelly, "Federal Aid to Oklahoma Region Ranks Last in Nation," *Sunday Oklahoman*, July 26, 1987.

21 David C. Nice, "State Participation in Interstate Compacts," *Publius: The Journal of Federalism* 17 (Spring 1987): 69.

22 Susan Welch and Cal Clark, "Interstate Compacts and National Political Integration: An Empirical Assessment of Some Trends," *Western Political Quarterly* 26 (September 1973): 477.

23 For changes in the uses of interstate compacts, see David C. Nice, *Federalism: The Politics of Intergovernmental Relations* (New York: St. Martin's Press, 1987), p.120; the total and state mean numbers of interstate compacts are reported in Nice, "State Participation in Interstate Compacts," p.70.

24 This discussion of the Interstate Oil Compact was drawn from Gibson, *Oklahoma*, pp.223, 227, and Keith L. Bryant, Jr., *Alfalfa Bill Murray* (Norman: University of Oklahoma Press, 1968), pp.198–99.

25 Oklahoma Department of Libraries, *Directory of Oklahoma 1985–86* (Oklahoma City: Oklahoma Department of Libraries, 1986), p.258.

26 Ibid., various pages in Boards and Commissions section of *Directory*.

27 "New Federal Law Usurps State Authority on Indian Gambling," *Stillwater NewsPress*, December 5, 1988.

CHAPTER THREE

1 See Arrel Morgan Gibson, *Oklahoma: A History of Five Centuries*, 2d ed. (Norman: University of Oklahoma Press, 1981), pp.1–27, for material on the prehistory and European exploration of Oklahoma.

2 Ronald N. Satz, *American Indian Policy in the Jacksonian Era* (Lincoln: University of Nebraska Press, 1975), p.2.

3 Gibson, *Oklahoma*, p.53. Historian Reginald Horsman argues that Jackson was confident about his removal policy in part because of his belief that In-

dians were of an inferior race. It was providential for the tribes to yield their land to the superior white race. This position is illustrated in the following selection from his second annual speech in December 1830: "What good man . . . would prefer a country covered with forests and ranged by a few thousand savages to our extensive Republic, studded with cities, towns, and prosperous farms, embellished with all the improvements which art can devise or industry execute, occupied by more than 12,000,000 happy people, and filled with all the blessings of liberty, civilization, and religion?" Horsman, *Race and Manifest Destiny: The Origins of American Racial Anglo-Saxonism* (Cambridge, Mass.: Harvard University Press, 1981), p.202.

4 Angie Debo, *A History of the Indians of the United States* (Norman: University of Oklahoma Press, 1970), p.108.

5 H. Wayne Morgan and Anne Hodges Morgan, *Oklahoma: A History* (Norman: University of Oklahoma Press, 1977), p.26.

6 Gibson, *Oklahoma,* pp.53–70.

7 Ibid., pp.71–75.

8 Jimmie L. Franklin, *Journey toward Hope: A History of Blacks in Oklahoma* (Norman: University of Oklahoma Press, 1980), p.4.

9 John W. Morris et al., *Historical Atlas of Oklahoma,* 3d ed. (Norman: University of Oklahoma Press, 1986), map 24.

10 Debo, *History of the Indians,* p.115.

11 See Gibson, *Oklahoma,* pp.117–29, for a useful discussion of the Civil War in Oklahoma.

12 Ibid., p.130.

13 Stan Hoig, *The Oklahoma Land Rush of 1889* (Oklahoma City: Oklahoma Historical Society, 1984).

14 Debo, *History of the Indians,* p.311.

15 Angie Debo, *And Still the Water Runs: The Betrayal of the Five Civilized Tribes* (Princeton, N.J.: Princeton University Press, 1940).

16 Danney Goble, *Progressive Oklahoma: The Making of a New Kind of State* (Norman: University of Oklahoma Press, 1980), pp.39–40, 166–67, and John Thompson, *Closing of the Frontier: Radical Response in Oklahoma, 1889–1923* (Norman: University of Oklahoma Press, 1986), pp.70–71.

17 Rennard Strickland, *The Indians in Oklahoma* (Norman: University of Oklahoma Press, 1980), p.36.

18 Article VI, Section 35, of the Oklahoma Constitution.

CHAPTER FOUR

1 Danney Goble, "Oklahoma Politics and the Sooner Electorate," chap. 4 in Anne H. Morgan and H. Wayne Morgan, *Oklahoma: New Views of the Forty-Sixth State* (Norman: University of Oklahoma Press, 1982), pp.134–35.

2 Ibid., p.140.

3 Ibid., p.141.

4 Angie Debo, *Prairie City: The Story of an American City,* 2d ed. (New York: Gordian Press, 1969), p.163.

5 John Thompson, *Closing the Frontier: Radical Response in Oklahoma, 1889–1923* (Norman: University of Oklahoma Press, 1986), p.193.

6 Angie Debo, *Oklahoma: Footloose and Fancy-Free* (Norman: University of Oklahoma Press, 1949), p.54.

7 Goble, "Oklahoma Politics and the Sooner Electorate," p.142.

8 James R. Scales and Danney Goble, *Oklahoma Politics: A History* (Norman: University of Oklahoma Press, 1982), pp.97–105.

9 Ibid., p.105.

10 Jimmie L. Franklin, *Journey toward Hope: A History of Blacks in Oklahoma* (Norman: University of Oklahoma Press, 1982), pp.142–48.

11 This account of Walton is adapted from Scales and Goble, *Oklahoma Politics,* pp.112–34.

12 Ibid., p.126.

13 Thompson, *Closing the Frontier,* p.214.

14 Douglas Hale, "The People of Oklahoma: Economics and Social Change," in Morgan and Morgan, *Oklahoma: New Views,* p.57.

15 Sheila Manes, "Pioneers and Survivors: Oklahoma's Landless Farmers," in Morgan and Morgan, *Oklahoma: New Views,* pp.127–28.

16 Franklin, *Journey toward Hope,* p.151.

17 H. Wayne Morgan and Anne Hodges Morgan, *Oklahoma: A History* (New York: W. W. Norton, 1977), pp.162, 161.

18 Manes, "Pioneers and Survivors," p. 127. The Dust Bowl inspired University of Oklahoma geography professor Paul Sears to write one of the classic early works of the environmental movement, *Deserts on the March,* in 1935. See Paul B. Sears, *Deserts on the March* (Norman: University of Oklahoma Press, 1935).

19 William S. Savage, "Rural Images, Rural Values and American Culture: A Comment," in Donald E. Green, ed., *Rural Oklahoma* (Oklahoma City: Oklahoma Historical Society, 1977), p.117. Oklahomans' attitudes about the Dust Bowl period may finally be changing toward acceptance. In 1990, civic leaders in Sallisaw held a Grapes of Wrath festival, and Okemah finally held a celebration for Woodie Guthrie

to recognize his musical contributions, though not necessarily his political views. See also the editorial "Steinbeck Forgiven" in the *Tulsa World,* July 12, 1990.

20 Manes, "Pioneers and Survivors," p.131.

21 Morgan and Morgan, *Oklahoma: A History,* pp.133–34, 137.

22 Ibid., p.135.

23 Scales and Goble, *Oklahoma Politics,* p.298.

24 Goble, "Oklahoma Politics and the Sooner Electorate," p.164.

25 Hale, "People of Oklahoma," pp.77–82.

26 Ibid., p.82.

27 Ibid., pp.82–83.

28 Mark Singer, *Funny Money* (New York: Alfred A. Knopf, 1985), p.27.

29 Donald A. Murry, "The Status of the Oil and Gas Sector," in *State Policy and Economic Development in Oklahoma: 1986* (Oklahoma City: Oklahoma 2000, Inc., 1986), pp.11–12.

30 "America's Oil States," *The Economist,* May 9, 1987, p.31.

31 Neal R. Peirce and Jerry Hagstrom, *The Book of America: Inside the 50 States Today* (New York: Warner Books, 1984), p.604.

CHAPTER FIVE

1 Albert Ellis, *A History of the Constitutional Convention* (Muskogee, Okla.: Economy Printing Co., 1923), p.40.

2 Danney Goble, *Progressive Oklahoma* (Norman: University of Oklahoma Press, 1980), pp.164–65.

3 Ibid., pp.202–3.

4 James H. Robinson, "The Original and Derived Features of the Constitution," *Annals of the American Academy of Political and Social Science* 1 (July 1890; June 1891): 208, 242. A good text for studying the original Oklahoma Constitution (as completed in 1907) is Charles Evans, *Oklahoma Civil Government* (Ardmore, Okla.: Bunn Brothers, 1908).

5 See Robinson, "Original and Derived Features of the Constitution," and A. E. Dick Howard, "State Constitutions: Pillars of the Federal System," *This Constitution* 17 (Winter 1987): 34–38.

6 See Ellis, *History of the Constitution Convention;* Goble, *Progressive Oklahoma;* and Arrell Gibson, *Oklahoma: A History of Five Centuries* (Norman: Harlow Publishing Corp., 1965), p.330.

7 True Emerson, "The Oklahoma Constitutional Convention" (Master's thesis, Oklahoma State University, 1931), p.26.

8 James Dealey, "Our State Constitutions," *Annals of the American Academy of Political and Social Science* 29 (Supplement, March 1907): 13.

9 Dealey, "Our State Constitutions," p.13, and Robert B. Dishman, *Shape of the Document* (New York: National Municipal League, 1968), pp.5–6. For a somewhat different view of the criticism of the length of state constitutions, see John Kincaid, "State Constitutions in the Federal System," *Annals of the American Academy of Political and Social Science* 496 (March 1988): 12–22.

10 Dealey, "Our State Constitutions," pp.14–16.

11 Walter Dodd, *State Government* (New York: Century Co., 1928), pp.94–101.

12 Frank P. Grad et al., eds., *Constitutions of the United States: National and State*, 2d ed., 6 vols. (New York: Legislative Drafting Research Fund of Columbia University, Oceana Publications, 1974).

13 Dodd, *State Government*, pp.24–25.

14 Ellis, *History of the Constitutional Convention*, p.162.

15 Dealey, "Our State Constitutions," p.50.

16 Ibid., pp.54, 45, 45, 49, 48.

17 Ibid., pp.31, 32.

18 Ibid., pp.33–35. See also Charles Adrian, "Trends in State Constitutions," *Harvard Journal on Legislation* 5 (March 1968): 315.

19 Dealey, "Our State Constitutions," p.36.

20 James Scales and Danney Goble, *Oklahoma Politics: A History* (Norman: University of Oklahoma Press, 1982), pp.8–16.

21 Ibid., pp.9–10.

22 Rennard Strickland and James Thomas, "Most Sensibly Conservative and Safely Radical: Oklahoma's Constitutional Regulation of Economic Power, Land Ownership, and Corporate Monopoly," *Tulsa Law Journal* 9 (Fall 1973): 189–90.

23 South Dakota (1898), Utah (1900), Oregon (1906), and Montana (1906).

24 Council of State Governments, *The Book of the States 1986–87* (Lexington, Ky.: Council of State Governments, 1986), p.18.

25 Jimmie L. Franklin, *Born Sober: Prohibition in Oklahoma, 1907–1959* (Norman: University of Oklahoma Press, 1971), pp.3–25.

26 Scales and Goble, *Oklahoma Politics*, p.26.

27 "No Constitution At All," *Daily Oklahoman*, August 25, 1907, pp. 1, 2.

28 "Bryan Speaks to Fully 10,000 Persons Here: Defends Constitution While Hearers Cheer," *Daily Oklahoman*, September 6, 1907, p.1.

29 Goble, *Progressive Oklahoma*, p.225.

30 Roger Thompson, "The Theory of State Constitutions," *Utah Law Review* 14 (September 1966): 551.

31 Scales and Goble, *Oklahoma Politics*, pp.31–32.

32 Peter S. Onuf, "New State Equality: The Ambiguous History of a Constitutional Principle," *Publius: The Journal of Federalism* 18 (Fall 1988): 53–69.

33 Francis Thorpe, "Recent Constitution-Making in the U.S.," *Annals of the American Academy of Political and Social Science* 2 (September 1891): 166.

34 H. V. Thornton, director, *Oklahoma Constitutional Studies* (Guthrie, Okla.: Cooperative Publishing Co., 1950), p.29. See also *Directory of Oklahoma 1987–1988* (Oklahoma City: Department of Libraries, 1988), pp.667–737.

35 "Leaders Discuss Proposals for Constitutional Changes," *Tulsa World,* October 17, 1987, p.1C.

36 Frosty Troy, "Con Con Lousy Idea," *Oklahoma Observer,* November 10, 1987.

CHAPTER SIX

1 Citizens Conference on State Legislatures, *The Sometimes Governments: A Critical Study of the Fifty American Legislatures* (Kansas City, Mo.: Citizens Conference on State Legislatures, 1971), pp.30–33.

2 Council of State Governments, *The Book of the States 1986–87* (Lexington, Ky.: Council of State Governments, 1986), pp.95–97.

3 Samuel Kirkpatrick, *The Legislative Process in Oklahoma: Policy Making, People, and Politics* (Norman: University of Oklahoma Press, 1978), p.42.

4 The major source for the discussion of the 1989 change in Oklahoma house speakers is Elizabeth Hudson, "Sacking the Speaker: A Quick, Clean Political Revolt," *Washington Post,* June 8, 1989. See also the clipping files on Jim Barker at the State Capitol Library. As a postscript, we note that the new Speaker kept his promise not to hold onto his new office and left the legislature to run, unsuccessfully, for governor. Jim Barker and Guy Davis also decided not to run for reelection. On the other hand, the leaders of the revolt apparently will relinquish their influence over the house, as a strong Barker supporter, Okemah Democrat Glen Johnson, who also served as majority leader during the Lewis speakership, assumed the top house post for the 1991–92 legislature. His strongest challenger and one of the major leaders of the revolt, Cal Hobson, recognized Johnson's imminent victory and decided to run for the state senate instead. As for the Tulsa–Oklahoma City coalition, it seemed greatly weakened after the 1990 session by the opposing positions that the two cities took on major reform issues in the session.

5 The source of the information on Senator Stipe and his campaign is Randy Ellis, "Reputation for Patronage Has Kept Stipe in Senate," *Daily Oklahoman,* October 20, 1988.

6 Citizens Conference on State Legislatures, *Sometimes Governments,* pp.39–42.

7 Ibid., p.282.

8   Commission on Reform of Oklahoma State Government, *Report and Recommendations to Governor George Nigh* (Oklahoma City, 1984), p.56.

9   Citizens Conference on State Legislatures, *Sometimes Governments*, p.81.

10 Adapted from Anthony Brown, "Oklahoma's 41st Legislature: A Review and Analysis of the First Session," in Larkin Warner et al., *State Policy and Economic Development in Oklahoma, 1988* (Oklahoma City: Oklahoma 2000, Inc., 1988), pp.59–65.

11 Kirkpatrick, *Legislative Process in Oklahoma*, pp.22–35.

12 Midwest Political Research, *On the Record: A Guide to Oklahoma Legislators and Districts* (Oklahoma City, 1989).

13 Ibid.

14 Oklahoma Department of Commerce, *Demographic State of the State: A Report to the Governor and Legislature on Demographic Trends for the State of Oklahoma* (Oklahoma City: Oklahoma Department of Commerce, 1987), p.v.

15 Kirkpatrick, *Legislative Process in Oklahoma*, pp.235–46.

16 In an unpublished poll conducted by Oklahoma political scientist Thomas Kielhorn, the public's opinion of the Oklahoma legislature was assessed. According to this poll, conducted in August 1987 after a very difficult session, only 1 percent of Sooners ranked the legislature's performance as excellent, 20 percent as good, 41 percent as only fair, 31 percent as poor, and 7 percent as uncertain. Telephone conversation with Thomas Kielhorn, March 22, 1988.

17 John Wahlke, Heinz Eulau, William Buchanan, and LeRoy Ferguson, *The Legislative System* (New York: John Wiley, 1962), p.272.

18 Ibid., p.276.

19 Kirkpatrick, *Legislative Process in Oklahoma*, p. 205.

20 Joe Westphal, unpublished survey of Oklahoma legislators conducted by a political science class at Oklahoma State University (spring 1986).

21 Alan Rosenthal, "The Legislative Institution—Transformation or Decline?" (Paper prepared for State of the States Symposium, Eagleton Institute of Politics, Rutgers University, December 1987).

22 The summary of Senator Riggs's position is drawn from "Rotten, Rank Spoils System," *Oklahoma Observer*, September 10, 1988.

CHAPTER SEVEN

1   Larry Sabato, *Goodbye to Good-Time Charlie* (Lexington, Mass.: D. C. Heath, 1978), p.8.

2   Terry Sanford, *Storm over the States* (New York: McGraw-Hill, 1967), p.184.

3 In some of the discussion to follow, the pronoun *he* is used in referring to the governor. Although this designation is correct historically in Oklahoma and makes for a less cumbersome use of the language, we recognize and support the position that pronouns should be gender-neutral where possible.

4 Thad L. Beyle and Lynn R. Muchmore, "Governors in the American Federal System," in Thad Beyle and Lynn Muchmore, eds., *Being Governor: The View from the Office* (Durham, N.C.: Duke University Press, 1983), p.12.

5 *Governing the American States: A Handbook for New Governors* (Washington, D.C.: National Governors' Association, 1978), p.277.

6 Ibid., p.3.

7 Tinker Air Force Base, with about twenty thousand employees, considers itself the largest "single" employer in the state.

8 Telephone interview with James Thomas, administrator of the State Office of Personnel Management, September 1, 1987.

9 Jack W. Strain, Leroy Crozier, and Carl Reherman, *An Outline of Oklahoma Government* (Edmond, Okla.: Central State University, Bureau of Governmental Services, 1987), p.38.

10 Article VI, Section 11, of the Oklahoma Constitution.

11 Ibid., Section 7.

12 David Osborne, *Laboratories of Democracy: A New Breed of Governor Creates Models for National Growth* (Boston: Harvard Business School Press, 1988), p.4.

13 Lynn R. Muchmore and Thad L. Beyle, "The Governor as Party Leader," in Beyle and Muchmore, eds., *Being Governor*, p.50.

14 Coleman B. Ransone, Jr., *The American Governorship* (Westport, Conn.: Greenwood Press, 1982), p.84.

15 William H. Young, "The Development of the Governorship," *State Government* 32 (Summer 1959): 183.

16 Richard E. Neustadt, *Presidential Power* (New York: Signet, 1960), pp.43–44.

17 Robert A. Dahl, *Who Governs?* (New Haven, Conn.: Yale University Press, 1961), p.204.

18 Quoted in Osborne, *Laboratories of Democracy*, pp.139–40.

19 This number includes the three-member Corporation Commission, which is more regulatory and quasi-judicial than administrative.

20 Joseph A. Schlesinger, "The Politics of the Executive," in Herbert Jacob and Kenneth Vines, eds., *Politics in the American States* (Boston: Little, Brown, 1965), pp.219–28.

21 Thad L. Beyle, "Governors," in Virginia Gray, Herbert Jacob, and Kenneth Vines, eds., *Politics in the American States* (Boston: Little, Brown, 1983), p.459.

22 James R. Scales and Danney Goble, *Oklahoma Politics: A History* (Norman: University of Oklahoma Press, 1982), p.214.

23 Ibid., p.216.

24 Ibid. The quote is taken from James A. Robinson, *Anti-Sedition Legislation and Loyalty Investigations in Oklahoma* (Norman: University of Oklahoma, Bureau of Government Research, 1956), p.26.

25 Jean G. McDonald, "Oklahoma Patronage, the Political Parties, and State Elective Officials" (Ph.D. dissertation, Michigan State University, 1972), p.214.

26 Quoted in David Zizzo, "Roads Often Serve as Currency of Power, Officials Find," *Daily Oklahoman,* November 21, 1988.

27 Wayne F. Young, "Oklahoma Politics with Special Reference to the Election of Oklahoma's First Republican Governor" (Ph.D. dissertation, University of Oklahoma, 1964), pp.190–200.

28 Ibid., p.207.

29 Arrell Morgan Gibson, *Oklahoma: A History of Five Centuries,* 2d ed. (Norman: University of Oklahoma Press, 1981), p.249.

30 Ibid.

31 This count was made from Appendix F, "Executive Branch Agencies," in Oklahoma Reorganization Council, *Comprehensive Plan for Executive Branch Reorganization* (Oklahoma City: 1987).

32 Ibid., p.3, quoting from *Problems in State Government* (Norman: University of Oklahoma, Bureau of Government Research, 1957).

33 Ibid., p.1.

34 See Kenneth J. Meier, "Executive Reorganization of Government: Impact on Employment and Expenditures," *American Journal of Political Science* 24 (August 1980): 396–411.

35 *Daily Oklahoman,* October 26, 1967.

36 *Oklahoma Statutes,* Title 74, Section 10.3.

37 The following account is adapted from *Norman (Okla.) Transcript,* April 3, 1987, and June 26, 1987; and *Daily Oklahoman,* October 3, 1987.

38 *The Bailey Oklahoma Poll,* January 17, 1987.

39 David R. Morgan, "Assessing Changes in Gubernatorial Power," *International Journal of Public Administration* 5 (4) (1983): 429.

40 Patricia Caperton and Michael T. Moore, "The Formal Office of the Governor: A Comparative Analysis of Variations" (Paper presented at the annual

meeting of the Southwestern Political Science Association, Dallas, Texas, 1987), p.15.

CHAPTER EIGHT

1 G. Alan Tarr, "Court Unification and Court Performance," *Judicature* 64 (March 1981): 358–64; James A. Gazell, *State Trial Courts as Bureaucracies: A Study in Judicial Management* (Port Washington, N.Y.: Dellen, 1975), p.145.

2 Henry Robert Glick and Kenneth N. Vines, *State Court Systems* (Englewood Cliffs, N.J.: Prentice-Hall, 1973), p.12.

3 Elmer E. Cornwell, Jr., Jay S. Goodmen, and Wayne R. Swanson, *State Constitutional Conventions* (New York: Praeger, 1975), p.27.

4 "Trouble on the Bench: The Impeachment of a Justice," *The National Observer*, May 17, 1965, p.7.

5 Supreme Court of Oklahoma, Administrative Office of the Courts, *State of Oklahoma, The Judiciary: Annual Report for Fiscal Year 1986* (Oklahoma City: Administrative Office of the Courts, 1987), p.43.

6 *Oklahoma Statutes*, Title 21, Section 2.

7 Calculated by the authors from data presented in Supreme Court of Oklahoma, *The Judiciary: Annual Report for Fiscal Year 1986*, p.42.

8 Robert A. Kagan, Bliss Cartwright, Lawrence M. Friedman, and Stanton Wheeler, "The Business of State Supreme Courts, 1870–1970," *Stanford Law Review* 30 (November 1977): 121–56; Robert A. Kagan, "The Evolution of State Supreme Courts," *Michigan Law Review* 76 (May 1978): 961–1005.

9 Richard A. Watson and Ronald G. Downing, *The Politics of the Bench and the Bar: Judicial Selection under the Missouri Nonpartisan Court Plan* (New York: John Wiley and Sons, 1969), p. 353; Herbert Jacob, "The Effects of Institutional Differences in the Recruitment Process: The Case of State Judges," *Journal of Public Law* 13 (1) (1964): 104–19.

10 Based on 1969–84 annual editions of *State of Oklahoma, The Judiciary* (see note 5) and questionnaires distributed to some members of the trial division of the court on the judiciary. See Marilyn Mollet, "Judicial Selection and Retention in Oklahoma" (Senior honors thesis, Department of Political Science, Oklahoma State University, 1985), p.20.

11 Thomas A. Henderson, Randall Guynes, Carl Baar, and Neal Miller, *The Structural Characteristics of State Judiciaries* (Alexandria, Va.: Institute for Economic and Policy Studies, 1981), p.11.

12 Article VII, Section 6, of the Oklahoma Constitution.

13 George B. Fraser, "Oklahoma's New Judicial System," *Oklahoma Law Review* 21 (November 1968): 386.

14 Oklahoma Department of Libraries, *Directory of Oklahoma, 1985–86* (Oklahoma City: Oklahoma Department of Libraries, 1986), pp.169–82.

15 Glick and Vines, *State Court Systems,* p.79.

16 See Ronald K. L. Collins, "Models of Post-Incorporation Judicial Review: 1985 Survey of State Constitutional Individual Rights Decisions," *Publius: The Journal of Federalism* 16 (Summer 1986): 111–38; Ronald K. L. Collins, Peter Gaile, and John Kincaid, "State High Courts, State Constitutions and Individual Rights Litigation Since 1980: A Judicial Survey," *Publius: The Journal of Federalism* 16 (Summer 1986): 141–61; John Kincaid, ed., "State Constitutions in a Federal System," *Annals of the American Academy of Political and Social Science* 496 (March 1988); Elder Witt, "State Supreme Courts: Tilting the Balance toward Change," *Governing* (August 1988): 30–38.

17 *Umholtz v. City of Tulsa,* 565 P.2d 15 (Okla., 1977).

18 *Centric Corp. v. Morrison Knudsen Co.,* 731 P.2d 411 (Okla., 1986).

19 *Vanderpool v. State,* 672 P.2d 1153 (Okla., 1983).

20 *Franco American v. Oklahoma Water Resources Board and City of Ada,* 58 Okla. Bar Journal 1406 (1987).

21 Alex Adwan, "Lawsuit Crisis: Real or Imagined?" *Tulsa World,* August 17, 1986, p.8.

22 Ken Neal, "Redistricting Needed to Provide Better Justice," *Tulsa World,* August 17, 1986, p.9.

23 John B. Doolin, "Oklahoma Courts in Crisis," *Oklahoma Observer,* March 25, 1987, p.6. In a June 1990 speech to the Oklahoma Bar Association Board of Governors, District Judge Gordon R. Melson, the president of the Oklahoma Judicial Conference, indicated that caseload disparities were not so extreme (between 1,394 and 2,834 in 1989). He still contended that the crisis in the court system was serious. See David Averill, "Oklahoma's Judicial System Overdue on Reform," *Tulsa World,* July 8, 1990.

24 Ibid.

CHAPTER NINE

1 Timothy J. Conlan, "Federalism and American Politics: New Relationships, A Changing System," *Intergovernmental Perspective* 11 (Fall 1985): 33.

2 Seymour Martin Lipset, *Political Man: The Social Bases of Politics* (Garden City, N.Y.: Anchor, 1963), p.187.

3 John Naisbitt, *Megatrends* (New York: Warner, 1984), p.179.

4 Ibid., p.193.

5 Stanley Scott and Harriet Nathan, "Public Referenda: A Critical Appraisal," *Urban Affairs Quarterly* 5 (March 1970): 313–28.

6 David S. Broder, *The Party's Over: The Failure of Party Politics in America* (New York: Harper, 1972).

7 *New Republic,* May 4, 1987, p.7.

8 Thomas E. Cavanaugh and James L. Sundquist, "The New Two-Party System," in John E. Chubb and Paul E. Peterson, eds., *The New Direction in American Politics* (Washington, D.C.: Brookings, 1985), p.55.

9 Austin Ranney, "Parties in State Politics," in Herbert Jacob and Kenneth Vines, eds., *Politics in the American States* (Boston: Little, Brown, 1965), p.64.

10 The Ranney index for 1974–80 appears in Virginia Gray, Herbert Jacob, and Kenneth Vines, eds., *Politics in the American States* (Boston: Little, Brown, 1983), p.66.

11 William Flanigan and Nancy Zingale, *Political Behavior of the American Electorate,* 3d ed. (Boston: Allyn and Bacon, 1978), pp.69–70.

12 Samuel A. Kirkpatrick, David R. Morgan, and Thomas Keilhorn, *The Oklahoma Voter* (Norman: University of Oklahoma Press, 1977), p.45.

13 A. James Reichley, "The Rise of National Parties," in Chubb and Peterson, eds., *New Direction in American Politics,* p.177.

14 Kirkpatrick et al., *Oklahoma Voter,* p.50.

15 Dorothy K. Davidson and Deborah Rugs, *Election '84: The Oklahoma State Party Convention Delegates* (Norman: University of Oklahoma, Bureau of Government Research, 1985), p.18.

16 *Oklahoma Observer,* August 10–25, 1979.

17 Kirkpatrick et al., *Oklahoma Voter,* p.44.

18 *Tulsa World,* September 10, 1988, and *Daily Oklahoman,* October 27, 1988.

19 V. O. Key, Jr., *Politics, Parties, and Pressure Groups,* 5th ed. (New York: Thomas Y. Crowell, 1964), p.316.

20 Conlan, "Federalism and American Politics," p.35.

21 John Gunther, *Inside U.S.A.* (New York: Harper and Brothers, 1974), p.880.

22 Stephen Jones, *Oklahoma Politics in State and Nation* (Enid, Okla.: Haymaker Press, 1974), p.174.

23 Sarah McCally Morehouse, *State Politics, Parties and Policy* (New York: Holt, Rinehart, and Winston, 1982), p.109.

24 Senate Bill 383, passed in the 1988 legislature, changed the name of the State Ethics Commission to the Oklahoma Council on Campaign Compliance and Ethical Standards.

25 Morehouse, *State Politics,* pp.103–4.

26 Jones, *Oklahoma Politics*, p.175.

27 *Washington Post*, August 29, 1986.

28 Taken from Kay Scholzman and John Tierney, "More of the Same: Washington Pressure Groups' Activity in a Decade of Change" (Paper presented at the annual meeting of the American Political Science Association, Denver, Colorado, September 1982).

29 Chris Casteel and Paul English, "Political Groups Seek Influence with Dollars," *Daily Oklahoman*, October 23, 1988.

30 This testimony is taken from the transcript of a case before the District Court of the 23rd Judicial District, Pottowatamie County, January 27, 1987.

31 Senate Bill 383 (1988) provides that the Council on Campaign Compliance and Ethical Standards may adjust the reportable daily amount lobbyists may spend to take account of changes in the cost of living.

32 *Daily Oklahoman*, October 31, 1986.

CHAPTER TEN

1 *Oklahoma State Expenditures in Brief* (Oklahoma City: Kerr Foundation), for 1988 and 1978. Unless otherwise noted, all comparisons of Oklahoma state revenue and expenditures over time come from these two sources. These reports rely on figures obtained from the state office of finance, but certain revolving funds (e.g., higher education auxiliary enterprises) are not included. Throughout the chapter when a year is provided, it is the fiscal year, which in Oklahoma begins on July 1 and ends June 30.

2 U.S. Bureau of the Census, *Government Finances in 1987–88* (Washington, D.C.: Government Printing Office, 1990), p.23.

3 Ibid. All revenue figures are for general revenue, which excludes receipts from utilities, liquor stores, and insurance trusts.

4 U.S. Advisory Commission on Intergovernmental Relations, *1986 State Fiscal Capacity and Effort* (Washington, D.C., 1989), p.87. See also John Kincaid, "Fiscal Capacity and Tax Effort of the American States," *Public Budgeting and Finance* 9 (Fall 1989): 1–23. The figures presented in this chapter support the position that Oklahoma's tax burden is relatively modest. A report released, however, by the Tax Foundation, a nonprofit organization in Washington, D.C., suggests that the state and local tax burden of Oklahoma is the ninth heaviest per $10,000 of individual income for 1990. The rankings are based on the foundation's revenue *estimates* for 1990. The most recent reliable figures for a fifty-state comparison are for fiscal year 1988, when total state and local revenues collected in Oklahoma were approximately $4.5 billion. The Tax Foundation estimates an incredible $2.4 billion, or 52

percent increase for the two-year period, leading one to conclude that the ranking is unsupportable. It is true, however, that Oklahoma's tax burden appears higher when based on income instead of per capita because of the much lower than average wealth of Oklahomans.

5 "Shifted Burden," *Norman (Okla.) Transcript,* March 28, 1988.

6 This account comes from Bill Johnson, "State Learns Bitter Lesson When Oil Boom Goes Bust," *Norman (Okla.) Transcript,* November 23, 1988; Harry Culver, "FY-88 Offers Welcome Breather for State's Oil and Gas Industry," *Oklahoma Revenue,* October 31, 1988; "Oil Impact Fading," *Norman (Okla.) Transcript,* November 28, 1988; Robert J. Kleine, *U.S. State-Local Tax Systems: How Do They Rate?* (Washington, D.C.: Public Sector Consultants, 1988), p.20.

7 *Oklahoma State Expenditures, 1988,* p.4. The exact figure for 1987 is 42 percent.

8 U.S. Bureau of the Census, *Statistical Abstract 1989* (Washington, D.C.: Government Printing Office, 1989), p.140.

9 J.R. Morris, "America's Most Poorly Funded Higher Education System," *Norman (Okla.) Transcript,* June 21, 1987, p.7. The source of this information is *Higher Education Financing in the Fifty States,* published by the National Center for Higher Education Management Systems, Boulder, Colo. The data are for 1984.

10 Aaron Wildavsky, *The Politics of the Budgeting Process* (Boston: Little, Brown, 1964), pp.4–5.

11 John Wanat, *Introduction to Budgeting* (North Scituate, Mass.: Duxbury, 1978), p.10.

12 Quoted in Ron Jenkins, "Bellmon to Push for Two-Year Budget," *Tulsa World,* August 2, 1987.

13 This is an ex-officio board whose membership is composed of the governor, lieutenant governor, state treasurer, attorney general, state auditor and inspector, state superintendent of public instruction, and the president of the State Board of Agriculture (the only nonelective member).

14 Telephone interview with director of state finance, Alexander Holmes, August 4, 1987.

CHAPTER ELEVEN

1 Thomas R. Dye, *Understanding Public Policy,* 2d ed. (Englewood Cliffs, N.J.: Prentice-Hall, 1975), p.1.

2 Peter Bachrach and Morton S. Baratz, "Two Faces of Power," *American Political Science Review* 56 (December 1962): 947.

3 James E. Anderson, *Public Policy-Making* (New York: Praeger, 1975), p.3.

4 Bachrach and Baratz, "Two Faces of Power," p.948.

5 Ibid., p.949; see also E. E. Schattschneider, *The Semi-Sovereign People* (New York: Holt, Rinehart, and Winston, 1960).

6 This information is drawn from Paul English, "Bellmon Seeks Indians for State Posts," *Daily Oklahoman*, March 12, 1988.

7 Harry Culver, "Tax Exemptions: Who Gets What," *Oklahoma Observer*, October 25, 1987, p.5.

8 Enid F. Beaumont and Harold A. Hovey, "State, Local, and Federal Economic Development Policies: New Federal Patterns, Chaos, or What?" *Public Administration Review* 45 (March/April 1985): 327.

9 Craig St. John, "Growth and Development in Oklahoma," *Free Inquiry* 15 (November 1987): 231.

10 See Beaumont and Hovey, "State, Local, and Federal Economic Development Policies"; Barry M. Rubin and C. Kurt Zorn, "Sensible State and Local Economic Development," *Public Administration Review* 45 (March/April 1985): 333–39; Robert Goodman, *The Last Entrepreneurs: America's Regional Wars for Jobs and Dollars* (Boston: South End Press, 1979).

11 Beaumont and Hovey, "State, Local, and Federal Economic Development Policies," p.329.

12 "1986 Economic Barometers," *City and State* (January 1987): 14.

13 For 1986 rank, ibid.; for 1987 rank, "Coast to Coast," *Inc.*, October 1987, p.77.

14 "1986 Economic Barometers," p.14.

15 Deborah Kasouf, "State Economic Index Adds Fuel to Debate," *Public Administration Times*, April 15, 1987, p.12.

16 Neil J. Dikeman, Jr., Alexander Holmes, Donald A. Murry, Kent W. Olson, Stephen Smith, and Larkin Warner, *State Policy and Economic Development in Oklahoma: 1986* (Oklahoma City: Oklahoma 2000, Inc., 1986); Oklahoma Academy for State Goals, *Strategy for Economic Expansion in Oklahoma* (Tulsa: Oklahoma Academy for State Goals, 1987); Counsel for Community Development, Inc., *Oklahoma: Tools for a Global Competitor* (Cambridge, Mass.: Counsel for Community Development, Inc., 1987); Hudson Institute, *Oklahoma's Future: Strategy and Policy Options for the Year 2005* (Oklahoma City: Oklahoma Academy for State Goals, 1988); Oklahoma Futures, *Oklahoma's Strategic Economic Development Plan, 1988–1993* (Oklahoma City: Oklahoma Department of Commerce, 1988). See also annual updates to the five-year plan, also published by the Oklahoma Department of Commerce.

17 Unless otherwise noted, information for recent legislative actions is taken from Alicia Ramming and David Ligon, eds., *Highlights of Non-Appropriation Legislation Enacted During the First Session of the 41st Oklahoma Legislature*

(Oklahoma City: Research Division, Oklahoma House of Representatives, July 1987).

18 This paragraph is based on Larkin Warner with Cindy Maker, "State Policy toward Indian Tribes and Economic Development in Oklahoma," in *State Policy and Economic Development in Oklahoma: 1989* (Oklahoma City: Oklahoma 2000, Inc., 1989).

19 Counsel for Community Development, Inc., *Oklahoma*, p.S-15.

20 Smith Holt, "On Defining a University," *Oklahoma Observer*, October 25, 1987, p.8.

21 "New Hampshire, Wisconsin Tops with College Entrance Test Scores," *Stillwater NewsPress*, February 25, 1988.

22 Jim Killackey and Ed Kelly, "Oklahoma Slips in Three Areas of Education," *Daily Oklahoman*, February 26, 1988.

23 "Reform Package Designed to Simplify Property Tax System," *Stillwater NewsPress*, February 1, 1988.

24 J. R. Morris, "America's Most Poorly Funded Higher Education System," *Norman (Okla.) Transcript*, June 21, 1987.

25 State Policy Research, Inc., *State Policy Data Book, 1989* (Alexandria, Va.: State Policy Research, Inc. 1989), tables G-42, G-44, G-47.

26 *Oklahoma Observer*, March 10, 1987, p.7.

27 Ibid., January 25, 1988, p.7.

28 Ibid., January 10, 1988, p.9.

29 Frosty Troy, "They've Finally Got It Right," *Oklahoma Observer*, January 25, 1988.

30 David A. Penn with the assistance of Ramona Henry and Sheila Murray, *Oklahoma Infrastructure Study: Conditions, Needs, and Recommendations—Executive Summary* (Oklahoma City: Governor's Infrastructure Advisory Task Force and Oklahoma Department of Economic and Community Affairs, 1986), p.5.

31 Ibid., pp.3–4.

32 Alan Ehrenhalt, "Exploring ABCs of Federalism," *Governing*, September 1988, p.79.

33 St. John, "Growth and Development in Oklahoma," p.231.

34 See Rubin and Zorn, "Sensible State and Local Economic Development."

CHAPTER TWELVE

1 Richard Dagger, "Metropolis, Memory, and Citizenship," *American Journal of Political Science* 25 (November 1981): 715–37.

2   According to the Census Bureau, an official metropolitan statistical area (MSA) contains a central city of fifty thousand population or more and includes all the outlying counties that are economically and socially dependent on that central city.

3   This discussion draws from Samuel A. Kirkpatrick, David R. Morgan, and Thomas Kielhorn, *The Oklahoma Voter* (Norman: University of Oklahoma Press, 1977), p.38.

4   Title 11 of *Oklahoma State Statutes* is devoted to city government.

5   Bryan D. Jones, *Governing Urban America: A Policy Focus* (Boston: Little, Brown, 1983), p.206.

6   The following account is adapted from the *Daily Oklahoman,* May 5, 1985, and a telephone conversation with James Hamill, July 9, 1987.

7   U.S. Bureau of the Census, *1982 Census of Governments: Finances of Municipal and Township Governments* (Washington, D.C.: Government Printing Office, 1984), p.103.

8   The discussion of statutory forms of city government is adapted from Jack Strain, Carl Reherman, and Leroy Crozier, *An Outline of Oklahoma Government* (Edmond, Okla.: Department of Political Science, Central State University, 1987), pp. 128–34. This volume is updated periodically and is based on the text of the same name authored by H. V. Thornton beginning in 1954.

9   *Municipal Year Book 1989* (Washington, D.C.: International City Management Association, 1989), pp.xv, 307–8.

10   Jewell Cass Phillips, "The Operation of the Council-Manager Plan of Government in Oklahoma Cities" (Ph D dissertation, University of Oklahoma, 1935; privately printed edition), pp.19–24.

11   See Michael W. Hirlinger and Robert E. England, *City Managers and the Legislative Process: The Case of Oklahoma* (Norman: University of Oklahoma, Bureau of Government Research, 1986), p.29.

12   From records of the Oklahoma Tax Commission, October 1988.

13   U.S. Bureau of the Census, *1982 Census of Governments: Finances of Municipal and Township Governments,* pp.4–7. Municipal general revenue excludes utility, liquor-store, and employee-retirement revenue.

14   Ibid., p.103.

15   Herbert S. Duncombe, *Modern County Government* (Washington, D.C.: National Association of Counties, 1977), p.39.

16   *Reorganizing Our Counties* (Cleveland: Governmental Research Institute, 1980), p.30.

17   U.S. Bureau of the Census, *1982 Census of Governments: Finances of County Governments* (Washington, D.C.: Government Printing Office, 1984), p.4.

18   Ibid., pp.12–15.

19 This account of the county commissioner scandal is adapted primarily from Robbie Jameson, *The Oklahoma County Commissioner Scandal: Reaction and Reform* (Norman: University of Oklahoma, Bureau of Government Research, 1986), pp.19–25.

20 Charles T. Jones, *Sunday Oklahoman*, February 13, 1983, quoted in Jameson, *Oklahoma County Commissioner Scandal*, p.24.

21 Frank S. Meyers, "Political Science and Political Corruption: The Case of the County Commissioner Scandal in Oklahoma" (Ph.D. dissertation, University of Oklahoma, 1985), p.134.

22 This information on the reaction to the scandal is summarized from Jameson, *Oklahoma County Commissioner Scandal*, pp.28–63.

23 Phillip M. Simpson, "The County Government Scandals in Oklahoma: The Structure/Corruption Relationship" (Paper presented at the Southern Political Science Association Annual Meeting, 1982), quoted in Jameson, *Oklahoma County Commissioner Scandal*, p.59.

24 David R. Morgan, *Managing Urban America,* 3d ed. (Pacific Grove, Calif.: Brooks/Cole, 1989), p.48.

25 Quoted in Jameson, *Oklahoma County Commissioner Scandal,* p.27.

26 State Policy Research, Inc., *State Policy Data Book 1989* (Alexandria, Va.: State Policy Research, Inc., 1989), tables G-8, G-9, G-10.

27 U.S. Bureau of the Census, *1982 Census of Governments: Governmental Organization* (Washington, D.C.: Government Printing Office, 1983), p.5; *State Policy Data Book 1989*, table G-2.

28 *State Policy Data Book 1989*, table G-2.

29 U.S. Advisory Commission on Intergovernmental Relations, *American Federalism: Into the Third Century* (Washington, D.C.: Government Printing Office, 1974), pp.38–39.

30 *Rodriguez v. San Antonio School District,* 411 U.S. 59 (1973).

31 Jim Killackey, "Superintendents' Lawsuit to Seek Funding Change," *Daily Oklahoman,* June 28, 1990.

32 Special Joint Committee on School Finance, *Oklahoma School Finance: A Study with Recommendations* (Oklahoma City: A Report to the Governor of Oklahoma, the Speaker of the House of Representatives, and the President Pro Tempore of the Senate, December 1986).

33 Center for Economic and Management Research, *Statistical Abstract of Oklahoma 1988* (Norman: University of Oklahoma, 1988), p.226.

34 Special Joint Committee on School Finance, *Oklahoma School Finance*.

35 These data on special districts come from U.S. Bureau of the Census, *1987 Census of Governments: Government Organization* (Washington, D.C., 1988), pp.20–21, A175-A177.

CHAPTER THIRTEEN

1 John Kincaid, "Introduction," in John Kincaid, ed., *Political Culture, Public Policy and the American States* (Philadelphia: Institute for the Study of Human Issues, 1982), p.11.

2 Phillip L. Zweig, *Belly Up: The Collapse of the Penn Square Bank* (New York: Crown Publishers, 1985), and Mark Singer, *Funny Money* (New York: Knopf, 1985).

3 The following account is adapted from Singer, *Funny Money*, and Zweig, *Belly Up*.

4 Public Integrity Section, Criminal Division, U.S. Department of Justice, *Report to Congress on the Activities and Operations of the Public Integrity Section for 1987* (July 1988), pp.45–50.

5 Larkin Warner, Robert Danffenbach, and Tabitha Doescher, *Non-Energy Based Economic Growth in the State of Oklahoma* (Stillwater: Oklahoma State University, College of Business Administration), pp.27–29.

6 U.S. Bureau of Economic Analysis, *Local Area Personal Income, 1981–86*, vol. 5: *Southwest, Rocky Mountain, and Far West Regions; Alaska and Hawaii* (Washington, D.C.: Government Printing Office, 1988), pp.34–55.

7 The following is adapted from chapter 10, Hudson Institute, *Oklahoma's Future: Strategy and Policy Options for the Year 2005* (Oklahoma City: Oklahoma Academy for State Goals, 1988), pp.201–16. For some reason, the Hudson Institute Report on Oklahoma's future focuses on decisions that will shape Oklahoma in 2007, the state's centenary, but the title states that the report's contents are strategies and policy options for the year 2005.

8 Danney Goble, "Oklahoma Politics and the Sooner Electorate," in Anne Hodges Morgan and H. Wayne Morgan, eds., *Oklahoma: New Views of the Forty-Sixth State* (Norman: University of Oklahoma Press, 1982), p.174.

9 Angie Debo, *Oklahoma: Footloose and Fancy-Free* (Norman: University of Oklahoma Press, 1949), pp.65–73, viii.

Index

Other volumes in the Politics and Governments of the American States series include:

Alabama Government and Politics
By James D. Thomas and William H. Stewart

Arkansas Politics and Government: Do the People Rule?
By Diane D. Blair

Nebraska Government and Politics
Edited by Robert D. Miewald